THE BRITISH THEATRE
Its Repertory and Practice
1100—1900 A.D.

Illustration from Dick's edition of *The Infant Phenomenon* (1842)

This shows the development of pictorialism in the nineteenth century.
In addition to scene painting we have the "set" flowery bank down
stage left

THE
BRITISH THEATRE

Its Repertory and Practice

1100-1900 A.D.

By

E. J. BURTON, M.A.

Illustrations by Anne Brighton

GREENWOOD PRESS, PUBLISHERS
WESTPORT, CONNECTICUT

Library of Congress Cataloging in Publication Data

Burton, Ernest James.
  The British theatre.

  Reprint of the ed. published by Jenkins, London.
  Bibliography: p.
  Includes index.
  1. Theater--Great Britain--History. 2. Theater
--Production and direction. 3. Drama--Bibliography.
I. Title.
PN2581.B8 1977   792'.0941   77-22954
ISBN 0-8371-9739-2

Originally published in 1960 by Herbert Jenkins, London

Reprinted with the permission of Barrie and Jenkins

Reprinted in 1977 by Greenwood Press, Inc.

Library of Congress catalog card number 77-22954

ISBN 0-8371-9739-2

Printed in the United States of America

Preface

by

FRANCES MACKENZIE

Principal of the British Drama League Training Department

It is significant in an age when mechanized forms of mass entertainment are highly developed and daily increasing in scope and influence that there should be at the same time a corresponding development of intelligent interest in the live theatre. Playgoers are becoming more fastidious and critical and are more ready to accept "serious" theatre. Amateur drama enthusiasts are becoming more aware of the meaning of quality in acting and production, and appreciate the effort which its achievement will demand.

Nevertheless many people are still only dimly aware of the glorious heritage of their own theatre and all that has gone to create the richness and variety of tradition from which they are nourished. Of these traditions the creation and interpretation of character by playwright and actor have always been an outstanding feature of the English Theatre.

Visitors from abroad frequently express astonishment that they can find so few performances, either professional or amateur, of the English classics. More shame to us! But as far as the amateur theatre is concerned there is undoubtedly an iron curtain of fear based on ignorance which deters them from attempting plays of the past, which seem to them "difficult" mainly because of superficial differences in style and language.

Mr. Burton's most comprehensive book should do much to dispel this fear, and to stimulate and encourage people to explore the theatre of their forefathers. Most amateur producers and teachers have not the time for much historical research, or even for the wide reading of texts. Nor do they know where to look for the information they want for the production of a period play.

Mr. Burton's book on the British Theatre should fill a long-felt need. The book is eminently practical. It covers an immensely wide field, but succeeds in indicating the essential features of each period and acts as a sign post to further exploration.

The emphasis throughout is on the problems of presenting period plays today and on their validity as entertainment in our own times. I note with pleasure that Mr. Burton stresses the importance of presenting the *character* which lives beneath unfamiliar speech and manners, and he shows that plays of the past survive and are actable today only because playwrights present human beings in action who are as true for us now as they were for their contemporaries.

This book with its extensive bibliography and helpful illustrations should form an invaluable practical handbook for amateur producers, teachers and students of drama.

Contents

List of Illustrations

Introduction

THE purpose of this book is practical—to assist producers and designers of setting with their preparation and approach to their tasks, to give necessary basic information concerning the plays of various periods and their staging, and to indicate the wide variety of material available and its possible treatment on the modern stage. Further, the book endeavours to indicate where further information may be obtained. Necessarily the material given is highly selective and only that which in the writer's experience is most needed. Thus, for reference what may be called intermediate authorities, easily accessible, rather than those large and rare works which the scholar must study, are listed. At the same time, every effort has been made to suggest fairly the views of modern scholarship and recent research. Similarly, the lists of plays are those which could well be added to the repertory of modern theatre, and which in many cases still await revival; this does not prevent the reader going further, to other plays not listed.

Along with this survey of our existing dramatic heritage, the book endeavours to show the various forms of staging possible, to indicate when and why these arose, and to suggest, again, how in modern theatre these are being used at the present time. Many people today speak loosely of the advantages of the open stage, or the full arena; many again oppose these; others consider everything from their own limited experience—so that for them the Elizabethan stage is merely a box set "with something stuck on in front"—as a person once described it. To mediate amongst these conflicting opinions one must surely know something of the techniques of the varying stages, see why and how they developed, and the kind of dramatic conventions and disciplines associated with them. Loose advocacy of one or the other would then be conditioned by a careful study of the kind of dramatic presentation possible within its limits and effects—or the acting techniques and training needed by performers. Similarly a play text should be related to its theatre, and to assumptions in the writer's mind concerning its performance. Not that we have to copy slavishly—but we should at least know what the original *play* (not merely the *script*) was before we plan our own presentation.

The need for this book has been apparent from the questions and problems posed by students in drama and theatre—not only actors in training and producers, but those desiring to specialise in stage décor and set design. Again and again students have read the available books of reference and when asked can repeat aloud the facts about (say) the early eighteenth-century theatre. But immediately they set to work on the production of a play of this period, they begin with a neat box set and "realistic" interiors—and then complain that too many such settings are needed, that entrances are difficult (they won't fit the words and grouping), and, anyway, how can one secure scene change quickly enough? That this is not exaggerated may be gauged from the remark of a distinguished actor-manager a few years back; he attacked the appalling inefficiency of the stagecraft of Restoration dramatists, which, he said, bore no relation to the actual needs of theatre. His subsequent arguments showed that he was thinking in terms only of picture-frame, box setting, naturalistic and detailed solidity. Again, many students and workers will examine the illustrations and photographs in such standard works as Nicoll's *Development of the Theatre* and will fail to analyse or to understand their implications unless these are carefully shown. Simple line drawings are designed to abstract (from reliable contemporary sources) necessary details and significant information. We have not always succeeded in our intention—but we have tried hard. Again, my aim is to supply, as it were, mediation between the worker and the authoritative sources, to break down barriers which may hinder fuller theatre art. Obviously, the treatment is not complete. I have tried to choose from each period those plays and problems which may together best exemplify particular tasks.

Lastly, while this work does not aspire to originality, save in showing at times fresh significance and relationship between theatre form and dramatic expression, I have included original material from my own research work, more especially in the Georgian and Victorian theatre. Much more needs to be done—especially on acting styles and methods, and stage directions, of the nineteenth century; at every turn fresh information is found which may remove prejudice and misunderstanding, giving perspective and proportion to this most vital of all human activities. Thus, the producer will find that nearly all the tasks of "direction" are dealt with during the course of the book, as they arise historically through the developing drama. Such tasks can be seen more vividly in relation to the kind of drama in which they emerged as essential, and after can be blended with other aspects of the producer's work. So, too, with movements, entries, grouping, and properties, as these relate to the setting.

I leave my task at 1900. From then on the normal textbooks are at the service of the theatre worker; these deal exhaustively with the plays of our own day and their presentation—so exhaustively that the student, overwhelmed by technical detail, needs now and again to consider *the play in itself* as a basis for his production, acting, or stage design. I hope that this book will be a small help in this direction—at least for dramatic work and theatrical practice before 1900.

Ritual and Folk Drama

THE MATERIAL

THE so-called Dark Ages saw the meeting of barbarian cultures with the civilising influences of the Church, the inheritor of classical tradition and Roman organising ability. The new "nations" had their own religious beliefs and folk-lore, and, associated with these, rituals that were basically dramatic. As Christianity spread so these "folk-plays" changed their character—but were not necessarily lost. They continued as part of our own culture until recent times and have now been revived. Such folk-plays, the transformed descendents of fertility rites which enacted symbolically the death and resurrection of the life forces at the turn of the year, are found throughout England; the most widely spread is the *St. George and the Dragon* play, perhaps because it adapted itself to pseudo-Christian ideas, and, once started on this flexible career, later incorporated other popular figures as occasion arose. Here the death and resurrection theme is clearly seen in the revival of the Dragon and the Turkish knight. Children also preserve many folk games and playlets, some of them highly dramatic, and fairly easily arranged for present day performance—sometimes by children themselves, who with a little encouragement quite easily recreate a fuller form, nearer to the original. A striking example is the rhyme *Old Roger is Dead*. This is found not only in Yorkshire, where it is still played in the parks, but also, with slight change, in America. It involves the death and resurrection theme, and all parts are taken by all children in turn, the rest meanwhile forming an audience who stand round keeping time to recitation as the action is mimed. In *Mime for Schools and Clubs*, Miss Grace Brown tells how a group of children, without prompting from her (she did not know the rhyme) produced the play in a fuller theatrical form, as part of their normal school dramatic work. Many of the skipping games and recitations which children use can also be worked into simple and attractive programmes. You may present (quite simply) a "street scene", in which children meet and enjoy games, some measure of direction ensuring that the activities are played as rhythmically and efficiently as possible—as indeed they

15

are normally by children themselves. Alternatively, a single game can be "dressed" and the simple theme can be played out more fully. Further, our natural ability to compose simple dramatic rituals and games did not die out in later centuries—anonymous or acknowledged authors were still producing similar dance songs in later centuries. *Spanish Ladies*, an example of this, make an attractive dance mime. In a sense the tradition carries down to the present day, with such poems in traditional form as those arranged in *Speaking and Moving* (Frances Wilkins. Oxford University Press).

A fuller and longer embryonic dramatic form is the ballad, which suggests by its name the combination of dance movement, action, and story, which characterises the folk poem. In the true ballad you will

Fig. 1.—EARLY MEDIEVAL COSTUMES
(from Knight's *Old England*)

find a soloist telling the story, and becoming the various characters—their speeches are given directly; there is no "he said"—while the audience are also performers, joining in a refrain and moving rhythmically at the end of each stanza. Dance, music, character, action—theatre, even—are all potentially here. Small wonder that the ballad is used in many schools as a way to fostering pupils' experience of drama. The form encourages mime, while the narration is spoken; character emerges where pupils speak the lines of particular people; and a free presentation of the actions may afterwards be costumed and presented to an audience, while the ballad is spoken as appropriate, sometimes before the presentation of each episode, sometimes merely as linking commentary. It may not be irrelevant to note the number of plays that have been founded on the old ballad adventures, notably the Robin Hood series, which appear in straight plays, pantomime, and film.

From earliest times men have dressed up as animals, whether to secure the powers of the animal, or to represent the animal in magical rites—in either case a form of "characterisation". Maskings and mummings again continued in medieval times as part of our heritage; sometimes they retain an element of the old magical purpose, whether to ensure fertility and food, or with a more specialised intent towards witchcraft. The Abbots Bromley Horn Dance is perhaps an example of the former; the "ooser" or bull's head used at meetings of a "coven" of the latter. The animal disguise today is found often enough in the display by the local dancing school, where rows of little "rabbits" charm the assembled parents, in dancing routines for variety shows, and in pantomime and fantasy plays. The animal "disguise" is an element in dramatic training, developing and extending the flexibility and fluency of the actor. It enables the dramatist to communicate with his audience in a more imaginative way and to widen the range of dramatic expression. A sophisticated and lovely form of animal "impersonation" is found in such a ballet as *Swan Lake*. In a "straight" play animals, too, are used, especially when the action is devised with children in mind—Maeterlink's *The Blue Bird* is an example. While one can hardly, except as a curiosity, present an old "mumming" as an entertainment in itself, the possibilities of this enchanted world of fantasy and magic, which explores beyond the normal limitations of human experience, are obvious—in carnival, dance, pageant, and variety entertainments, the "mummers and maskers" will still appear. They formed an important part in the "masques" of Elizabethan and Caroline days, and in symbolic theatre down to the twenties of the present century.

Whether or not we believe that all ritual, religious or otherwise, is dramatic in origin, it remains true that in all forms of worship there is a "dramatic" content, since actions are performed which have a meaning and significance beyond the outward appearance, and those taking part represent beings and influences other than their own. The central act of the Church at worship was the Mass, basically dramatic, for, as the Anglican post-Reformation Liturgy states, it has amongst its purposes "to show forth the death of Christ". Beyond this, towards the end of the Dark Ages, events which were narrated in the Gospel read from the left of the altar moved gradually into dramatic form. The Easter Gospel's elaboration is known to most people. Three clergy move (possibly to a side chapel) where they are met by another in white robes, who asks them whom they seek, and on their answer tells them that Jesus has risen. The presentation was part of the whole

Mass, and gesture and movement were strictly controlled by ritual custom; at the same time this carefully considered use of movement and arms and hands was itself an elementary training in dramatic presentation. The movements of a priest during the Celebration of Mass today may profitably be studied by those who hope to present such ritual

Fig. 2.—MODERN ANGLICAN ALTAR

plays. The flavour of the "trope" as these dramatic extensions of the service were called may be studied from the precise directions given in a later ritual play.

> MAGDALEN: (*Here she turns to the men with her arms extended*) O my brothers! (*Here to the women*) O my sisters! Where is my hope? (*Here she beats her breast*) Where is my consolation? (*Here she raises her hands*) Where is my whole well being? (*Here, head inclined, she throws herself at Christ's feet*) O my Master!
>
> MARY MAJOR: (*Here she points to Mary Magdalen*) O Mary Magdalen, (*Here she points to Christ*) sweet disciple of my son (*Here she embraces Magdalen putting both hands round her neck*) weep with me in grief . . . (Quoted by A. Nicoll, *The English Theatre*, pages 23 and 24.)

Setting was suggested by a model sepulchre. Further, one may remember and again study with profit the existing remains of the "décor" of the Church—especially wall paintings—in addition to the architectural features of arches and rood screen.

As the plays become more usual their performance necessarily grouped itself round the major Festivals of the Church—Christmas, Whitsun, and Easter. Further, additional dialogue developed, and the vernacular was introduced. But when this happens we are perhaps moving away from the ritual play proper. More important was the gradual elaboration of the acting areas and method of presentation. From the simple Easter "trope" requiring perhaps one side chapel in addition to the main altar and the open space before it, more localities were brought into use, each of which was associated with a particular part of the ritual story, and therefore with particular characters. These *stations*, *mansions*, or *houses*—all terms have been used, although the anglicised form is better kept for later plays produced on this convention—might be at the side of the open space before the altar, and then within the nave or main part of the church. The sketch plan (Fig. 3) of the arrangement of such houses (based on a French manu-script of a ritual play of the twelfth century) shows the more developed form of setting. At the end of the plan we see the altar, and, to its left, perhaps the original "sepulchre" used in the earliest form of the Resurrection play. The later additions show how the story was developed until all the relevant events of the Gospel narratives were introduced. We shall see that this method of play presentation—the small mansions (whether platforms, booths, or curtained recesses) even though used also by the audience in conjunction with an open space or *platea* which can be any place at any given time—is typical of medieval theatre and has a long and lasting importance for later dramatic presentation.

APPROACH TO PRODUCTION

Clearly, one's attitude to such plays as those listed cannot but differ greatly from the approach one makes to a modern naturalistic play concerned with the struggles and business of everyday life. There the producer seeks to discover and to reveal in his direction the diverse characters and idiosyncracies of the people concerned. Here, in the play itself the issue is plain. It is part of a religious ritual, and the "characters" are determined by the appropriate response demanded by the ritual. They are not characters to be developed in their own right—they exist to represent humanity in its relations with God, and humanity sharing a Divine revelation. Their very gestures and move-ments are dictated for them by the overall intent and familiar story. On the other hand, the actor must have sincerity and an appreciation of the situation and article of belief which he helps to communicate through his actions. No priest would (ideally) ever sentimentalise his conduct of worship by adding a personal overtone; but he must show his respect for, and his understanding of, what he is about by the

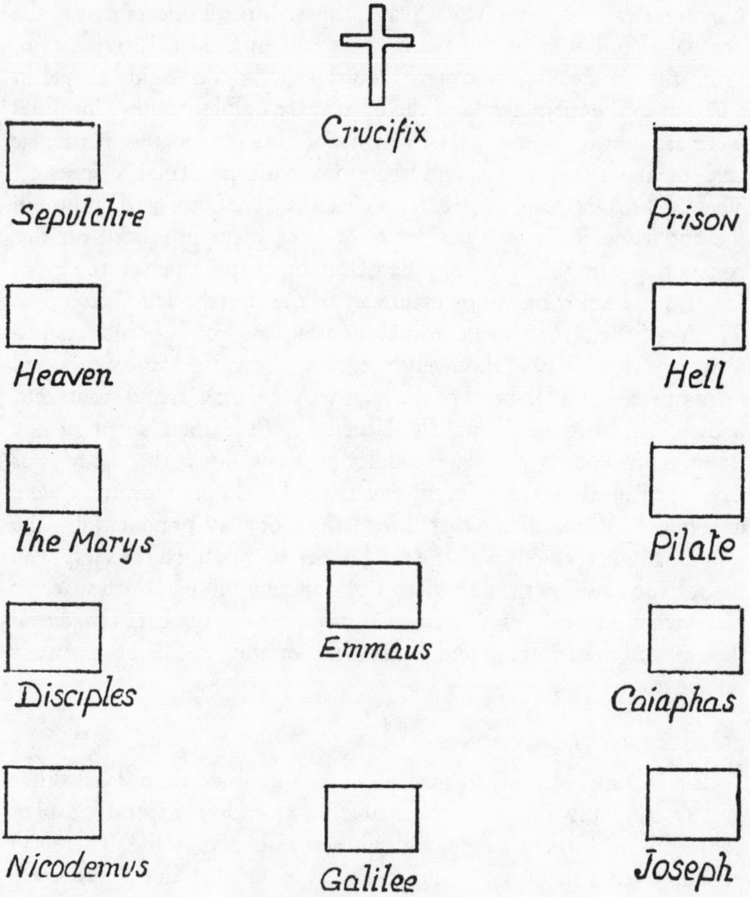

Fig. 3.—SETTINGS IN CHURCH
Plan of houses in relation to altar

careful movement of body, limbs, and head, and by the correctly varying emphasis and pitch of voice. The actor who does not really believe, or at least attempt dramatically to share in belief during his part in the play, will introduce discord. In his efforts to convey reverence he will almost certainly exaggerate and falsify the simplicity and beauty of the presentation. To guard against this danger, of course, the original performance was marked by the careful instructions which defined and guided every movement. It may be well to familiarise actors with the grammar of simple ritual movement and gesture required in these plays. The movements themselves will induce the mood of reverence and unconscious sharing of the belief which the plays perpetuate. Slow and steady movements at first should be followed by an attempt to pass easily from one attitude to another; there must be no jerking or ugly angularity. These ritual gestures are in some ways a valuable training in physical control and the development of bodily fluency. Their precise relation to the play is determined by the place and scope of action. Presented in a large Cathedral, the movement and gesture may be slower and more ample than when performed in a small hall or parish church. Clearly, too, just as the ceremonial of the larger building is richer and involves many more clergy, so greater numbers may be employed. Outside performance may also use much larger groups. At the same time, just as the celebrant in the Mass is marked out by his vestments and by his more elevated and central position, so the important characters must be thrown into positions of prominence, and never grouped too tightly. Even when they advance to embrace contact is made by a leaning towards each other, a stretching out of the arms, which still leaves space between them, and from which they can easily turn to separate and clearly defined positions.

Next, the producer must decide on the vital and important moments in the ritual. The study of one of these plays is, again, a valuable training in the elements of direction, in the perception of dramatic form. In the simple *Quem quaeritis* the dramatic moment is clear when the news is given, "He is not here; he has risen as he foretold", and this climax is resolved by the triumphant strains of the Easter anthem. Similarly, the shepherds are startled by the blaze of light from the heavens; there is the moment of awe when the heavenly host burst into song, and the subsequent steady progression to the final revelation when (after the shepherds have travelled to Bethlehem) they kneel in adoration. How are such climaxes marked? In the Mass, the priest elevates the host; the kneeling people bow their heads. In a ritual play, kneeling in worship will be found again and again the appropriate mark, naturally, of these moments when God reveals himself, serving to throw into prominence the angels or prophets who give the news. Clearly, too, there may be emphasis by silence—the pause, the seconds of silent prayer, which suddenly hush the whole congregation. In a ritual play it is perhaps better to formalise, so that the whole group is arranged in some significant pattern, rather than to allow more naturalistic grouping of shepherds or worshippers. Further, even when there seems to be no obvious instruction for a moment of reverent kneeling (for example, when the women leave the tomb and return to announce the good news of the Resurrection) it will be found that a genuflection before the "angels" at the tomb will pattern and point the action, and send the women more easily into their returning progress.

Again, climaxes in a play which is part of an act of worship are often marked by singing—praise in which the audience, or congregation, share. The anthem and the Christmas carol are a natural part of this kind of dramatic ritual.

Just as the priest's robes and those of the attendant clergy mark them out and make their function clear, so great attention must be given to the colour scheme and shape of clothes to be worn by the actors. They need not necessarily be accurate—it is rather the total effect and harmony which is important. Pseudo-Arabian costumes, shapeless and clumsily draped, are not the answer—looser, flowing garments which allow of easy gesture and the colours of which blend or contrast are more suitable. At this stage we are not very far removed from the early tropes, where the performers or ministers might be garbed simply in a white alb. Any over-emphasis on luxuriant feathered wings for angels vulgarises and throws the whole ritual out of balance. On the other hand, a long white dropping sleeve, as has a full cut surplice, may well help in the gesture and grouping of "angels" and even seem singularly appropriate.

Another important element in ritual drama is the procession. Any great festival has its procession, and the entry of actors through the audience (or congregation) is signified and in keeping with the nature of the presentation. The procession is in a sense an early dramatic form, preserving its theatrical character in the Lord Mayor's show, or in carnival floats and disguises. In the Church service it is a necessity to enable the clergy to reach their stalls. But it is more, for on great festivals the processional hymn, with the solemn bearing of the cross and the chant or hymn while choir and ministers progress round the interior of the church, is a dramatic act of witness and triumph. Further, the procession might well originally be made through the streets of the town. Such a procession was beautiful in itself and created an atmosphere of anticipation and attention. A procession may well start and conclude your own presentation.

In short, the whole play must be conceived as evolving from the ritual of the worshipping community.

SETTING

If you are presenting the drama in a church your setting is (in a sense) ready-made for you. The chancel will be your main acting area, and if you can contrive a higher acting level between the choir stalls, with the necessary additional steps down into the main aisle of the nave, you can still further increase visual effect. Side chapels, if there are such, provide additional "houses" from which entry is made on to the main acting area. The pulpit and reading desk (with its small rostrum) are available for figures of special importance, and further "houses" may be located in the side aisles, before pillars, or on small platforms, and reached by actors in procession from vestries or from the back of the church. If the church has a west tower, the ground level of this (which may already be used as a vestry) is an excellent starting point for processions. Your great problem, if the setting is so complex as to require various "houses" or acting spaces, is that of lighting. Most churches have fairly powerful lighting for the chancel and high altar, which are thrown thus into prominence in the ordinary services of which the ritual dramas are an extension. In the ancient services the processions were illuminated by the ceremonial candles borne by acolytes. Today a dramatic effect in a play (where candles would be dangerous, though still needed in the ritual of the church) can be obtained by carrying electric torches built into representations of old-fashioned flambeaux. Bulbs must be carefully concealed beneath thin paper or cellophane cut irregularly. It may be necessary to install extra spots and floods—and unless you are prepared to do this, you must constrict your acting areas accordingly. Even if you use merely the chancel you have at least four points of entry—to right and left of the altar, and to right and left of the chancel arch or from the choir stalls, where characters not required can remain immobile during action which does not concern them. Processions through the church will not necessarily be unimpressive if not lit brilliantly, but even rather more awe-inspiring as they emerge from half light into the illumination of the chancel and move to left and right. Normally the play will conclude with a final grouping of the actors, probably with the singing of a hymn or psalm of praise. The choir, displaced from their usual place in the chancel, may well be placed at the back of the church if there is no convenient side aisle or chapel, whatever complaint the organist may make. In any case, singing could, and maybe should, be unaccompanied—except for those parts of the service in which the congregation join.

The simplest form of ritual drama today consists in allowing a reader (who must have a due sense of pace and emphasis) to deliver portions of the scripture story while the actions are mimed by the actors. Thus the Christmas story is often presented—but there must be careful rehearsal. The reader's voice must not jerk—or drag—and when he ceases to allow more lengthy action to take place, his voice must seem naturally to die away, and to be taken up by the action, rather than suggesting an accidental break. At appropriate moments hymns and processions—e.g. of shepherds, wise men, and worshippers— gradually build the ritual drama to its climax where all kneel in adoration before the Infant. The positioning of the crib, Mary and Joseph and attendant angels, is sometimes difficult unless the space before the altar can be kept in complete darkness, and lights brought up on the prearranged group at the appropriate moment. The pulling of a curtain to reveal the nativity tableau is distracting. Such a device is out of keeping with the dignity of the ritual. It would be better to allow the angels to enter from each side, to move forward diagonally, spreading the wide sleeves of their robes to form a kind of screen. Mary and Joseph may then enter behind them, and be revealed as the angels move slowly to each side.

Incidentally, each church has its own architectural features, tombs, rood screen, steps, screens, which can be brought into the action as places of vantage, helping in grouping and movement, or adding functional beauty if you have lighting which can emphasise their mouldings and tracery.

If you are presenting a play of this kind in an ordinary hall or theatre, a setting which retains features of the church presentation may enable you to secure the necessary dignity and style, even with a picture frame stage as a start. The diagram (Fig. 4) shows the basic idea. Wings, draped and with some simple decoration, become "houses", and the backcloth has a large gilded cross of plywood hung before it. On each side of the proscenium, in front, is hung from a semicircular hoop light material which may represent a further medieval pavilion or house. Steps lead down to the auditorium as shown in the plan. The material of the larger and more complete pavilions in front is copied, to suggest further such pavilions, by the side wings. The action is conducted on the unlocalised space of the stage, brought forward on to the steps, or taken back to the platform before the gilt cross. With the possibility of processions through the hall, we then possess almost the original flexibility of staging and arrangement of houses indicated in the plan of the medieval French play. (Fig. 3.) Obviously, no suggestions will be given in detail for the exact décor, its colours, and its general effect—that will depend on the wishes of the producer. But something of the rich colouring of medieval stained glass might be kept in mind—with a light blue sky-cloth lit by a ground row behind the cross, and "houses" not too dark or definite in colour against which the rich colouring of the actors' robes may show to effect. It is by the grouping that the maxi-

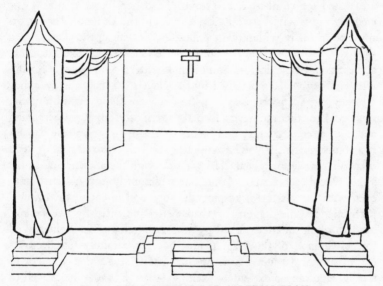

Fig. 4.—BASIC SETTING FOR A RITUAL PLAY

mum effect will be achieved, not necessarily by the setting itself, which may retain the grey of medieval stonework, though some may prefer to design gay pavilions, or suggest rich gold ornamentation.

FOLK-PLAYS

The folk-play, acted either on the village green or in the hall of the manor houses, had little formal staging. The actors moved and grouped as well as they could. This suggests that we might well adopt "arena" performance—that is, the action takes place in the middle of our hall, while the audience sit round. But whatever method you adopt, there must be careful planning. While the old actors had practical knowledge of how to secure and use a suitable acting area, being guided by careful traditions of grouping and movement, the present-day actor will find himself in rather a strange world unless an equivalent convention is provided for him. If you decide to act in the arena, you must secure two places of entry through the audience; you must see that the limits of the acting area are clearly marked—the boy with the collecting box in the old St. George plays may obviously leave the acting area for a specific purpose, as may any other character who has a direct relationship with the audience; but others should know the general boundaries of their territory, and, within it, the approximate areas used for combat, resurrection, and dance. Further, during the exciting fights (say) between St. George and the Dragon, other actors must be formally withdrawn to the sides, or wait in the alleyways to the stage, so as not to impede the audience's view or hamper the tactics and evasions of the dragon. Some simple pattern of movement for this purpose may well be practised by the players, so that wherever they are they can adapt themselves to the "rules of the game". Similarly, it is better for them to have a formal pattern of grouping at beginning and end, after their entry and before their exit—much as the dancers in a country dance. If you have to use a small platform stage at one end of a hall, let the main characters walk through the audience up to the stage, where each turns and announces himself boldly. You are thus, even with the platform, keeping the style and intent of the original performance. The dragon is perhaps better presented by two people, head and hind quarters linked by a covering cloth. The fight and all the movements of the dragon must be very carefully rehearsed. Its entry from the darkness of a village hall through the audience and on to the lit stage can be extremely exciting—though it may be as well to send two attendants along with it to see that it is not molested on the way by the small boys in the audience. Further, it may be a little chary of finding its own way—though my own "dragons" managed without any help and acquitted themselves well. For this kind of folk-play little is needed in the way of scenery or even rostra—instead you must see that you have a flat and uninterrupted level space for action. On a proscenium stage raised rostra might run along the back, on which characters not engaged in the immediate events may group.

ARENA WORK

In the arena any such varying levels of surface should be avoided—they are both inappropriate and dangerous. If, on the other hand, you attempt to present a ritual play in the arena, with pavilions around the walls of the hall (and behind the audience) a central raised platform, with approach steps on each of the four sides, will be very helpful. Clearly, you have to accept that the audience will gain varying views of the groups, and that often they will stare at the back of important characters. However, if you allow your characters to move with the slow dignity and ample gesture which is appropriate, you will find that the difficulty is less than might appear. However, the ritual play proper, even with "houses" around an unlocalised space, and although far from happy in a proscenium frame convention, has still a flow of feeling in one dominant direction—towards an altar; the dynamic of its action is from the altar which represents God, out through its actors to the audience, and back from the audience through the actors again to the altar as an act of worship. If you act in the arena this flow and pattern is lost, unless you ask them (by the suggestion of the steps which ascend in the centre) to direct their thoughts as it were upwards in adoration.

Miracles and Mysteries

As the ritual plays developed further, their elaboration and the crowds which attended at festivals really made them unsuitable for presentation in the church—the demands upon space, both for the actual "performance" and the audience, were too great. The churchyard, or the steps leading up to a great church in town or city, was an easy and natural extension of existing facilities. Few historians of theatre have noted that certain ceremonies (e.g. the actual marriage ceremony as distinct from the nuptial mass) took place at the porch of the church. Such use of the sacred precincts, and the ceremonial processions through the village or town, made the gradual move from church interior to open-air performance easy and natural. There was no abrupt break in tradition, only perhaps a shifting of emphasis. But when the plays had been taken outside, it was easier for the laity to take a fuller part; within the church itself, ceremonial must be controlled by the clerics. Again, this was not a revolutionary change. Church and State were closely identified; business life was hallowed by religion; the good subject of the State must be a member also of the Church; heresy was a crime not only against religion but against the civil authority. Whatever rivalries there might be between contending interests, all alike were within the Church, and the gradual development of the plays by the laity and the organised business life of the towns did not, in theory, mean that there was any lessening of the religious motive in their presentation.

What could be done to organise the presentation of the plays? Existing means had to be used—and the trade guilds composed the fabric of town life. Again, these, which regulated the conduct of each trade and craft, were quasi-religious bodies, with chaplain and charities for the well-being of their members both in this life and, through masses for the repose of souls, in the next. There was little separation in medieval life into sacred and profane—and this must be remembered when we examine the existing plays.

On the Continent plays were performed outside churches, in the great market squares in the middle of towns, round the village "green", but in England, in some places, the performance linked with the ceremonial procession of floats and wagons, and moved further away still from the actual church building. Again, although we have isolated mystery plays, the tendency was for a whole series to be performed on a great festival, just as (earlier) there had been a grouping of ritual plays around Christmas, Easter, or Whitsun. The inauguration of the festival of Corpus Christi (Thursday after Trinity) in 1311 helped again to provide a time when the weather was probably tolerable for out-door performance, and a popular holiday would set free peasants, workers, and merchants; there was no immediate pressure of work—harvest or sowing—to keep away those who might like to travel into towns which could afford to present the plays adequately. For the theatre, even in those early days, showed its later tendency to price itself out of existence. Once a really good "cycle" of plays had been presented the standard had to be maintained. Smaller towns, villages, and poorer communities, could not afford to produce "mysteries" in this way. Their inhabitants travelled to the greater towns, or were to be content with the simple additions to ritual which we have already noted; often they took a fresh delight in the old pagan maskings and mummings, which in actual fact did survive in the more remote villages. The mystery plays themselves were acted until the late sixteenth century. There is considerable evidence of dramatic activity of this kind during the first ten years of Elizabeth's reign even in smaller villages; but soon the great cycles of plays were discontinued in the large cities. One feels that, when the socio-religious establish-ment which had produced them was passing away, their vitality was lost. When the parent trunk was severed the dramatic branches withered. Further, other forms of theatre were rapidly developing. When, in the twentieth century, the performance of the mystery plays revived, it was naturally often by a return to their original home—the church—on the one hand, or by a corporate effort in such cities as had sponsored the full cycle of dramas, notably at York.

ORIGINAL STAGING

From the original trope or illustration of the ritual, we have now reached a full presentation of the Bible story—from Creation to Day of Judgement. Gradual additions—such as prophecies of Our Lord's coming as Messiah, stories which illustrated His work and mission, dramatisation of Gospel events—worked outwards from the two central points of birth and resurrection gradually to include all import-ant aspects of teaching. But these were not isolated from the whole attitude of the time to the presentation of religious truth—for example, there was necessarily a connection between dramatic performance and the wall paintings, statuary, and grotesques, of the medieval church.

The actual method of presentation may be termed "market-place theatre". The "houses" round the open square or green which was typical of some Continental performances do not seem to have been so general in England. True, we have our fairs with their booths and show tents. This does not preclude the performance of a particular play or episode in this way, when a village had (as seems to have occurred) a tradition, involving the acting of a special part of the Bible story,

Fig. 5.—A HELL-MOUTH WITH DEVILS
From Valenciennes mystery play illustration

while unable to attempt a full series of plays. One method used in the larger towns was, however, that of the pageant wagon. Each episode had its own "float" or wheeled platform. Instead of the spectators watching performance emerging from various "houses" on to the open space, the "houses" were brought round to them in various suitable open sites. In order, the episodes (each with its stage equipment and actors) were given before the crowd assembled in one place. It would be wrong, as some, to regard this change simply as placing "mansions" on wheels. A new technique in production is involved. Each of the pageant wagons might represent two or three localities if necessary, at least in the more developed plays; shepherds move from the open hillside to the manger, Herod's knights leave his court for Bethlehem. In essence we have a raised platform surrounded by an open space, which contains the audience, and may also be used (as the "platea" with "houses") as an acting area. Further, this "stage" is well equipped with effects, smoke, flames, and fireworks. It may be regarded as possessing more than one "level" of acting. The floor in front of the stage could be used in various ways, and was suitably the normal place for the inhabitants of hell; on the other hand the structure which was erected on the wagon might be substantial enough possibly to bear an upper platform for the throne of God. The actual appearance of the completed portable stage is doubtful. Some think that material was fastened round the sides of the acting area so that actors were seen only from the waist up as in earlier outdoor ritual plays; illustrations which support this theory may be of puppet stages. Clearly, at some time (as in the shepherd plays) performers made their way through the audience and climbed up on to the wagon. Herod leaves the "pageant" and "rages in the street". We have to suppose that arrangements were flexible—according to the nature of the play to be shown. Certain principles emerge: (a) An acting area which includes platform and the area around; (b) the use of the platform to represent differing places in the same "episode" without change of setting beyond different properties; (c) startling and broad effects, sometimes quite elaborate as shown by the accounts of the guilds which were responsible for production; (d) subsidiary "houses" such as hell mouth on ground level; (e) a free use of the imagination and the co-operation of the audience, while at the same time vivid and grotesque detail was added where possible and popular; (f) Rich and varied costume, with little historical accuracy—it was that of the medieval scene; Jewish priests were garbed as bishops, soldiers had medieval equipment. The relevance of all this to later Elizabethan theatre is fairly obvious. This was not the only, or even general, method of staging. The Cornish "rounds" use houses in a circular space, with probably a raised platform as a focal point to one side, round which the audience stood, on the raised bank, or (according to Southern) into parts of which they descended according to the action. Experimenting with this form of staging, I found that anticipated difficulties vanished, and that the general effect was most striking. The *Castle of Perseverance* manuscript shows a similar circular acting space, with a high central raised stage. The use of this, with a parallel consideration of the Cornish Rounds—our only actual medieval theatres surviving—is considered by Mr. Southern in his *The Castle of Perseverance: Medieval Theatre in the Round* (Faber). One of my students, Miss Joan Cook, who has been working on a study of medieval drama in Leicestershire has discovered references to "mystery" towers which seem to have been linked traditionally with some such form of presentation. Information may be found in a book *Some Ancient Mystery Towers Remaining in England*, published by the author S. Smallwood, and printed by William Carling and Co., Hitchin (1916).

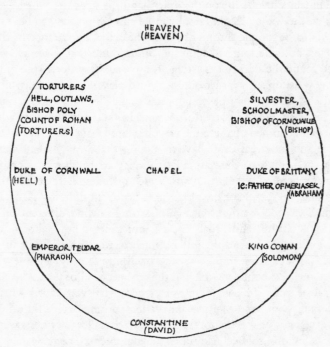

Fig. 6.—"HOUSES" IN A CORNISH ROUND

The use of a raised stage, with different acting levels in association with some part of the surrounding ground, seems to be established in various parts of the country.

Further research shows the use, not of "ambulatory stages", but of the fixed platform with various levels, in some cities. Mr. Glynne Wickham's work, *Early English Stages*, should be studied on these matters. F. R. Halliday in *The Legend of the Rood* suggests that the acting area and platform of the Cornish plays are to some extent typical of presentation through the country and an influence on Elizabethan theatrical practice. Fig. 6 shows the position of houses in two Cornish plays, the miracle *St. Meriasek* and (in brackets) for *Origo Mundi*.

Certain elements recur in the apparent diversities which we have noted: the use of varying levels and acting areas, the open stage with use of the "platea" when needed, and the retention of methods, assumptions, and conventions, inherited from the ritual play. We should, also, note carefully the difference between medieval "theatre in the round", so-called, and modern "arena" presentation. The medieval round in Cornwall has several houses in addition to one main focal point to one side, and the audience may station themselves to see more closely particular sequences of action. Even if they do not move thus, the formal house convention clearly differentiates medieval practice from the usual central unified setting and acting place of modern arena work. Then, too, the "platea" or open space was in origin the "place" used by the audience, to be invaded by the actors when needed. "Platea" is still the equivalent in some Mediterranean languages of our word "pit". Again, the greater flexibility of the medieval acting area is indicated.

APPROACH TO PRODUCTION

The motive behind the plays is still primarily religious—but the content has expanded to cover all aspects of human activity. These plays were one of the few means that the people in general had of expressing themselves, and like the Greeks of old they had the sanction of religion to allow this. The god protected them. So that the plays include: (1) daily life and customs—cooking, housework, and local reference, as the shepherds' supper and their allusions to Conway, Clyde and Lancashire; (2) political and social allusion—the diatribe against social abuse, enclosures, and the unofficial tax collectors and civil service set up by local lords, in the second Wakefield Shepherds' play; (3) everyday grudges and grouses of the English—the weather, for example, which, even in the fourteenth century, was the worst ever known; (4) barely veiled satire and burlesque of contemporary institutions and classes—the "knights" of Herod, who slay babies, are driven off by a mob of stalwart peasant women brandishing pots and pans; (5) surviving ritual—in dogmatic statements by prophets or by God himself; (6) passages of intense religious drama and devotion— when the central themes of Nativity and Crucifixion are reached. But, more. Each event suggested expansion. Original mimetic improvisation was developed into words. Ideas spread from one community to another. More and more original material was added. From the natural

c

unwillingness of Noah's wife to entrust herself to the ark we can trace the expansion to a vivid scene of farce and knock-about in which Noah and his wife become characters in their own right, quite apart from the Bible narrative. Other figures who relate closely to the life of the Middle Ages—e.g. the shepherds—are similarly developed and made the subject of original dramatic action. (Note that the Wise Men remain ritual figures.) Finally, the everyday experience of the dangers and adventures of the shepherds' life, border raiders, sheep-stealers, and medieval rogues, is developed into the play of *Mak and the Shepherds*, a lusty and amusing farce of theft and ingenuity—Mak uses everything from magic spells to native wit—which in no way detracts from the sincerity of the visit to Bethlehem which follows. But original action has developed from bald paraphrase of the Bible narrative in earliest mysteries until it constitutes approximately nine-tenths of the content of the second Wakefield Shepherds' play.

We must admit, too, that we are now dealing with a more mature form of theatre in which we can detect (and must allow for) differing styles and drama. There are—as in ancient Greece—the two major aspects of man's dramatic activities: (i) tragedy, which concerns itself with the ultimate and basic experiences of life, birth, death, hate, love, ambition, pity, and all those things which will for ever remain, in the end, beyond our power of ordering, however complex our social structure; and (ii) comedy, the exhibition of follies, mistakes, and wrong relationships, in communal life. So we have the sentimental "tragedy" of the Brome *Abraham and Isaac*, the full tragedy of the Crucifixion and the chief actors in the events which surrounded it. True, here death is swallowed up in victory—but that might be said of *King Lear* or *Macbeth*, though in differing relation to the protagonists. In *Macbeth* evil is overcome, the people cleansed; Lear passes beyond the power of earthly suffering; while Christ and his followers pass through death to the new life. Comedy emerges more freely—for social readjustment, mockery, and that half sad, half gay, quality that we call humour, are in the immediate experience of the actors, while the larger issues they cannot develop so freely or with such immediate confidence. Farce is there, too, with its reduction of living entities to automata, completely at the mercy of the forces around them—whether it be in the overthrow of each shepherd in turn with machine-like inevitability by the young boy Trull, or in the devils panicking as they struggle helplessly against the forces of God—"Out, harrow, and wel-away," they lament, grotesque clowns caught **by** the scheme of things, ferocious, confident, and yet absurdly stupid, amid the jeers of the audience, who rejoice in the overthrow of their own fears and weaknesses which the devils objectify.

With all this rich variety of style, theme, and event, we have to consider the medieval theatre and its conventions as a whole. Was it, for example, like Chinese "opera"? Was it nearer to modern Western naturalistic theatre? I cite these two examples, for, if the choice has to be made, it was probably much nearer the first than the second. And I choose this illustration, because so many producers still approach these plays with the second in their minds as the norm for presentation. In the medieval plays we have masks, grotesques, violent effects, vivid colour, intrusion upon the audience (where characters run among the onlookers), a non-pictorial background, wrestling, songs, god-like visitants and supernaturals, abrupt transition from mood to mood—and unless all this is faced, the presentation will be only a false and sentimental shadow of the real play. The incongruities of the medieval script, as they seem to us, must be accepted—and appreciated. A shepherd may give a ball to the infant Christ, and tell him to practise at tennis. The surrounding text shows the complete devotion and sincerity of the action. It was the kind of thing they themselves would do if they wanted to worship the infant; they would bring what they had. There was no false piety, no sense of pretended reverence; all life belonged to God—Mak, the bunch of cherries, the tennis ball, and all. Accept, too, and see that your actors speak, the words (still quaint and fresh even when "modernised") with sincerity and an appreciation of what they meant to the original actors. Any precious or sentimental rendering will wreck the rough beauty. Accept the whole medieval angularity (as it may seem to your actors) of phrase, action, costume, gesture. Do not try to smooth it out or weaken it. Have confidence in the dramatic impulse which formed the play. You will find that study of medieval buildings, drawings, costumes, attitudes, will help you greatly. It may be objected that an actor cannot put himself back into the medieval period. Curiously, the people who say that would probably have no hesitation about casting an actor for an even more complicated role in a Shakespearian play, which would involve not merely putting oneself back into the general situation and attitudes of a period, but also "building" a complicated character in controversial situations. For the actor in the medieval play has little to do in detailed character building. These plays are sufficiently near the ritual drama for finer points of individuality to be irrelevant. They represent, are typical, of shepherds, nagging wives, brutal knights. So that once the central situation and attitude has been grasped the actor (so long as remains within the medieval picture) is free to build his own character study round the lines and events he shares—but always within the overall pattern of the play, which must be appreciated and directed with care.

The producer's first task is to decide what particular elements of the whole dramatic experience are involved in the play he wishes to produce. Clearly comic situation, adventure, and suspense, and the resolution of human annoyance by the Christmas babe—the rough shepherds, their anger forgotten, kneeling before the child—all these must be considered if he wishes to produce the second Wakefield Play of the Shepherds. If, on the other hand, he has the Coventry Nativity Play in mind, his material is different in character. This treats only in passing of human comedy and social problem; all the events centre upon the Nativity; the dramatic development is consistently and sincerely religious; there is a sense of awe and an apprehension of beauty throughout, and these find expression in the Coventry carol. This particular play is necessarily popular for performance in church. Yet perhaps to recapture the sincerity and impact of the original play is not easy, despite its apparent dramatic consistency. Believers may overdo the devotion and sentimentalise. Even in his devotions medieval man was practical, because the events were simple facts. There was no need for undue emotional excitation to secure their acceptance. Non-believers may find it difficult to establish contact with the events, as presented. Yet the good director and the willing actor will be able sincerely to attempt the task, after due study and exploration, and with the use of sensible conventions of presentation.

Next, the producer must seek to find points of contact, not only (i) between characters and events in the play, but (ii) between his own experience, the experience of his actors, and the experiences shown in the play. As an example of the first, we desire to link the farcical episode of Mak with the religious devotion of a Nativity scene. Some producers avoid the task; they omit the Nativity scene; so do some versions of the play. To do so is to destroy a work of art, however unconsciously the original begetters of the play moulded it as a unity. In performance gradually some thread would be woven. If he reads the play again, the producer will note that the original ferocity of the shepherds is tempered by genuine kindness when they discover that (as they think) they have misjudged Mak. One insists on returning to give a coin to the new-born babe. The common human respect for the helpless child, and all its potential being, is there. Then from the disappointment of the false baby, the shepherds come naturally to the birth of the real child. The rough humanity which they showed in dealing with Mak (in true Christmas spirit he is merely tossed around as a punishment) leads them to worship with their simple gifts (all of a piece with their general attitude) the true baby and hope of the future. Some have seen in the first part a kind of sacrilegious parody of the worship at the manger. But look again at the development of the "shepherd" plots in other plays; the emphasis is continually on further relating the shepherds of the Bible story to the real shepherds of the English uplands, and the Mak episode is all of a piece with this—it is an easy development which accords with the main theme. One might (if one wished to be ingenious) see the shepherds as the guardians of Christ's flock, from whom the evil one snatches the stray, so permeated is Bible imagery with the idea of the shepherd and Christian symbolism with the Lamb of God. Such an ingenious intellectual approach, not unknown with interpreters of Shakespeare, whether in conscious parody or mystical symbolism, seems unnecessary and foreign to the whole spirit of the play seen in its dramatic context and the overall content of medieval theatre.

An example of the second necessary contact is the establishment of a reverent and sincere approach to the religious events of the play. How can a twentieth-century materialist, to take an extreme case, link himself with the shepherds who kneel and worship? There is no human being, however, who does not feel what some call "awe" and others "respect for the creation", or sometimes "humility" and "wonder", when he enters a great building, looks at the immensity of the night sky, or examines the intricacies of life through a microscope. That is the feeling with which the shepherds approach the child; he symbolises to them all these things—and more. At least we can all share this sense of our own weakness and stand rather humbled—scientists most of all—before the vistas which discoveries today disclose. Again, there are suggestions of simple characterisation in these plays which give a kind of mental "grip" to the actor who seeks to embody them. The dialogue shows clearly that shepherd 3 is sceptical and soured, while 1 is rather kind-hearted, always thinking the best of people. Here are the embryonic elements of characterisation which later become the great talking points in dramatic study—especially (unfortunately) among those who are less practical in their approach, and who argue on theoretical issues from the text without the test of actual performance. The producer will (with his available cast in mind) arrive at some pattern or relationship amongst the characters, following suggestions given in the text where these are found—for these have been developed in the original play which he seeks to present—and adding legitimate detail (with or without the actor's co-operation) where necessary. Faced with three equally burly actors for the shepherds, he may have a little difficulty in securing dramatic distinction amongst them on the stage, for even if they are only "types" they should present different facets of the type. However, there are burly men who are fierce, and there are burly men who are gentle, by nature. Normally one finds that one's actors differ from one another in voice, build, and attitudes. Then one can begin to choose the cast with characterisation (however simple) in mind, and arouse interest through the presentation of different kinds of people in the same situation. The greater then the chances of the audience's recognising among the shepherds their own attitudes and emotions, and so sharing the action of the play in their own being —which is what the producer hopes his audience will do. Just as the worshippers in the ritual drama participated in the events through prayer and corporate devotion, so the audience in later theatre "participates" in the actions and emotions of drama. Don't, however, "type cast". It may be that the ferocious shepherd may be best presented by a little man who will reveal when he acts that truculence and inner assertion which smaller men often possess; this, released, shapes the character to something real and vital. On the other hand, do not allow the characters to be mere comic exaggerations; they are real, if simple, people; their beliefs and attitudes may seem to us grotesque, as may the whole medieval scene; but that is quite different.

SETTING

The producer's next task is to consider his method of presentation. Yes—this is the producer's task, and no one else's in this kind of drama. He knows the play, he knows what he has to communicate to and share with his audience, and he must be allowed to indicate the general requirements of his production. He will plan in such a way as to secure the maximum participation by his audience. They will not necessarily speak, move, or find themselves involved in unofficial crowd scenes, but they must be helped to the full experience of the play. Further, the producer has certain mechanical processes in his mind—the moving on and off stage of actors, the arrangement of properties, the necessary rearrangement of some part of the setting while action is proceeding elsewhere, the need to avoid any wait which will interrupt the dramatic flow of action and wreck his intended climax. Lighting resources and sight lines will be kept in mind constantly; he will instinctively avoid stage planning, however effective, if it conflicts with his knowledge of the general possibilities. Sometimes an inexperienced producer will err here; often, though, the less experienced director tends to be unadventurous and to follow some already established pattern.

It is on the fundamental shape of the play, the problems involved in the simple presentation of its action, that the producer will first concentrate. Either before, or at the same time, he will consider how the play was originally presented, because the methods then used are part of the real play, the play for which, the conventions out of which, his performance has to be devised. He will not follow these slavishly; he is not, presumably, an antiquary who wishes to recreate the past. What he does want to recreate is a *play*, for his actors and his present-day audience, in whatever building is at his disposal. And to give the same dramatic impact, emphasis, and experience, as was afforded by the original performance, he may have to use very different methods. None the less, he will start by examining the original methods of setting, for some of them may well be absolutely integral to the play itself, and these he cannot neglect. A "picture-frame" or naturalistic approach is ruled out by the nature of the plays. True, there are opportunities at times for more static picture making (as in the Nativity tableau) but for the rumbustious mixture of acrobatics, music, dance, and masking, which he may have to present, some of the original conventions are essential.

First, he needs room for movement. The unlocalised space may be retained. His thoughts may turn to arena production, or he may use the gangways or aisles of his hall for processions, entrances, and exits. What of scenery? He knows that he is supposed to build an ark within the short time of action; animals enter it, floods encompass it, doves fly away. As in Chinese classical theatre, so in medieval—much has to be imagined by the audience. He can do no more than symbolise these things. Elaborate naturalistic setting is out of the question, holds up action, and destroys the original play. He has, of course, more technical equipment than had the old performers—flexible lighting— and he will not scruple to use it; the small group bathed in light and surrounded by darkness can be anywhere he asks the audience to suppose; around them in the darkness are the cliffs of Mount Ararat, the temple walls of Jerusalem, or the horrors of hell.

What of the stage itself? What is his equivalent for the pageant wagon, the raised platform, or the mystery tower? Unless audience be raised above the level of the actors, the actors themselves must have some kind of elevation. This elevation is common to nearly all types of theatre except the most primitive. Most producers will look immediately to the platform at the end of the hall where they are to play. If you do decide to use the existing stage, remember the dramatic pattern and nature of your performance. Do not allow yourself by association to assimilate the whole thing to a modern one-act play set in a drawing-room or farmhouse kitchen. Remember the unlocalised space in front. Remember the imaginative use of lighting. Keep the bold gestures and movements demanded by the original script and outdoor performance. For example, a performance of *Noah's Flood* which I saw. The hall was in darkness. Actors entered from a door at the back, to the sound of a pipe and tabor, carrying their simple scenery and properties with them—the side of the ark, carpenter's tools, animal heads on poles. As they walked through the audience lights came up on the acting area of the curtained stage with rostra (as steps) in front. The action of "erecting" the ark was positioned on the main stage, and other events moved around this, up and down the stepped rostra. The animals were represented simply by the poles with typical animal masks which were carried in regular order by the assistant actors. Lights dimmed for the long voyage, only the heads of Noah and his family being outlined by spots. At the conclusion, the team took down their equipment, and marched away as they had come. They had, as it were, first "acted" themselves into the position of a team of medieval workmen, and then, that situation established, had acted the play itself—using such modern helps as might be available without infringing the spirit of the presentation. The lighting effect, for example, helped the modern audience considerably in their imaginative sharing of the Flood. To the medieval audience this would have seemed possibly an unnecessary elaboration. Another team could have followed the first. Such a method of staging can be used flexibly so that a play can be taken round various halls.

Alternatively, rostra can be built against the long side of a hall or large room, and the audience seated around in a semicircle, leaving a gangway for the approach of actors. If there is a convenient door in the side wall, so much the better. The rostra represent the original pageant or platform, and poles at the side carry a canopy and a back curtain or drapery. Again, lights must be available so that this platform stage and the floor space around it can be adequately lit. A series of plays from a mystery cycle can thus be presented quite simply, each team bringing its own equipment and setting its stage. Clearly, too, you are not bound to make just a simple platform. You may have steps all round, and a still higher stage at the back of the first, on which you can group the inhabitants of heaven. Hell mouth on floor level must be provided for the devils if you are attempting a full presentation. The simplest "hell mouth" (and the most practicable) I have ever seen was devised by drama students. It was merely a large box frame of wooden battens, about twelve feet long, five feet high and a similar width. The top was hinged half-way along, so that the front part could be pushed up. The end facing the audience was the mouth. So described the contrivance sounds square and unexciting. Naturally, however, canvas was draped and rucked around the battens, cotton-wool stuffing was built up over the hinged head, monstrous eyes were added, and red fangs of felt hung across the mouth. At the rear loose canvas led to the back stage. Devils crept through into the body and erupted as required, with billowings of smoke. Some of the actors found the monster's interior very snug and made themselves comfortable with cushions for most of the performance. The advantage of such a frame foundation is its lightness and portability. But the actual joints, especially those battens supporting the hinged roof, must be sturdy to stand up to constant wear and possible knocks from clumsier devils.

An outdoor performance against the wall of an old house or in a walled garden can be contrived in much the same way, a stepped platform, with a further higher rostrum at the back, and a blue hanging with cut-out silver stars for the heavens as a final background. On this upper stage is placed God's gilded throne. On ground level is the hell mouth. Entrances are flexible. If no doors are available, actors may come in procession through the audience, and retire in that way. Again, we have the typical three-level setting. (See Fig. 7 and 8.)

Some producers may like to try to approach even more closely to medieval conventions by using a platform more or less surrounded by the audience. This may sound attractive; it is in the nature of a small arena performance. Care is needed with lighting, and the actors must perform in the round; they must abandon the subconscious tendency to play out towards an audience on two or three sides (as in the previous setting and as in the original ritual dramas); the audience is now completely around. Once the convention has been accepted, masking (and resulting attempts to move so as to form a two-dimensional picture, peculiar to the picture frame stage) ceases to worry either actors or audience. But grouping and movement must be fairly "loose"—i.e. actors must be further spaced than in "facing one-way" productions. Such a "tight" grouping (to point relationship between two actors at a given moment) is effective only from one or two directions. Momentary "masking" of one actor by another does not worry—but the complete "blackout" of one performer, which occurs when actors are too close, really removes him from the stage so far as a great part of the audience is concerned. Step rostra can, of course, be provided to secure access from, or use of, the ground level.

In his attempt to produce for the modern audience dramatic impact equal to the original the modern director may well develop some aspects of the plays. In such an episode as *The Harrowing of Hell* he can seize upon the opportunity for movement of "devils" and "souls" in large crowds, using appropriate music. Whether he envisages this as free movement to background sound, or whether he rehearses the movements to and with the music until he has arrived at the verge of

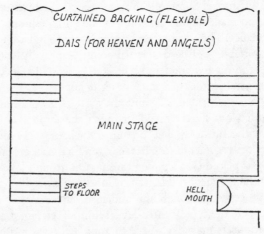

Fig. 7.—BASIC SETTING FOR A MEDIEVAL RELIGIOUS PLAY: PLAN

dance drama is his own concern. Such a scheme of production is probably within the convention and style of medieval drama, and it secures for the audience the general experience and assumptions of the medieval onlookers. In the Middle Ages wall paintings would sufficiently set the scene in the minds of the audience. From early years they were familiar with the agonised faces, the drifting crowds, and the contorted faces of the thwarted demons, if not from an actual picture of the "harrowing", at least by association with other pictures around them. Such elaboration is justifiable, even on the most strict principles of production, to secure the total effect of the original play. Care is necessary, however, to "key in" such elaboration with preceding and subsequent episodes (unless it constitutes an "act" in itself).

Finally, the problem of a play which requires two or three different localities, or rather groups of actors. Mak and the Shepherds need the moorlands, the interior of Mak's cottage, and the Nativity scene. The cast, dressed in simple tunics or robes, may go in procession to the "pageant". There the shepherds can proceed with their drama. Meanwhile, Mary, Joseph, and attendants, can put on the additional costume necessary. How can we show movement from one locality to the other without scene changing? "Use lighting—black out, regroup, and bring up the lights again", is one answer. Yes, it's possible, but dangerous; the audience hear what is happening, even if they don't see the scufflings in the semi-dark. Better to do the scene change openly—this

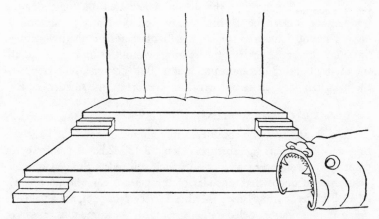

Fig. 8.—BASIC SETTING FOR A MEDIEVAL RELIGIOUS PLAY: ELEVATION

kind of compromise does not perhaps fit in with the style of the play at all. On the other hand, the Middle Ages was well acquainted with the use of a dropped curtain to mask off or reveal the altar. The church at Stebbing in Essex has one of the pulley blocks remaining. The draping of a curtain before the rostrum at the back of the stage, and the arrangement of Mary, Joseph, and the angels there, seems to me quite in keeping with the general nature of these plays—provided that the curtain is of worthy material and is drawn back not too quickly, not too slowly, but in accordance with the dignity of the occasion and the general tempo of production. The shepherds may leave the stage and progress round the ground area to indicate their journey, singing as they go, as indicated in some scripts. What of Mak's cottage? Remember we must have some kind of cot at least, however rough the benches and other furniture. We have to start with the bare stage (with its curtained backing) for the action of the sheep-stealing. The shepherds are left asleep and Mak walks down from the stage with his prize and then reapproaches the stage, now to represent his cottage. A possible solution is the use of small and light subsidiary curtains placed diagonally from the front corner poles of the stage to the middle back of the setting. These are quite different from the ceremonial curtain across the back. When Mak leaves, the sleeping shepherds are, say, stage R. The curtain is drawn concealing them. The curtain running diagonally on the other side is drawn revealing Gil at work. This remains the setting until we return to the moor. At the end of the Mak episode the curtain is drawn to conceal Gil and the cot; these are removed, and by the time the shepherds are back on the moor the whole stage is clear for the final "draw" on the Nativity tableau. Of course, if you have a fairly large area of stage and sharply defined lighting, you could achieve this staging without using curtains at all, merely by lighting the appropriate part. But "scatter", reflection, and the like, hamper a clean and satisfactory effect on the smaller stage.

COSTUME AND COLOUR SCHEMES

These must always be considered in conjunction with the basic setting and its colours (or absence of colours). Medieval paintings, or paintings of a slightly later period which still reflect the general conventions and devotional attitudes of the period, e.g. *Adoration of the Magi*, by Hieronymus Bosch (Medici Society card 729), are a valuable guide and inspiration. Select rather freely from costume illustrations of the period. Work from reproductions of original drawings and illustrations; these will give the flavour of movement and gesture to be associated with the costumes, and indeed with the whole production, for all must be a unity. Costume books are valuable, but a careful study of those contemporary clothes which best suit your purpose is much more helpful—and remember you can select. The medieval presentations were anachronistic, and while it might be safer to keep to one limited period, by the time you have garbed your dignitaries—in dress that is almost timeless—constructed your masks for devils (for whom coloured tights and leotards suitably trimmed will suffice) and put your shepherds into rough medieval garb (which remained unchanged in essence for centuries) you may wonder what else there is to do, or what relation to period can be further achieved. It is rather in the feel and set of the costume that this emerges—the draping of angels' robes, the angle of a page's hat, the lifting of a long robe with the thrust forward hips. There is a great variety of costume possible, and in a sense you are more free in these plays, than in many later, to select and combine ideas, designing for the overall effect that you need in your play. Some producers like to work from a particular picture, trying to "realise" this at some point in their play, especially in nativity tableau. This is valuable for colour—but sometimes results in a static beauty which is not quite consonant with the warmth and vitality of the original play. If you are so fortunate as to have a large open-air site where there are medieval buildings, whether ecclesiastical or civil, for your purpose, your presentation will naturally become larger in scope. You may use crowds, pictorial effect, movement; within the ruins of an old Abbey, with different levels available, your imagination can play with the floodlit groups of angels looking down on the earthly action. In a sense, the play then returns within its original ritual pattern, larger and stronger than when it first emerged. Remember that movements must be at once more stylised and controlled and dignified; the massive effects of colour and grouping must be realised with care in relation to proportion and distance. And you will certainly need a chorus or crowd master to superintend and marshal your actors. But something is lost from the mystery play by such presentation—the robust and complicated form with its bustle, beauty, vulgarity, and moments of revelation (as through a kind of angled squint), is somehow softened and sentimentalised into a spectacular and slightly insincere ritual play, glorified by lighting, crowds, and well trained "leads".

Moralities

IN the teaching and thought of the medieval church qualities good and bad assumed almost a personal being. All creation spoke with meaning—allegory and figurative interpretation of every actual visible creature and event accustomed them to thought, as it were, on two levels. The reverse process was only a natural corollary—abstract qualities could easily assume bodily and visible reality. Virtues and vices looked at them from the wall paintings, the images of saints, or leering devils of gargoyle and misericord. Even if each individual devil did not itself suggest a particular sin or temptation as one looked at a mystery play, or picture of hell-fire and its torments (perhaps even one's own particular failing), some became more specifically known— the Seven Deadly Sins. These qualities, real as Bible characters, began to enter into the religious plays once the personal problems involved were more fully dramatised. So the devil tempts Noah's wife to resist her husband. In later plays the particular kind of temptation—Pride or Gluttony—is named and introduced as a character. Further, as interest moves to the individual struggle, and the personality of a man is analysed in its earthly warfare, the other powers and abilities appear on the stage—Strength, Discretion and Wisdom. The whole experience of humankind is shown, with its struggles and problems, on the stage. This is the first consistent effort to show the complexities of character —but instead of presenting the action of contending individuals, the warfare within man and woman, and the forces in operation against them, are dramatised. Since the aim of faith was to enable each to work out the salvation of his soul, this was still in the tradition of the religious drama. Further, images and assumptions were those upon which this had been founded. The medieval concept of Deadly Sins, the fear of Death, the urgent quest of right relations with the whole supernatural world, must be kept in mind as you study and produce the plays and, further, the visual images with which the characters and motive forces are linked. Many of your problems in costume and décor will be solved once you place the plays securely in their context.

The plays which most clearly encouraged this study of the strife of the individual were the "miracles" based on the lives of saints; we have few of these in Britain and it is only to be expected that the development of the morality play owed something to influence from the Continent. Indeed, our greatest English morality is based upon a Dutch original. None the less, once the form was established it became a major dramatic influence and style, which existed not only in its own right, but shaped and entered into other drama in various ways, down to our own time, when there seems to be a revival of this kind of dramatised personal struggle.

One must differentiate the various "actors" in the morality plays. First there are those which typify qualities—Good Fellowship, Mammon, Pleasure. Then come the "divisions" of man's personality, his own possessions as a thinking and feeling organism—Strength, Beauty, Five Wits, Discretion—which (put together) represent the whole man, the entire character. Finally, there are the "superhumans" —God, Death, and angelic visitants. The form is found early in Germany where a twelfth-century "Ludus de Antichristo" includes characters who represent paganism, hypocrisy, and the synagogue. The same tendency is found in the mystery plays—those of the Coventry cycle introduce truth, mercy, and peace—but a Norwich play of the fourteenth century, including allegorical characters, indicates that the morality play made possible, and fostered, a new development in theatre, for to this play is added the note "ix may playe it". We envisage a team of actors, who perform such a play perhaps in the halls of the nobility and on village greens. The morality encouraged the start of professionalism in theatre because it was a fairly short play which could be toured and which was satisfying and complete in itself. Dramatists could construct their plots with symmetry round their theme; they were not hampered by irrelevancies which had to be inserted because part of Bible narrative or Saint's life. They could deal with the character and adventures of mankind as best suited (a) acting space and resources, (b) the personnel of the group, (c) the considerations of balanced plot—with due regard for humour and effect, costume and dance. Approach these plays with the realisation that they are skilled dramatic work—for a theatre whose conventions differ from ours, but all the more valuable on that account, not to be cast aside as outmoded and quaint. For the morality contains within itself the future developments of British theatre, and its effects are still with us. Indeed, we might claim that many dramatists are returning to the morality play and the dramatic presentation of the strife within the individual. Nor is this a matter of script only; in style, setting, make-up, movement, the patterned angularity and conscious formalism, as well as occasional strident realism, plays of our time return to "morality" theatre.

During the later fifteenth and early sixteenth century this form, which was so urgently concerned with the individual struggles and dilemmas, naturally explored more and more carefully and in further detail the life around it, so that gradually "naturalistic scenes" from everyday life occur, as in *Wealth and Health*. Again, as the power of the Church and its scheme of man's salvation was questioned and challenged by other possible bases for individual struggle, so these other "philosophies" (however embryonic) began to fill the background and to relate to the soul's adventures. Science and travel, politics and controversy, are introduced in personification. So we find the anti-Catholic *Lusty Juventus* or such themes as Redford's *Wit and Science*. In the sixteenth century, again, men's minds were busy with examination of their own past and its relevance to present arguments. History, too, was therefore incorporated. Looking back on Bale's *King Johan* we may be tempted to see it as a history play into which some morality elements were incorporated. From the viewpoint of its own time, it was probably an established form of theatre, into which historical figures now entered, naturally and inevitably. As time went on, dramatists smoothed out the varied pattern by allowing "real" characters to speak the sentiments uttered by the old morality figures. "Popery" was supplanted by a historical legate, and "everyman" time and again by the characterised commentator who (more or less powerless in the great matters of state which are now the subjects of the play) is the "average person"—for the emphasis has moved from individual salvation to the welfare of states, as nationalism supplants the old medieval ideal of Christendom.

We must take this form of theatre seriously, and try to appreciate its variety and excitement. It is different from our preconceptions of theatre —but it exists in its own right, not merely as an imperfect ancestor of our own. How far it influenced the Elizabethan theatre is apparent immediately one glances at *Dr. Faustus* or the allegorical plays and figures in later Jacobean drama. The grotesques, the essentially "theatrical" figures, are still there. So, too, are song, dance, spectacle, and supernatural beings.

ORIGINAL STAGING

Some think that (ideally) a three-level acting area was used— the lower level representing hell, or the grave; the middle, earth; and the upper, heaven. The analogy of the mystery plays, with their hell mouth on ground level, would suggest some such arrangement. In addition, one would normally try to place God and His angels on a higher level to secure authority and clarity for His pronouncements. On the other hand, pictures of performances in halls during the later Middle Ages show the use of a simple platform with curtained entrances—an easy and logical use of existing conventions. One calls to mind the pageant wagon—which was a raised stage. One remembers the "mansions" grouped around the open space used by all. On the simple platform the entrances (labelled with the names of the appropriate characters) are the "mansions" from which actors emerge on to the "platea"—big or small according to the size of the hall. Admittedly the plays thus depicted are often of a more secular character—revivals of Roman comedy for example—but the morality itself was merging with secular interests, and clearly uniting in performance with the interlude played in noblemen's homes. Ways of presentation would spread, merge, and compromise, as they did finally in the Elizabethan theatre itself. The use of such a convenient curtained stage would not preclude the use of a lower (or floor) level, or of a higher speaking place in a gallery above for God. The problem is well illustrated by *Everyman*. Towards the end, he gazes into the grave, and the text might be interpreted as indicating the need for a lower level. Yet the words "into this cave" are not quite decisive, even if we accept the literal Latin sense of "cava"; even "sinks into his grave" is perhaps more suggestive of prostration on the stage, rather than a physical descent, especially as soon afterwards an angel enters to elevate Everyman to Heaven. The time interval in the text suggests rather a mimetic death than a physical descent to a lower stage, followed by a rather hasty (as those who have produced the play know) ascent nor merely to the original, but the heavenly, stage. The full three-tiered scheme of presentation is eminently suited to elaborate and spectacular productions in large open spaces or town squares, such as are found on the Continent. When *Everyman* has been thus produced it has often been with additions and a general broadening of the whole scope of the play—the simple outlines have been filled. Small troupes of semi-professionals would, however, find the available platform and hangings of a hall the normal and obvious way of staging. Out of doors the elevation provided by trestles and planks might well afford all they really needed. Some drapings for the back, and perhaps the sides, would be provided, in the style of the pageant plays. The association of such presentation with *Everyman* is indicated by a surviving illustration of an Everyman group of characters, seated on a curtained platform barely distinguishable from a pageant wagon. In fact, the first professionals might well (where roads were good enough) have pulled their belongings from village to village in a cart and have used this in performances. The smaller moralities, of the British tradition, would, I think, have some simple method of performance.

But simplicity of staging does not preclude elaboration of costume, make-up, and calculated effect. The five virgins in white kirtles, with "wigs and chaplets" who enter and sing in *The Morality of Wisdom*, the masquers and dancers who may be added at the end of such a play, all indicate the tendency to fuller expression where possible, and to develop the dramatic genre to its uttermost. Simple plays (almost stark in theme and character planning) could always be the centre-piece of carefully organised spectacle—especially when transferred to Court or the hall of a powerful nobleman. Further, as time went on, the morality (attracting to itself as the most typical theatrical form all the other and newer tendencies in dramatic expression) could become almost overwhelmingly ornate—especially when some compliment was to be paid or some controversial subject to be treated. Processions, courtly rituals, and dances, could be incorporated. Later court moralities merged almost imperceptibly, with a change of emphasis, into the Court mask. Best known, of such elaborate and developed moralities, is the mid-sixteenth century *Satire of the Three Estates*, where the title indicates contemporary struggle. The issue is amongst the great powers, although poor John Commonweal is given ultimately a place of honour. For such productions all the resources of the acting place could be used; Tyrone Guthrie's production for the Edinburgh Festival followed fittingly the original emphasis of presentation. But, after all, the typical morality is best remembered from the conversation when the wandering players visit the home of Sir Thomas More in the play of that name:

MOORE: Whom doo ye serve?
PLAYER: My Lord Cardinalles grace. . . .
MOORE: I pre thee tell me, what playes have ye?
PLAYER: Divers my Lord: The Cradle of Securitie.
    Hit nayle o'th head, impacient povertie,
    The play of four Pees, decies and Lazarus.
    Lustie Iuuentus, and the mariage of witt and wisdome.
MOORE: How manie are ye?
PLAYER: Foure men and a boy, Sir.
MOORE: But one boy? Then I see
    Ther's but fewe women in the play.

APPROACH TO PRODUCTION

What is the *essential* theme of the play? This question, which the producer has always to decide for himself, is nowhere so clearly answered as in the morality—for it is a play on a theme, an idea, round which the various forces are grouped, and to the exposition of which each makes his essential contribution. For a young director the morality play is a valuable experience; here is a pattern of action, and through it all is a theme, a linking thread, Moreover, in the earlier moralities this is expressed in simple and direct statement. Yet because of the difference in attitude between our own age and that in which the play was first presented, the theme is often today confused or weighted and lost beneath an overlay of twentieth-century assumptions. The producer should make out a simple plan before he starts his detailed work, a kind of skeleton which may afterwards be clothed with detail and gradually shaped into a living body, to receive his particular adornment and clothing.

It is for lack of this essential consideration that so often such a splendidly constructed play as *Everyman* is muddled in presentation, and the producer feels bound to add all kinds of "gimmicks" in a vain effort to interest his audience. In some productions the only real climax occurs at the start, when after a long and often badly delivered address by "God", Death appears; here the moment of horror is seized and exploited. But after that action tails away—and the final scene of dissolution is garbled with naturalistically grouped "entities" cluttering the stage. Construct your plan. (i) God's statement. (Study the speech and you will see that this falls into various parts, all clearly to be marked by vocal change.) (ii) the summoning of Death and the commission: (iii) Death fulfils his commission to Everyman: (iv) Everyman is appalled by the message: (v) he turns to Good Fellowship: (vi) to his relations: (vii) to his possessions . . . He is now in complete despair. Then comes the turning point of the action: (viii) he turns to his spiritual assets—first, his Good Deeds: (ix) Knowledge and wisdom come to his aid. Now the upward path is begun: (x) he begins to cleanse away his faults; he goes to confession: (xi) he fulfils his penance —the correct ecclesiastical procedure is indicated: (xii) his duty done, his Good Deeds can now help him: (xiii) he is ready to go on the journey —the climax approaches. The coming of death in actual event is presented with complete and accurate detail. The whole man is shown, with his physical powers, his outward beauty, his five wits, and his faculty of judgment. He lies sick; the essential being is, of course,

Everyman who stands and moves; although the naturalistic "fact" would be shown by a man "lying sick", the morality presentation shows the complex *reality*, with actors who move and argue. His physical strength leaves him. In real life he goes to his couch, exhausted, as one does at the start of an illness. He loses his good looks. In "reality" he is wasted by disease as it gains hold on him. Gradually, he loses sight, taste, hearing, sense of smell, and touch, so Five Wits departs. His power of judgment goes—on the stage, Discretion leaves him; he is no longer able to decide and think for himself. But the soul remains, living. The character of Everyman is still before us. Only two things are with him—the Knowledge that has guided him to do the right things in time, and the Good Deeds he has achieved. (xiv) The moment of dissolution comes. Everyman commends his spirit to God. He is seen no more—Knowledge points the moral. Only Good Deeds is with Everyman now. (xv) The moment of triumph— Everyman appears in glory. Before and after the play the moral is introduced and pointed by prologue and epilogue. The statements are quite clear. But unless the players observe the plain purpose of the play, their work will be wasted. If they cannot accept its actions and theme and "over-motive" they might as well not try to act it—or any other play for that matter which they would present only with reservations. It is curious that actors are often willing to act in a naturalistic play which contains events and characters far removed from their own opinions and tastes, yet cannot approach a period play in a similar spirit, accepting it as something which has to be sincerely presented, but not necessarily representative of their own views. Understand the assumptions of the play; whether you agree with its theology is irrelevant. For the purposes of presentation you are willing to identify yourself, temporarily at least in the process of production, with Lear, Cordelia, Ariel, Bottom, Pastor Manders, Mother Courage, Thomas Becket. Yet some seem at times unable to accept the morality on its merits as a dramatic work for presentation in theatre.

There is the simple plan of action. The theme is the salvation of Everyman, his triumphal progress through the experience of Death. The climax is not the arrival of Death's summons, but the successful vanquishing of the danger. The moment of crisis is the actual deathbed scene, drawn with all its detail to show the breaking up of the whole human personality. Consider carefully how you will make this experience, which they are going to suffer themselves, absolutely clear to the audience. See that their interest is held, and successfully led to the happy denouement, with its warning of dangers scarcely overcome. For the play aimed to impress by its "realistic" presentation of human death. The appearance of "Death" as a separate entity is only a preparation for that, the real strife.

So the producer marks out the pattern of action—the first summoning, the increasing anxiety with the small intervals before each new attempt to find aid—and the final despair. Then, by pause, attitude, lighting, he marks the "turn":

> I think that I shall never speed
> Till that I go to my Good Deeds. . . .

From then on, through succeeding stages of effort, the way opens more and more clearly to final success. How do we mark the actual death process? The complete man must be indicated by some patterned grouping, from which various attributes detach themselves. Further, the "man" must be separated from the "heavenly qualities"— Knowledge and the Good Deeds—which alone will survive with the essential being of Everyman. For clarity, ritual and stylised grouping is here appropriate. This is the simplest form of stage grouping; normally, actors are positioned in asymmetrical positions, to secure emphasis and an overall "picture". But it is often useful, even when producing a naturalistic play to start with actors arranged symmetrically, and then to ask yourself how best you can disarrange the regularity to secure emphasis and dominant placing of key figures. The morality is a useful starting point for production technique here also.

How can the real quest and mounting fulfilment of the play be emphasised for the audience today? If you have a large cross suspended by thin wires (see the suggested setting, Fig. 9) this can be used as a visual accompaniment to the voice of God, being brightly lit while He speaks, and then left in darkness as we move to earth where Everyman has forgotten him. Directly Everyman begins to turn to Him, a little light glows upon the Cross. The turning point is marked —and the light gets stronger and stronger until the moment of death when the Cross is bright against a dark background. When Everyman reaches Heaven the whole area round it is lit showing Everyman and the angel kneeling before it. Thus lighting intensifies and points the quest and triumphant conclusion. Again a simple exercise—which can be kept in mind when more involved modern plays are produced.

Thus start and end are linked. God calls—and Everyman returns to God. The essential crisis is shown.

Gimmicks are sometimes used in presentation. One suggestion has been (copying a much longer and more sophisticated version of the play) to have the figure of Death hovering around all through the play. The producer finds the first shock of Death's appearance—complete with skull-like face and bony skeletal make-up, white bone shown on black background which merges into dark hangings, or unlit darkness—so dramatic that he cannot bring himself to dispense with the figure. But, surely, this is to mistake the whole purpose of the play? The thought of death comes to Everyman. He knows he is to die—and the whole intent of the play is to show

Fig. 9.—BASIC SETTING FOR *EVERYMAN*

death, the real thing, not the bony bogey, but the reality, moment by moment. To keep the almost naturalistic depiction moving around is to destroy the play and to admit that its conventions and methods are for you ineffective.

Another suggestion is that one can show the universality of the play by costuming in modern dress. But what of the language? Surely that remains medieval, and demands medieval moves and gestures by its very rhythms? And is not medieval costume associated in our mind with the timeless dogmas and faith of the Church? However, the transposition into a form of modern attire may well enforce some aspect of the play. By distortion of this kind a new vision may be gained or the audience alerted. Choose for the right reason, that thus you hope to present the play better, not merely for novelty. At least, however, try to be consistent. If the characters are dressed in jeans and sweaters, do not bring on medieval angels laden down with massive feathered wings. Let the angels be, as their name indicates, simple "messengers", clad unobtrusively in modern style. *Everyman* has been taken as an example because of its popularity and perfection of construction (despite some apparent deviations—e.g. the conversation on the morals of contemporary clerics, actually delightfully fitting the moments while Everyman is off stage). All moralities must be studied fully, and their action and theme settled before the start of production. The *Morality of Wisdom* moves from dignity and ritual grace to a wild and jarring rout of revellers—and the essential tragedy of the transition must be emphasised. Don't pull your punches, if you wish to deal honestly with the play. Again, the desired centrality and importance of John Commonweal in *The Satire of Three Estates* must be marked, despite the allure of the pomp, circumstance, and subsidiary episodes. The producer's problems become more complex in such a very elaborate play; he may find that he has to choose what theme (or themes) he will present—the original text may be too involved for the modern audience to absorb—or the author may have too many characters and subordinate considerations for clarity in modern production. Cutting may be essential. Admittedly the *whole* play will not be presented, but, curiously, the essential play may be, if the cutting is wise. Script is subordinate to performance. The producer's concern is to use it to present the author's intention as far as he can. If this involves omitting certain parts, we accept the need. On the other hand, omission which purposely distorts and alters can never be accepted. Omission need never do this. The normal short morality invites addition rather than cutting, a temptation usually to be avoided. Clarifying through movement and lighting and grouping is not addition, but revelation, unless it gets completely out of hand. The wild dance at the conclusion of *The Morality of Wisdom* could become a mask in its own right with further allegory; such a development would distort and lessen the impact of the play as a whole.

SETTING FOR MODERN PRODUCTION

Movements and grouping of characters suggest at once the desirability of using different levels and/or rostra. Consideration of the original staging supports the idea. Obviously where it is feasible to employ, without obvious antiquarian rather than theatrical choice, some of the physical features of the original performance one is able to present more quickly and easily the essential drama—for it was with such a stage in mind that the whole was contrived, written, or improvised. Next, the patterned action, with forces acting one way or another on the human being, and the formal plotting, with the need for clarity in establishing the semi-ritual figures, leads one at once to suggest curtained entrances or perhaps arches as methods of access to the stage, since each can be associated with a certain character or group of characters. Again, this naturally accords with medieval convention. The brevity with which the abstractions establish themselves, using a few simple words, really presupposes some such method—the script demands the setting. The audience can be helped by décor that communicates, and sets attitude and atmosphere—whether in the hangings, colour, shape of arches, or imaginative backcloth with medieval lettering or formal emblems. See the setting for *The Interlude of Youth* in Nicoll's *Development of the Theatre* (Fig. 164). For such imaginative décor reproductions of medieval manuscripts and altar pieces can be studied. In costume the flamboyance and conscious angularity of medieval presentation should be remembered. The individual mattered little as a separate human being in this world. There is little or no portraiture between the Greco-Egyptian mummy portraits and the dawn of the Renaissance. What does matter is his soul—and the tangible and intangible forces which strive around him, against him, and for him, in the world. Naturalism—the insistence on beguiling personal characteristics, the little details of everyday domestic warmth and humour—is out of place. Effects are broad. But this is by no means to say that this drama is an unworthy form or lacking in subtlety; it is just different, and perhaps the most delicate means of expressing some of the living experiences and problems of man that has yet been devised. Costume should be planned in accord with general background and the movements characters have to make. Once again, illustrations and illuminations from the period aid you. Consider grouping—what shapes of headdress and costume will be seen together? You have a rich variety to choose from—even within the medieval period itself accurate concord of style was not demanded in costume. Clothes lasted longer, and the "fashionable" and "out-of-date" could be seen together. Further, in your designs there may necessarily be an element of fantasy, and the special message of these strange incarnations of the subconscious or the superhuman. Suggested books of reference are given in the appendices.

A possible setting which combines medieval conventions with an attempt to secure relation to the dogmatic assumptions and attitudes of the play *Everyman* is shown. (Fig. 9). In practice this proved very flexible and allowed clear portrayal of events, distinction of characters, and smooth flow with easy pointing and emphasis when necessary.

Further, the units can be taken down and erected on platforms or stages of varying size, since the backing is a cloth which can be made the maximum width and length needed and arranged to fit smaller stages; there are no flats to be fitted, simply standing arches. Equally, such a setting can be used without any pre-existing platform or picture frame, and is possibly better thus. In this case, the stage is placed along one wall of the hall, or against the side of a house during outdoor performance, and aisles are provided through the audience by which actors reach the stage.

For those whose thoughts turn towards "theatre in the round", a compromise may be suggested—so called "avenue arena", which accords with the processional and ritual nature of much early drama. For many morality plays also the idea of a journey through life can well be represented with such an "avenue". Briefly, a small stage or platform exists at each end of the hall. One can be used for Heaven, the other either for the ordinary world, or the lower regions. Through the hall from one platform to the other stretches an uninterrupted "avenue". In the middle, rostra may be placed to facilitate grouping and pointing of events and characters. In *Everyman*, one platform might well represent Heaven. Here God's voice is heard, and from here Death sets out. Here, too, Everyman ends his journey. He enters on the other platform—after Death has made his own journey from God through the hall, reminding each member of the audience of their own danger. Main action may take place in the "avenue" and round the central rostra, while the discarded helpers, Fellowship, for example, return to the second platform and the darkness. Such a setting can be highly symbolical, reinforcing the whole pattern of action.

While the settings discussed have particular reference to *Everyman* the requirements and action plans of the ordinary Morality plays are basically much the same. They were designed and acted on much the same stages. Where a hell-mouth is needed the same scheme may be adopted as for Mystery Plays. With the more developed and formal style of the morality, however, it might be suitable to provide two "devils' entrances", one on each side of the platform. This will at once give greater flexibility in grouping and movement. There is the possibility of reversion more completely to that form of medieval staging indicated by *The Castle of Perseverance*, and described by Richard Southern in his book *Medieval Theatre in the Round*. The use by the morality of this fairly generally accepted method of presenting religious plays is clearly established, and in open-air performance, with adequate space, might well be revived today. In the previous

chapter I have tried to make some suggestions, based on practical
experiment in this convention of presentation, which may help the
producer who intends to attempt it. Disciplines of grouping and
moving, ritual attitude, and the formal significance of the "houses"
and acting areas, must be agreed and accepted. Colour schemes and

Fig. 10.—CORONATION OF HENRY IV
Based on an illustration in Knight's *Old England*

crowd effects will require equally careful planning and realisation. So,
too, will the seating and demands of the modern audience.

Finally we must still recall the essential dignity of medieval ceremonial and gesture. Fig. 10 showing the Coronation of Henry IV,
illustrates grouping and attitudes—and interesting architectural features.

Interludes and Variety Entertainment

WHEN the established companies of actors found regular employment failing in the fifth century, when barbarian invasions and disorganisation prevented the leisure and taste which allowed audiences to assemble, they had to adapt themselves to changing conditions. None the less, the professional is a tenacious being—and performances were still being given in Rome up to the time of the Lombard invasions. In the Eastern Empire the mimes continued. In the West they could hope only for the rich patron, whose villa or "castellum" might furnish the security and audience previously found in the great cities; alternatively they could tour from place to place, gathering audiences as they went. Thus in the villa of Sidonius at the threshold of the sixth century, performances of Terence were still given. The opposition of the Church has probably been exaggerated. Although such cultured and classically-minded ecclesiastics as Sidonius were increasingly rare, the tradition of "Romanity" survived, and never really perished, in France. The fulminations of more Puritanically-minded priests are not really any more violent than those directed against the flourishing Elizabethan theatre, and serve the useful purpose of witnessing to the survival of secular drama. The professionals who sought food from the great lords tended to be more and more absorbed into the general body of retainers, from which the professional companies were later to emerge nearly a thousand years later. Only one or two held a specialised position— the court jester or fool may be the descendent of one of the Roman mime characters. He alone could preserve the satiric thrust or pointed buffoonery of the old classical comedy in the real Dark Ages which were yet to come when the Danes and other Northmen—surely almost the most unpleasant people the world has yet seen—were to wreck with their truculent barbarities the re-emerging civilisations of Europe. Only the clever man, regarded as a fool and using the protection of his guise, could survive. On the other hand, those who went on tour naturally worked with diminishing personnel. Death, illness, hardships, thinned the numbers as they toured from town to town. The fewer, the more mobile. Again, entertainment had to be varied to suit their audience—the Roman theatre had its animal acts, jugglers, rope dancers—and it was this kind of entertainment that kept the attention of the country people. From being the petted darling of a generous state, kept by government funds, the actor had become almost the "rogue and vagabond", outside the normal plan and pattern of society.

As secular elements entered the miracle plays in France, and as the

Fig. 11.—LATER MEDIEVAL COSTUMES
Based on an illustration in Knight's *Old England*

morality encouraged the growth of a regular troupe with a repertory of such plays, the existing entertainers, survivors of the old professionals, could merge with them. Yet the secular drama had survived. Even in Britain there is a remnant of an Interlude concerning "a cleric and a girl"—an old, old, story. Small wonder that we have few existing manuscripts, when the Church had (in this country) a kind of monopoly in setting down written records. The performance of such secular pieces was possible on "feast" days, on the one hand, in the market-place or fairground; on the other, in the hall of a great person. The social occasion is for ever linked with the "variety turn" to which such "interludes" were doubtless a support. What was an interlude?

When it emerges into recognisable form at the Renaissance it is a playlet—not very long—presented at a feast or banquet. Whether it is so-called because it is an "entertainment" (ludus) played between the courses or ceremonies of a banquet (other entertainers might also be there—singers and dancers, story-tellers and musicians), or whether it derived its name from the "ludus" (game) between ("inter") two speakers, seems undecided. In medieval times the talking of one person against another was a well known diversion—a half serious, half comic, exaggerated "back-chat" act, ancestor of all the double acts of quarrelling comedians. By the early sixteenth century it had added further

Fig. 12.—TUMBLER

characters, though the "double act" was still common. As it thus developed, and added content from current affairs, it gradually approached the morality form, which was abandoning the narrowly religious theme for a much wider contemporary interest. The two forms ultimately coalesced or became lost in the welter of varied and infinitely ingenious dramatic activity of the mid-sixteenth century. But the interlude at its best has vivid appeal, a strong and attractive theatrical style of its own, and seems to have returned today in the rumbustious comedies of social comment and outrageous frankness sponsored by our more advanced theatre groups. Again it is one of those uninhibited and comparatively uncomplicated forms in which the actor and director may learn some of their business. A great difference between the interlude and the morality proper is that the former introduces real characters—even if they are types, a typical housewife, parson, pardoner, schoolmaster. This is the stuff of what we have come to call "music hall", with vivid relevance to the life of our time, the everyday events, vulgarities, stock situations, and annoy-ances—women's talkativeness, man's hypocrisy, the squalling child, the "over-the-garden-wall" gossip. The form is absorbed at times into other and more important dramas, as were the interludes into "moral interludes", then into involved pseudo-historical moral plays, which yet kept the comic scene almost detached from the rest of the play, and so into the Elizabethan drama proper. One must add that the knock-about act (which is distinct) came rather from the horseplay of the mysteries than from the "society entertainment" of the interlude.

THE PRODUCER'S APPROACH

No need here to construct a carefully worked plot of the action. There is one simple point—and the conversation which works up to it is in itself the plan of action. There is much greater need to under-stand and appreciate the points made, and to secure clear well delivered

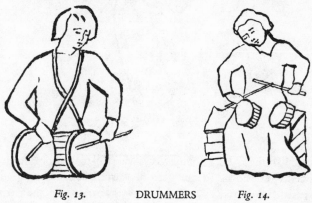

Fig. 13.   DRUMMERS   *Fig. 14.*

speech, with a strong sense of character. Quite simply, the producer has to discover exactly what the joke is. To what point does the course of conversation and action lead? Heywood was the most famous writer of interludes—a professional entertainer. He held a place, we learn, under Henry VIII as one of the "lusores regis". Here we see the re-emergence of the professional troupe in the court of a ruler—with whose representative a thousand years before their forerunners had taken refuge. The interlude form reached its greatest popularity during this period of re-emergence. Soon, the professionals would have their own theatres and be presenting full-length dramas, and at court itself the more elaborate presentations would oust or incorporate the simple short interlude. Theatre would exist in its own right, not only as part of a variety entertainment at a time of festivity. Let us look at Heywood's best known piece—*The Playe called The foure P.P.* True to its genre, this interlude presents four typical characters, everyday yet of unfailing interest to the people of later medieval and Tudor times—a pardoner, a "potycary" (apothecary), a palmer (or pilgrim), and a pedlar. Briefly, they enter upon a contest to see who can tell the biggest lie. When the palmer announces that he has travelled all over the world, but he has never seen a woman vexed or out of temper, the others concede victory to him. The common (or accepted) differences in behaviour as between men and women are a fundamental theme and assumption in such entertainments as the interlude, as they are in "music hall" and all folk entertainment. (Recall the additional material which attached itself from the imagination and experience of the actors and audience to the story of Noah, or to the conversation of the shepherds.) There is nothing subtle, but commonly observed and accepted characteristics, which (and this is the test of their validity in face of all psychological argument and theory) find immediate response and "acceptance" by the audience, both male and female. Nor is there any controversial issue—all enjoy the presentation of their own weakness or faults, and welcome a little extra ammunition for the sex-warfare which is part of the pleasures of living and loving. That is not to say that there is not developing subtlety in character presentation—as in *Johan Johan*, also probably by Heywood. On the whole, however, effects are broad and rather in the convention of the "variety" stage than of straight theatre. This should, perhaps, be the producer's first consideration. He may afterwards modify as he and his actors work on the play. Costume, gesture, dialogue, grouping, should be bold and free. Further, the essential jest must be carefully contrived and pointed—even if it doesn't seem at first very amusing. If played with zest and the determination to "believe" in the importance of the situation or comic issue, the play will live and, moreover, the audience will accept it as genuinely entertaining. The interlude for younger and less experienced actors gives valuable training in the disciplines of the stage. When actors are led too soon into modern naturalistic plays, they sometimes complain that they do not believe in the character, or that they themselves would not have behaved in that way, and despite all help and encouragement go through the part in a way that indicates their lack of real co-operation with the dramatist or the producer. Yet they do all that is required of them—externally—in moves and vocal expression. The actor's task is not to agree with the behaviour of his character or expressed opinions of persons in the play—his task is to enter imaginatively into the situations and attitudes, to share and to portray, whatever means he may use to achieve this end. Unfortunately, the issue is obscured in more developed plays—and the fundamental discipline of acceptance and sincere co-operation is lost in a welter of "rationalising" about motives, probabilities, the merits of the producer, or the general content of the play. Of course, there are good scripts and bad scripts. But once a part has been accepted, the actor must do his best with it, however weak or improbable it seems. Because even the worst "part" has emerged from human experience and observation he will find necessary points of contact in his own experience. The producer must clear this matter with his actors at the first examination of the play. Curiously—or not—when the interlude is played for all it is worth, it will be found, even by the supercilious, to be worth a great deal!

It may be better not to start with a reading of the text, but after a few indications of the characters and the general style of the play, to have some preliminary practice in movement and character, in a general sense. Speech emerges from character and situation, so let the actors try out some possible movements for the confident pardoner who hawks his spiritual wares from town to town, and can speak so eloquently and persuasively as a salesman at a country fair, a sharp practitioner with an appearance of generosity and simplicity, but always with inner knowledge (which he cannot quite conceal) that he is really concerned for his own monetary advantage. The pilgrim is sincere and slower of speech and movement—he walks through strange lands and has seen strange sights—a man of persevering if somewhat obtuse purpose and sincerity. The pedlar is concerned with all the petty affairs of his trade, rather brash and bold. The apothecary is sharper; a man of scientific practicality and precision, who knows his power. These are mere suggestions—for the apothecary might well be a rather dreamy muddle-headed alchemist. When some such character work has been tried, the actual speeches are studied. Sometimes these fit the elementary characterisation. Sometimes, there is clearly a discrepancy. The very discrepancy indicates the kind of character basis which was in the writer's mind as he wrote. But the fact is that study of the text first will reveal little of the individual physical or mental attributes of the characters, however such a "soaking" in the script is essential (as we shall see) in longer straight plays of character. Even here, however, we can see how various comic actors are able to interpret quite differently lines given to (say) Sir Andrew Aguecheck, Bottom, or merely suggested characters (such as Benjamin in the Quinteros'

Peace and Quiet), revealing possibilities which are equally valid and yet amazingly diverse. Lines have real power only when studied as spoken by an actual human being. Vastly different characters may make the same statements, and yet the statements will have quite a different impact according *to* the character, and will only have impact as proceeding *from* character. They will have *none* if merely recited clearly. Thus preliminary character work is needed, especially when the text gives little definite guidance towards character. Yet the writer (and his audience) had some quite definite assumptions in their mind about the people on stage. One has not necessarily to accept these—so long as one attains some basic concept of the person who speaks the lines.

The producer's further task is to consider the moves and attitudes in relation to costume and the fashion of the time. Contemporary illustrations and modern books of costume will help again. Consider the kind of grouping you will use. Relate the placing of the characters to stage depth, remembering arm positions and costume—the long sleeves of a doctor's gown as he raises his arms upstage towards a focal point, the stylised and comic effect of characters in a straight line gazing rigidly in the same direction, or the grouping of two or three in opposition to the one isolated figure (which can be used in *The Four P's* when each gives his particular statement). Such simple and perhaps rather angular effects are suitable for the interlude.

Here we may mention (though all plays need this care) that the producer should give some consideration to dance and processional movement. The interlude, which is part of a general festivity, can obviously employ such musical introduction or dance conclusion. Moralities and (to a less extent) the earlier mysteries and miracles may also involve the use of dance and secular (as opposed to religious) procession. Information on suitable recordings and reference books for dance patterns will be found below.

The climax should be marked by careful grouping, preparation, exact timing, and vocal pointing. For example, the palmer's winning line will be anticipated by his dominant position on stage, by the anxious attention of the three listeners, and by a slight pause in his delivery (accompanied by a raised hand and arm to enjoin careful listening) before he actually utters the important words. Here, as always, consider restraint as a method of emphasis. It may be that a hushed, almost whispered, utterance, accompanied by a look of bland, pious, innocence, will be much more effective (and create a stronger impression) than a bold, brassy, delivery. Again, the climax must be followed by a moment of shocked immobility. The other characters look at each other

Fig. 15.—PLATFORM STAGE WITH CURTAINED BACKING
Based on a print by Jean de Gourmont

—and their eyes turn slowly to the audience as if to involve them in the whole business of choice. Then, decisively, they concede victory.

ORIGINAL SETTING AND APPROACH TO MODERN SETTING

The simple hall platform, with its curtained entrances for background, is clearly appropriate. An existing picture-frame stage can be adapted. Preferably an apron stage or rostra in front will allow that closer relationship with the audience desirable in plays and sketches of this kind. (It should be noted that some modern revue sketches— such as Harold Pinter's *The Last One* in *Pieces of Eight*—are in fact modern versions of the interlude.) Further, the side wings which are part of a much later style of presentation should be angled, or draped back (as suggested for ritual drama) to give the impression of curtained entrance rather than open alleyways. The backcloth must be considered in relationship with the costumes and grouping. Fundamentally, the interlude setting (although it may obviously be further decorated with hangings or painted devices—just as the old music hall stage with more or less relevant backings and draperies) is really something adapted from the circumstances and locality of a larger festivity; in its original presentation this was simply the platform, gallery, or floor space of the Great Hall or Banqueting Room. When it merged with the morality play, or was taken on tour to towns and villages, it would accept again the simplicities of its environment. The raised

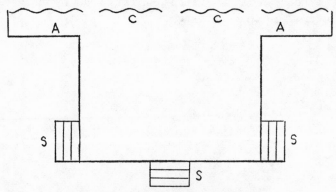

Fig. 16.—INTERLUDE BASIC SETTING (1)
S. Steps to auditorium. C. Decorated Curtains.
A. Small side stages; on these musicians may sit.

platform and simple draped backing would, one assumes, be all that was possible—as in the fair booths and hustings of the sixteenth century and later periods. None the less, or perhaps because of this essential

Fig. 17.—INTERLUDE BASIC SETTING (2)

simplicity, the producer can, with his helpers, devise some very pleasing effects of colour, shape, and atmosphere. Figs. 16 and 17 show a basic setting. Entrances are made between curtains. Performers move freely on the patform or down the steps to the audience when more direct address seems useful. The setting can be built by adding rostra to an existing picture-frame stage.

Renaissance Drama

THE revival of interest in the cultural heritage of Western civilisation, leading back through the Latin authors to Greek thought and literature, had naturally an important influence on the development of drama and theatre. First, there was the realisation that the comedies of Plautus and Terence could, and should, be acted, and the broader outlook, the keen interest of scholars, nobles, and churchmen alike, in the new era, made this possible. Next, the publication of the treatise of Vitruvius on Architecture, including his account of the classical theatre, inspired designs for theatres on the classical plan, as understood or misunderstood by his readers and those interested in restoring something of past grandeur and scope to theatre. At first, this kind of enterprise was not in any way connected with the equally active and changing professional theatre and players. It was the concern of wealthy amateurs, scholars, courtiers, and nobility. In Italy the munificence of the great churchmen helped to restore the theatrical elaboration (for better or worse) which their forerunners had despised or opposed. One was praised for having introduced the "pictured scene"—I quote in literal translation, for the exact meaning is dubious; the exploitation of perspective fascinated the Italians of the period, and we can date the development of "pictorialism" in the theatre from the early sixteenth century. Yet so distinct at first was this theatre from the popular professional troupe, that the latter were proud to call themselves the "commedia dell 'arte" in distinction to the "commedia erudita"—the "professional" rather than the "learned" theatre.

In England, as elsewhere, however, it was not long before interaction and creative compromise encouraged and widened the range of dramatists and actors, professionals, and amateurs alike. Just as in practice a way was found to combine both classical and medieval concepts of theatre building and presentation, so the small bands of professionals soon participated in the new Renaissance drama, and mingled with the learned and the cultured. Clearly, the two or three "professionals" in a large establishment would now be expected to take part in, and to superintend in some measure the technical side of, the more "scholarly" entertainments presented. While the touring "morality" company might visit and perform at the house of a nobleman—as for example Sir Thomas More's home—the great nobility and princes of the church would follow the example of the monarch in developing their own resident company of "lusores". As we know, the fiction that all professional companies were the "servants" of the Lord Admiral, or the "Chamberlain's" men, was kept up—and the actors of Drury Lane at any given time are still technically the "servants" of the reigning monarch. The resident "company" would still be expected to perform moralities, even if

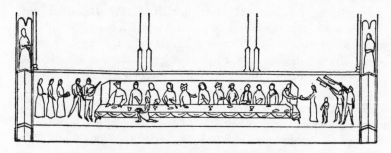

Fig. 18.—A FEAST AT A HIGH TABLE
Based on a brass illustrated in Knight's *Old England*

these were gradually altered in flavour by the new knowledge and outlook. So that a gradual rapprochement became possible between dramatic forms and the professional theatre also acquired something of the "scholarly" heritage for its drama. At the same time, the more ambitious and consciously classical productions remained the responsibility, naturally, of the professional scholar and the amateur production, whatever help might be hired to assist in the donkey work of the presentation.

A striking example is furnished by the work of Henry Medwall, whose play *Fulgens and Lucrece* may serve as a specimen of this early Renaissance drama in England. Medwall was chaplain to Cardinal Morton, and this play was probably written for performance in the cardinal's palace at Lambeth, previous to Morton's death in 1500. Medwall also wrote a morality play, *Nature*, which itself indicates the widening interests of the morality drama in humanistic and scientific themes. In *Fulgens and Lucrece* he uses a story derived from a treatise by an Italian humanist, and translated first into French, and later into English, printed by Caxton. Lucrece has two suitors, one rich and pleasure-loving, the other of humble origin. While the issue is left doubtful in the treatise, Medwall shows how Lucrece chooses the man of virtue rather than the wealthy Publius Cornelius. Although the theme has a morality flavour, the story is purely secular, and the problems of individual and distinctive characters, Fulgens, who though anxious leaves his daughter free to choose, and Lucrece's own act of judgment, are clearly developed. Further, although the story is fictitious, the dignity and authority of classical antiquity is perhaps suggested to predispose the audience to accept the play. Here, too, is something that will be used freely as the new century goes on—a story or plot from any available source which will be reordered to furnish suitable dramatic material. Yet again, Medwall adds a comic underplot, in the tradition of folk comedy, a knock-about episode in which the servants of the suitors contend for the love of Lucrece's hand-maid—the "echo" plot or comic relief to be employed often enough by later dramatists.

That "professionals" were at this time recognised in some sense is indicated by the opening dialogue between *A.* and *B.*

> *A.* Nay, I mock not, wot ye well,
> For I thought verily by your apparel
> That ye had been a player.
> *B.*   Nay, never a dell.
> *A.* Then I cry you mercy . . .
> Amongst these gallants nowaday
> There is much nice array
> That a man shall not lightly
> Know a player from another man.

There was, soon, however, another "professional" element in theatre. Children of the "Chapels Royal" were accustomed by their participation in the ceremonies and festivities, not only of the Church's year, but also during visits by foreign grandees, to "drama" in the broad sense of the word—procession, song, ritual, symbolic enact-ment, and thus could with some ease proceed to present (almost as part of their normal activities) the more formal morality plays, led and encouraged by their "master", who would himself take part. Material or plays specially suited for such young actors developed. Reference may be made to Mr. Philip Coggin's *Drama in Education*, especially chapter IX, "The Humanist Schools". From the amateur side came a similar use of children. Schoolmasters who wished to extend the classical knowledge of the pupils might well encourage them to act Latin plays, where these were within the capabilities and experience of the boys. Drama was seen as a valuable educational aid. From the performance of Latin plays, or new plays in Latin on the classical model, Udall turned to providing his pupils with a vernacular play, *Ralph Roister Doister*, which presented under an English guise some of the typical characters of the Roman comedy. Again, the English taste for compromise and adaptation started a new and fruitful dramatic *genre*. The *commedia erudita* (Roister Doister may well be the *miles gloriosus* of Plautus) merges into the native farce form in the battle between his followers and the household of Dame Custance. Again, the purpose of the play is "mirth"—"Mirth prolongeth life and causeth health" says the prologue. The constant mingling of diverse forms of dramatic activity is realised when we find that Udall contributed to a pageant in honour of Anne Boleyn's coronation in 1533, while Queen Mary in 1554 directed the Office of the Revels, the body responsible for the oversight of play presentation at Court, to supply him with costumes needed for Christmas entertainments. In passing, one should note that in all the plays acted by children, or in the use of drama in school work, the needs and abilities of the children were constantly studied—there was no indiscriminate attempt to exploit children as unpaid actors, or in their school work to do more than to involve them in the kind of situation, play, song, and honest mirth that they themselves would appreciate, either within their own experience or from the work which they carried out as choirboys, ceremonial and festivity which all people knew and accepted.

The first half of the sixteenth century shows increasing compromise and merging of forms—especially in the more popular drama and clearly in plays presented at Court. The titles indicate this, to us, incongruous mixture. Biblical plays, representing the more developed form of mystery, merge into morality, and add farcical comedy. The following titles are typical of the turn of the century, though the plays were actually not printed until a few years later: *The Commody of the most vertuous and Godlye Susanna* uses the Bible story as a basis for morality—the Devil, Ill Report, and Voluptas, all appear in person; *A Newe Enterlude of Vice, Conteyninge the History of Horestes*, by John Pickeryng, indicates the flexible use of the term "interlude" and the merging of the form into the longer play; here we have classical story joining with the medieval "Vice" of the mystery or morality; and finally, *The Lamentable tragedie, mixed full of pleasant mirth, containing the life of Cambises, King of Persia* gives us a typical example of this hybrid drama, later to be satirised by Shakespeare (among others) in the title of the *Pyramus and Thisbe* entertainment before the Duke in *A Midsummer Night's Dream*. Here we have ancient history, with a scholarly and secular origin, alongside morality abstractions—Councell, Murder, Cruelty; and some good native rustic fun in the comedy team of Huf, Ruf, and Snuf, who accompany Ambidexter the Vice; the professional "angle" of the play is apparent when we read the note that although there are thirty-eight roles, six men and two boys may play the whole piece.

On the other hand, plays of "unmixed" erudite style and origin continued. The learned benchers of the Inns of Court sponsored such presentations. Two important developments may be noted. While drama in general used the rhymed verse familiar from the mystery plays, the first attempt at serious native tragedy in what was thought (by the example of Seneca) to be the correct classical mode, was written in the more dignified blank verse—so as to follow, even at some remove, unrhymed classical lines; further, George Gascoigne presented in 1566 his version of Ariosto's *I Suppositi*—using prose as the medium for his comedy. The use of prose by Lyly, by Shakespeare, by Jonson, for comedy was thus anticipated. Meanwhile the more popular drama continued to use the long rhyming lines which it had inherited. Marlowe was to protest from the stage against such "jigging veins". Finally, this aspect also of the "learned" drama would combine with, and condition, the work of popular professional entertainers.

THE PRODUCER'S APPROACH

The producer must be willing to accept the play as it exists and not to demand, or try to achieve, a form of drama more familiar to modern taste. Incongruous and bizarre as the mixture of grave, gay, naturalistic, fantastic, secular, and sacred, may be, this mixture is the play, just as Chinese "opera" mixes conventions and actually contradictory modes of presenting action (e.g. through acrobatic symbolism and subtle stylised mime to music). Curiously we are familiar with, and more or less accept, a similar incongruity in, say, musical comedy of the old Edwardian style—where the transition from seriously emotional and almost tragic conventions to knock-about burlesque is achieved almost instantaneously. There is something of the variety show (from the interlude and court entertainment) in the more typical plays of the period—which is not without effect on almost completely "scholarly" productions. Just as a producer of a modern "pantomime" has to accept all the hodge-podge of contradictory components—farce, solo turn, morality play, fairy-tale, fantasy, and serious emotional situation—so must the producer of the more popular British Renaissance drama accept this as a different style of theatre. Don't reject it because it is different, or attempt to bowdlerise it into something more assimilated to modern expectation. Its success will depend upon your boldness. If you shrink from the play as it stands, you will succeed only in presenting a shadowy and bloodless travesty of real drama.

Play, then, the moral scenes in all their seriousness and with the same sincerity that you bring to a full morality play of the *Everyman* genre. Play the comic scenes for all their robust fun as you would the "Mak and the Shepherds" episode. Play the type characters and caricatures as if they were a variety "interlude". What, then, will unite these apparently diverse elements and dramatic flavours? The period itself united them in its own peculiar experience of drama— and in the sense of period you will also find binding and unifying power today. Not that a meticulous attention to all kinds of minute period detail in gesture and costume will achieve this—but rather the general "remoteness" and "otherness" of the whole theatrical presentation, its pervading style. We do not want to suggest an antiquarian quaintness, but, as before stressed, a different kind of theatre fully accepted.

Look at the woodcut title page of *Fulgens and Lucrece* with its blackletter inscription. "Here is co(n)tenyed a godely interlude of Fulgens Senatoure of Rome, Lucres his doughter, Gayus Flaminius & Publi(us) Corneli(us). of the disputacyon of noblenes. & is deuyded in two ptyes to be played at ii tymes. Copyied by mayster Henry medwall, late chapelayne to t(he) right reuerent fader in god Johan Morton cardynall & Archebyshop of Cau(n)terbury". Many producers realise that such a title copied as faithfully as possible and set out in some way on the programme may help an audience to readjust their dramatic vision, and thus place them in a receptive mood for some different experience. But study further the woodcut below. (Fig. 19.) Note the late "medieval" robes of both man and woman, the increasing squareness of shoulders in the man, and the stiff lines of the heavier material flaring and widening from the waist. Study again the typical ornamentation and the semi-pictorial quality in the decoration of the robes. There is something here of conscious theatrical exaggeration and elaboration as the artist seeks to communicate the pomp and importance of the two characters visually. Just as in words the title page "puffs" the play, so the wood-cut arrests attention by the same means as the theatre itself. This is an example of how the age emphasised and held attention. We shall not be far wrong if our production uses the same trends—the definite shoulder line, the stiffer, angular robes, especially as the Tudor period progresses, the almost symbolic and heavy embroidery. We see, too, the rather striking head-gear, and the very impressive plume—surely a worthy anticipation of the ritual headdress worn by the tragic hero down to the mid-nineteenth century.

Fig. 19.—COSTUME IN A RENAISSANCE PLAY
Based on the title page of *Fulgens and Lucrece*

In grouping, in costume, in general design and pattern, this sense of heaviness and richness can be kept. Most important, the gestures of the characters, weighted by heavy material, show, as the illustration indicates, the same definite and stylised quality. Here we have, from left to right, the hand poised on hip, sleeve well out, the hand raised in protestation almost to the shoulder, the deprecating and warning hand, with index finger pointing at waist level, the hand raised in supporting gesture near the heart. Finger positions also are worth noting and of course the set and poise of the bodies. Although something may be due to the artist's distortion, even the distortion indicates the approach and ideal of the time, which the actor will not fail to use.

As regards the pattern of action, the producer will examine each part of the play, each "plot", and allow these to follow their own course. Comic "interludes" (as we shall see clearly later) are often complete in themselves and are inserted as a recurrent relief to more serious action. These, then, present no problem, so far as overall pattern and presentation are concerned. Where, however, there are two plots the producer may find himself wondering whether the two movements to climax may act in phase or not. If there are apparently conflicting rhythms, clearly the less important must be played down until it becomes a comment rather than a complementary action. The problem may be considered more fully in Shakespeare's plays. The plan of *Fulgens and Lucrece* will serve as an example for earlier Renaissance drama. After the general conversational introduction (in place of the direct moral warning of earlier drama) which discusses plot and theme, we enter upon the main action with the coming of Fulgens. After a little exposition of the main plot, the two argumentative gossips who introduced the drama converse further, rather in the way that comedians will interrupt, from a stage box, the action on stage, pretending to be members of the audience—which is exactly what "A" and "B" do, but purpose also to intrude upon the action itself later. The main action resumes. When Lucrece goes out, "A" approaches Gaius and offers him advice and help in the wooing. "B" also is enlisted. What follows in conversation between the two is almost pure "interlude" with the usual discussion on women and marriage. The maid, looking for Gaius, for whom she has a message from her mistress, is soon chatting with "B", who woos her. As he manages to kiss her, "A" enters, and the two compete for her favour. Wrestling, singing, and finally a comic contest with whatever utensils they can find, do not decide the issue—for the "flower of the frying-pan," the maid, beats them both and goes out. After a further conference with Gaius, the two servants decide that the play must stop for a while—for the sake of the people who sit in the hall

> We may not with our long play
> Let them from their dinner all day.

So the first part ends.

The second half uses the same technique, but is concerned far more with the serious disputation, the long speeches in support of their

wooing by Gaius and Cornelius. The servants come and go, and comment, but their own "wooing" has been played out, and they are left
at the end to make some more earthy comments on love and marriage
(with special reference to the audience), and to point the dual purpose
of the play

> Not only to make folk mirth and game,
> But that such as be gentlemen of name
> May be somewhat moved
> By this example for to eschew
> The way of vice and favour virtue,

and finally to make the usual apology for the actors. What danger
will the producer face? Clearly, that he will allow "A" and "B" to
dictate matters too much. They have a great deal of conversation with
the audience, they have a really comic scene, they are in their own right
amusing characters, and he may feel (with his actors) that the serious
episodes are dull and lifeless compared with this robust and still
topical comment. He had therefore to work deliberately and with
care on the serious passages, to study the rhetoric, the real purposive
argument, urgency, and reasoning, that underlies the long speeches.
Further, by gesture, by costume, and by grouping he must stress the
importance of this main plot and not be diverted into an over-
emphasis on the things that he can easily appreciate. For, and this is
the real point, the comic bye-play and comment will be appreciated
only in its full effect if it serves as a foil to the more serious episodes.
As the anti-mask to the mask, so this is truly entertaining and satirical
when seen as the more "earthy" and time-serving man's reaction
to attempts to live by more enlightened faith and principle. The
same danger is found in the earlier religious plays, where only the
evil qualities sometimes attract, and the good are too often colourless,
only notable for absence of any evil qualities, instead of possessing
the majesty, authority, and compelling force, that the action demands.
The modern presenters have failed to share the assumptions of the
medieval dramatists and audience—and have "produced" the one
part of the play which they found agreeable material, for the depiction
of evil is easier than that of positive goodness. The issue is shirked.

The overall pattern is sufficiently definite in *Fulgens and Lucrece* and
there is no other clash. The main comic action is concluded before the
real climax of the drama. A further entertainment—the entry and dance
of mummers—is introduced in the second half; again we have the
typical appeal to various tastes and the use of different dramatic forms

but as in the later Elizabethan drama this is made to serve as an introduction to important action, a kind of ceremonial prelude to the
solemn disputation, a ritual in itself which must be presented with due
solemnity and the keen attention which the playwright and audience
gave to such discussions. The same general approach, and awareness
of possible distortion, will guide the producer through other plays of
this period, varying though the material is.

ORIGINAL SETTING

The easy interchange of speech with the audience or supposed
members of the audience in *Fulgens and Lucrece* suggests that the
performance was in a cleared space, probably on the floor level of
the banqueting room. This is the view of Dr. Boas in his edition of
the play. At all events such productions would have to be adapted

Fig. 20.—A HALL AND "MINSTRELS" GALLERY
Based on an old view of Leathersellers Hall

fairly easily to the circumstances of whatever locality the players used,
without any elaborate requirements in the way of staging. Further, the
rhetorical nature of much of the script obviates the need for careful
or "critical" grouping. Long solo speeches or duologues take up
quite a large part of the "action", and even where (as in the "wrestling
match") violent action is needed it is between two only. In other

words, these plays were developments of the occasional entertainment or solo speech technique of the "interludes". Only a space for standing is required—not an imagined setting or demands for differing localities and houses. On the other hand, it is hard to imagine, if a dais or raised platform were available, that this would not have been used—unless, of course, it was occupied, as might well be the case, by the chief guests. (See Fig. 21.) The actors would then be on a *lower* level and the sightlines, at least as far as the important visitors were

Fig. 21.—COURT MUMMERS
Based on an illustration in Knight's *Old England*

concerned, would be satisfactory. Again, even then some method of formal entry upon the stage would be almost essential, as the actors announce the coming of the chief characters. With such an early and simple play as *Fulgens and Lucrece* the producer is clearly at liberty to devise his setting as he pleases, remembering that simplicity and directness, and close relationship with the audience, will probably achieve a much more striking result than elaboration. The arguments are appeals to those sitting around rather than to other people on stage; the servants emerge from the bystanders; and the final moral statements are again meant for the audience who have so closely shared the action and enjoyed the song, dance, and wrestling.

Later and more elaborate plays developed, but being intended for performance in hall and house, must still have utilised fairly simple setting. The platform with curtained entrances, the gallery above where available, the emergence into the hall floor when the action suggested the use of a wider space—these things must have been basic possibilities. So, again, the producer should dress his stage rather with the costumes, attitudes, and movements of characters than with

Fig. 22.—STAGING A RENAISSANCE DRAMA
Setting based on the Lyons Terence—1493

elaborate décor. Better if he suggests the period by curtains, devices, and a chair or platform. We may note how little "furniture" is ever required. The bare floor space, an unlocalised "stage", is assumed. The pomp of the original hall, with tapestries and banners might be imitated, but this is rather to create atmosphere and period, not to supply "setting". In general the "erudite" plays followed this simple platform suited to rhetorical delivery, as can be noted in some earlier plays of the University Wits. On the other hand, when needed, devices from the earlier mysteries—such as hellmouth, or the use of a gallery for angels, could be inserted. (See Figs. 20 and 22.)

Elizabethan Theatre

THE building of The Theatre in Shoreditch in 1576 by James Burbage may be regarded conveniently as a significant date in the secure establishment of the professional theatre. From now on the players had their recognised and settled acting places. Further, these "theatres" were specifically for the professional company. This may seem obvious—but we must remember that for years the professionals had been accustomed to borrow or to share accommodation. Certain inns had become theatres in all but name. The inn-yard was a convenient acting place—it provided an open space surrounded by covered areas from which spectators could witness the action. The entry to the yard could be fairly easily controlled by reason of the narrow archway for horse or wagon which led to the street beyond. Thus the casual spectator was discouraged; people could not so easily drift round the acting area and then walk smartly away when the time for payment arrived. There was an enclosed space. Further, the innkeeper was amply repaid by the custom of a thirsty audience, and perhaps even more thirsty players. The gallery on the first floor gave the actors an upper storey from which to work—while a curtain could be draped across the ground level stabling below it. In front, a trestle stage could be erected. Thus the conditions paralleled those already obtaining in the hall and were easily adapted to the performance of morality and interlude. For the companies who travelled, the inn-yard, provided that no authority interfered, was an obvious choice. To prevent the action of civic authority, the troupes retained the protection of some important person. In earlier days, a lord might well give permission for his "servants"—those who normally concerned themselves with the entertainment of his guests—to collect some money for themselves by performances in the villages and towns near his "estate". From such occasional "tours" the companies gradually became almost entirely occupied with making a living by touring their plays. They soon found, however, that local burgesses regarded their occupation unfavourably. Any crowd of people brought together by a play might be unduly

rowdy; in any case, there were puritanical objections to the content
of the plays themselves; players, too, did not belong to the neighbour-
hood and were a dubious and dangerous element. So the travelling
companies had to retain the protection, however nominal, of some
aristocrat or high official. When permanent theatres were set up and
the companies became larger and more powerful, there was still the
same need of status and protection. Thus all Elizabethan companies
were someone's servants—in theory. Proudest of all were His
Majesty's servants—Shakespeare's own company in later Jacobean
times. The custom survives today, and the actors currently performing
at Drury Lane are the servants of the reigning sovereign.

From what models were the early Elizabethan theatre buildings
derived? Many historians have linked them immediately with the
inn-yard, and have based their interpretation of play scripts and
Elizabethan acting methods directly on this assumption. But just as the
plays themselves were of mixed form and reflected several earlier
conventions, so the theatres might exemplify the varying theatrical
practices outlined above, in the section on the Renaissance theatre.
Recent writers have felt that there was no typical Elizabethan theatre
and to interpret plays too narrowly, as if the Elizabethan dramatists
wrote for one particular physical setting, is to destroy the imaginative
richness and flexibility of the Elizabethan drama. Nicoll has linked the
Elizabethan playhouse with the conventions and characteristics of the
pseudo-classical Teatro Olimpico—and indeed the interchange of
travellers, the enthusiastic interest of scholars, might well have influenced
theatre ornament and emphasis of setting towards this Italian model;
Halliday attempts to show that the Elizabethan theatre could have
been derived from a normal medieval method of staging with a fixed
platform and "pavilions" in a circular space. The octagonal shape of,
say, The Globe, and the convention of three levels—upper gallery,
Heaven, platform, earth, and lower level, ground or trap, Hell—has
much analogy with medieval methods, even if not precisely those of
the Cornish "rounds" which Halliday has in mind. Again, we do
know that staging conventions varied. In indoor performances the
"house" convention remained. Sometimes the label or signboard
associated with later medieval methods was used. In the public theatre
the larger area and the two main doors of entrance which appear in the
De Witt drawing of the Swan might indicate a simpler and more
direct approach to the stage—though clearly one side of the stage, or
one door, could be associated (for convenience) with a particular
party or locality. Just as the plays themselves, so the practice of the

theatre at this time inherited from morality, interlude, and drama of mingled conventions; it added rhetorical style from the simpler and dignified erudite theatre of the cultured; it retained all the varied elements of dance, song, physical prowess, and spectacle, which have ever been popularly associated with dramatic occasion and festival; even its personnel was varied—the boy actors who were proving so popular maintained (nominally) a "private" performance in the favoured house—while the professionals in the large open-air buildings necessarily could perform other plays and use more expansive methods than the witty, imaginative, and whimsical, approach of the dramatists who wrote specifically for the children's theatre.

Yet all this need not cause us surprise—though it may demand that we abandon the neat formula and notes dictated to us at school under the heading "Elizabethan theatre". Just as today, the theatre had at its disposal many ways of presentation, varying conventions, and used these as it saw fit.

With the establishment of a permanent theatre and companies, playwrights could hope for surer reward. Theatre was now a commercial and potentially prosperous business. Before this, the professional companies had acquired their scripts or kept to various stock themes, as well as they could. The scholars had written for University and school. The master of the Children of the Chapels Royal had devised his entertainment. But what rewards there were came, as it were, to the whole presentation—not specifically to the author. With the need to attract an audience constantly to one centre came the accompanying need to put on new plays; and attractive plays, too. By the end of three performances the potential audience was almost exhausted; a new entertainment must be supplied. Clearly, it was impossible to give entirely new material—so we find frequent revival —but usually with some new attractions, additional scenes, and embellishments. The characteristic Elizabethan attitude to playscript endured from the days of the touring companies; it was the property of the company, the raw material of their performance, and could be used as they pleased—chopped, changed, rewritten, or thrown away. Yet with all this, new plays must be had—full length, substantial and exciting. There was demand for the professional dramatist. On the other hand, the needy scholars sought an outlet for their talents, and here in the theatre was a possible answer. It is the meeting of popular and erudite theatre that gives the peculiar flavour of early Elizabethan drama, and affords the modern producer and set-designer their ample opportunity. Further, it was the cultured courtiers and

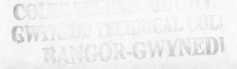

the ordinary people who loved and encouraged the drama. Many of the middle classes tended to be indifferent. Again, therefore, in the audience requirements, there was the same trend towards both the popular and the scholarly. How the Elizabethans met and solved this apparent contradiction is the measure of the universality and dramatic impact of their work. Again, the production of today has somehow to keep the original scope and strength of the action.

At first the scholars took a somewhat superior attitude. Marlowe proclaimed his intent:

> From jigging veins of rhyming mother wits
> And such conceits as clownage keeps in pay
> We'll lead you to the stately tent of war. . . .

From the ordinary vulgar material and hack writers of old professional troupes, and the improvised frolics of the vice and his associates, we shall move to a loftier dramatic theme—and we shall employ, too, that more dignified verse which, for the scholars, was a conscious approach to the grandeur of the unrhymed classical metres. Blank verse will supplant "rhyming mother wits", the uncultured who rely simply on their native understanding. But soon the gradual merging into, and inspiration from, live professional theatre, alter this attitude. Forms and themes were fround which satisfied both scholar and actor, with both popular and scholarly appeal. Thus Seneca, regarded by the scholars generally as the model for tragedy, gave sanction to the violence, bloodshed, and vengeful intrigue, which roused the excitement of the unlettered spectator, linking easily with the virtue and vice, the tyrants and hell-fire of earlier drama. The theme of revenge (familiar in modern drama in the never-ending feuds of the Western films and television plays) was just as popular—it is a basic human situation—in Elizabethan days. Perhaps the most constantly revived play in the earlier period (before 1600) was Kyd's *Spanish Tragedy*—with its ghosts, murders, and the employment of the solitary figure of the Senecan chorus—survivor, in name only, of the original classical "choros". Other blendings of new and traditional followed. Bible stories—Peele's *David and Fair Bethsabe*, folk stories —Peele's *Old Wives' Tale*, Green's *Friar Bacon and Friar Bungay*, and, most typical of all, Marlowe's own *Doctor Faustus*. Yet newer and more topical elements of Renaissance thought constantly found expression in theatre. The beginnings of social comment found in the mystery plays now develop into a fuller expression of·man's relationship with his times and society; while the "tragic" aspect, by which man is set in relationship with the universe, is more fully used now that the dramatic situation and experience is not bounded by the brief and more limited statement of accepted Christian morality and belief. Not that such belief is necessarily challenged; it is rather the development of perception and argument within the confines of that belief, and a constant relating of all this to the individual, that constitutes the poignancy of the tragic drama. So we find the Machiavellian prologue to Marlowe's *Jew of Malta*, the same dramatist's exploration of humanity's desire to be as God in *Tamburlaine*, the interplay of politics with religion in English history—as in *The Troublesome Reign of King John*—and national feelings and interests in the succession of history plays, mere chronicles at first, but becoming more and more fully devised dramatic statements, through the actions depicted, of man's essential and tragic failings, as in Marlowe's partially successful *Edward II*, or the much better conceived and more boldly executed *King Richard III*, whether its sole author was the young Shakespeare or not.

Yet this period, with all its possibilities in imaginative staging, its opportunities for fantasy, its fascinating freshness, has been neglected by modern producers, or when attempted has not yielded its real dramatic wealth, usually because the theme and assumptions of the original play received inadequate consideration, or staging was based simply on a picture-frame convention, restrained and naturalistic. Just to play on an open stage does not give us anything necessarily resembling the real dramatic emphasis of the period. It may hamper us still further! There is not, of course, any completely right or wrong interpretation of any one of these plays. But it is necessary that producer, set designer, and actors, shall approach their task with due thought and real effort to understand the theatrical conventions and methods of the drama they intend to present.

APPROACH TO PRODUCTION

All the plays noted above are worthy of constant revival—difficult though some may be. For purposes of attempting to establish some of the characteristic possibilities in the theatre of the time, briefly study one of the best known. *Dr. Faustus* blends Renaissance and medieval, morality, mystery, popular farce, and developed Elizabethan drama; it includes dance and spectacle, music, grotesquerie, hell-fire and classical beauty, fireworks and high tragedy, piety and the desire of Renaissance man to acquire the power and abilities of God for himself. Some of the most spiritual and developed concepts of evil are placed

alongside crude objective devilry. Whether a great play or not, it
amply illustrates all the varying elements in the drama of the period.
And, like *Everyman*, all too often it fails in performance because the
producer has not attended sufficiently to all the dramatic essentials of
its presentation. Like *Everyman* it can flag in mid-course. The opening
scenes of choice are exciting. The advent of Mephostophilis and the
sealing of the bond, the intervention of Good and Evil Angels, supply
the dramatic clash and resolution which hold the audience, and excite
the producer and actors at first reading. But once Faustus has decided,
what can retain interest? There appear to be somewhat dreary episodes
of wonder working, which, since we accept these as simple stage
actions and not really as magic at all, have little real vitality for us.

Fig. 23.—ELIZABETHAN STAGE
From a sketch of Swan Theatre by De Witt

We look forward rather eagerly to the inevitable—and thrilling—end;
probably all the more because it has been cited to us as something
we should admire, even from our schooldays; and it is good theatre—
rarely do the admonitions of our teachers so coincide with our enjoyment; we feel a sense of achievement and self-satisfaction as we antici-
pate the close of the play. Such an attitude indicates the constant danger
which hampers our efforts to produce plays from an earlier period—
we tend almost automatically to approach them with preconceived
notions and the partial knowledge of school days. We lose focus, we
see only part, and that imperfectly. We ignore the manifold appeal and
varied conventions used in Elizabethan theatre. We forget the love
of spectacle, procession, colour, and costume. It is there that the
Elizabethan audience had their satisfaction as Faustus travels round to
emperor, pope, and duke—it is futile to attempt to produce these
scenes with cheap effect and few actors. The final disaster at least

awakens response. But in mid-course, as Marlowe leads his hero towards his doom, what? Are these scenes meaningless or merely repetitive? On the one side we have the earlier religious plays, with full pomp and ceremonial; on the other the more detailed and better preserved scripts of later Caroline plays which evidence the same almost overwhelming love of procession and regal display, with careful consideration of court ritual and etiquette. Our view of *Dr. Faustus* may surely be guided by this knowledge. The ceremonious conduct of the scene at the Pope's court is hinted at, and is in fact essential if the real farcical point of the action—the complete breakdown of all ceremony—is to be achieved. Again, the court of the Emperor —that semi-mythical figure—is a place of enchantment and significance for the Elizabethan audience. The glory of the earthly ruler is a necessary reference point in the action—here Faustus triumphs, here he conquers all the power in the world—yet he is to be shown cowering and helpless in the realm of the spirit, where "Christ's blood streams in the firmament". The more domestic scene with the Duke and Duchess of Vanholt finds its place in the framework of action. Again we have the pride of the world; but it is the simple and whimsical taste of a woman that is to be gratified; no forts are to be taken, kingdoms destroyed; yet the scene must accord in style and sincerity of purpose with the others we have mentioned. A couple of chairs, a table, and Mephostophilis producing rather miserable fruit, before we hurry on to more exciting matters—I have seen this kind of presentation; and my whole recollection of the production has been by the years reduced to this one irritating scene, which fell away from the rest of the action so gravely. Let there be attendants, ceremony, maids-in-waiting: aggrandise the Duchess and build her personality; let her request come clearly, and with some indication of its difference from the kind of demand she could have made. Above all, let the exit and return of Mephostophilis indicate that he is carrying out a command, one that is part of his solemn agreement; and let the gift be made with due sense of occasion. Whether the scene be treated as semi-comic (I can imagine some Elizabethan performances taking this line) or as tragically solemn, is not the issue. Within a play actions may have varying significance. What is important is that the approach to any one shall be in accordance with the overall style, intent, and pattern, so that Elizabethan full-blooded ceremony, dignity, and sense of dramatic importance, shall not suddenly fall into triviality.

Similarly, the comic scenes must receive care. Play them delicately and with a sense of apology and you deviate from drama into the

tentative reading of an old-fashioned book. Equate them with the
approach of a modern clown or revue comedian (both elements are
found in *Dr. Faustus*) and you will find you have vital, vulgar, and often
incredibly entertaining, theatre. But you do need to "improvise"
the necessary gesture, audience awareness, and store of comic business
which underlie (by common consent) any written script provided for
low comedy. If you look at the actual words set down for a modern
"variety" team, you will understand this at once. The way in which
the clown and Wagner played their scenes is sufficiently indicated by
topics and remarks to the audience. I can think of some music hall

Fig. 24.—ELIZABETHAN COSTUME

comedians (of the twenties and thirties) to whom the script provided
by *Dr. Faustus* would have been a mine of golden comedy, probably
lauded by more intellectual critics. There must be no sense of
apology as you approach these scenes. Admittedly they are different
in atmosphere from the more serious parts of the play—but, as we
have seen, it is just this mingling of conventions that is so typical of
English theatre, both in medieval and later times, which recognises
that life is multiform, and not subject to any rarified abstraction which
leaves men and women as bloodless ideals. So annoyed are some
critics by the intrusion of these scenes that they are tempted to ascribe
them to some other hand than Marlowe's. They may well be—the
play was constantly revised, and "adicyones in fostes" (as Henslowe's

diary has it) were made even by Ben Jonson. Play script was (as we have seen) a "property" to be used as theatrical necessities demanded—cut, altered, adapted. But these scenes are part of the accepted play, whether by Marlowe or not.

The producer may also be confused by the differing versions of the play. These are partly explained by the facts noted above. Further, Elizabethan and Jacobean editions (in general) might be authorised or unauthorised (as in the case of some of Shakespeare's plays). A popular play might exist in several acting versions in script; a publisher might attempt to sell his publication of the play by virtue of its fuller and more recent text. The producer today must accept this Elizabethan flexibility—and use it. Through all the recensions the theatrical sense of the actors retained the essential play—and the modern director, availing himself of the Elizabethan attitude, will select and adapt his own acting version in accordance with his particular needs, so long as he presents the general aspects and import of the drama. The dangers that he may incur if he cuts the very items—spectacle, diablerie, and humour—which the Elizabethans regarded as part of their theatre have been suggested. He will then present nothing convincing or engaging at all. He must accept Elizabethan theatre in its fullness, and then attempt to mediate this fullness and vitality to the modern audience by whatever means he can devise or discover.

Finally, he must try to ascertain what the dramatic point of all the action was. The intellectual aspect, the erudite, is still there in the plays of the popular theatre. There are the incredibly moving and subtle remarks of Mephostophilis—"For where we are is hell." "This is hell"—to be set beside the physical devils and whirling bodily presences of sin. The appearance of Helen is no mere pleasing wraith, no parade of female allure. To some degree it may be the Renaissance concept of beauty—that pagan beauty that dangerously challenged the beauty of holiness and led men away from their faith and Church. But one thing it certainly is—the supreme sin of Faustus, leading to his death and destruction. For Helen is not Helen—she is a devilish appearance, and by intercourse with a devil Faustus commits the most damnable sin. The producer can only see the real impact of the action of Elizabethan tragedy if he studies as carefully as he can what this action meant to the men of the time—and then, again, tries, however he may, to indicate this balance and focus of attention to the modern audience. Not that he explains laboriously, or lectures. But clearly he can so prepare and emphasise the significance of the Helen episode to show the breathtaking lure which Mephostophilis has prepared as Faustus once more seems likely to repent, Faustus' satisfaction, wonder and trepidation, lost in ecstasy at Helen's beauty, and the final quiet satisfaction of Mephostophilis as the loveliness of Helen overcomes Faustus. It is this constant attention to the dominant theme of the play, the strife of Good and Evil, the progress of "Everyman" Faustus towards his fate, that will secure the successful and perhaps terrifying production, with its pomp and worldly display, its visible forces of evil, that intrigued and held audiences in the early theatre.

ORIGINAL SETTING

Whether or not one can specify any constant features for the early Elizabethan theatre, the script of *Dr. Faustus* presupposes at least three

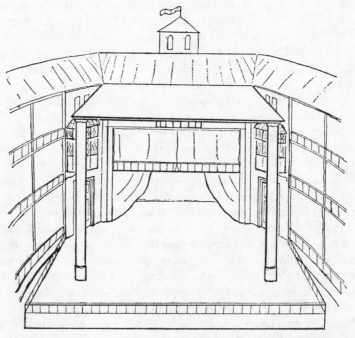

Fig. 25.—POSSIBLE RECONSTRUCTION OF ELIZABETHAN THEATRE

elements—corresponding to the conventions of medieval drama in some ways: an open acting space for procession and larger groups, a fairly massive trap-door for the entry and return of the hosts of hell, and some kind of an inner stage where Faustus may sleep, study, and keep his magic equipment, writing materials, and books. Though these may be carried on to the main stage, there seems the necessity of a table to which they may be returned. Otherwise the actor becomes hopelessly laden for succeeding action; and such an "inner stage" seems indicated by the scene with the horse courser, although, of course, this comic scene may be one of later embellishments of the script.

That these three acting areas were present in early Elizabethan theatre seems fairly certain from contemporary drawings and references. Their relation to earlier forms of stage has been suggested above. The importance for the set designer and producer is obvious; these three areas set the plan of action and the relation of the various scenes. In addition, we may I think postulate the two doors of entrance, one on each side of the inner stage, and a balcony or balconies above the doors and this curtained recess; a second "level" for acting, in fact. As one studies the text, some scenes place themselves at once in the relevant place. Fittingly, for an early play, there is no formal division in existing texts into "Acts" or scenes in the modern sense. This prime consideration must be remembered. Action can flow on continuously—only when the actors feel a "breather" is necessary is a halt made. Naturally such a halt is better made on what we have come to call a "natural break", but there is no carefully contrived working towards that "tableau" curtain, which alters in the nineteenth century the whole pattern of dramatic construction and scene termination. Modern editions which attempt to regularise the script for performances insert scene divisions in diverse places, which indicates that each producer must, in effect, decide for himself where there shall be such a break or pause in action.

For the larger scenes we may assume (again from contemporary illustrations and comment) that servants would set tables and seats on the large platform; ceremonial entries and processions would emerge from the formal doors. (Note the necessarily winding path that such would take to reach any prescribed place, unless the procession broke, and each moved helter-skelter to his place—an effect of comedy); devils come up on the large trap-door, which makes a focal point for the start and end of their dances; Faustus can deliberate and read within his study—but probably comes forward from it necessarily to greet those who enter, either from the side doors, or from the depths by the trap. All these localities are used at times in one action sequence, with Faustus on stage throughout. What, then, of the Good

and Evil Angels—who belong, again, to slightly different convention
from the devils of mystery plays, or rhetorical Renaissance drama?
There is an element of ritual and pattern here which would seem to
indicate that the two figures come in from similar entrances—the
old symbolism of right and left, or "right and sinister". Further, the
Evil Angel can hardly tangle with the devils who utilise the large
trap—she would lose significance. The dramatic "feel" is of pressure
on Faustus, from this side and the other. Each could enter from one
of the stage doors. But here their appeal would be less and their
function obscured. The obvious place for them (from the acting
viewpoint) is on the balconies above these doors. Faustus does not
address them. He is concerned solely with his own thoughts, breathed
into him, as it were, by the two angels in turn. The audience witnesses
them. Faustus does not. The text comes to life best if this arrangement
is followed. Is it in accordance with Elizabethan custom? Probably.
Being sensible and practical people they used their playhouse as seemed
best for any particular play—just as the modern producer does. This
upper gallery has caused controversy just because scholars have
wished to state categorically how it was used. Any director knows
that he uses the physical equipment of the theatre at his disposal in
the way that suits his immediate purpose. Thus this gallery or balcony
could be used for musicians, spectators, or for the action of the play—
as desired. Later, even with further balconies added, there is still the
same flexibility of use. The suggestion that an angel shall come in at
the higher level of heaven links with the earlier mystery or morality
convention. The only moot point is whether the evil angel can legitimately come in "above". We may note, however, that in some earlier
church plays there was the simple opposition of sides, heaven to one
side, hell to the other, presumably often almost on the same level.
Further, the curtained entrances of interludes with characters emerging
on opposite sides but the same level suggests that this convention might
well have been adopted. Finally, if you mark out in a hall a space to
represent the front stage, placing an imaginary trap-door in the middle
and a space representing the inner stage at the back, you will see at
once how the addition of the upper side galleries uses the whole
dimension of the auditorium and acting arrangements. We shall note
later how easy speech was in the Elizabethan theatre; how intimate
the relationship between performers and audience; how unified the
total arrangement. With these considerations the producer may
reconstruct, to his own satisfaction, the original method of presentation
—not forgetting the possible use of the centre balcony above the recess,

later an important area known as the "tarras". Characters emerge from, and retire to, the side doors; come forward into visibility on the upper levels, and can fade away as easily; devils arise from the centre stage around which Faustus constructs his charmed circle; the rear curtain can be drawn back to disclose the study or resting place. Further, there is no absolutely fixed pattern; different occasions and revivals probably altered the acting areas to suit local conditions and actors. For example, Helen might well first appear above on the "tarras", or come in to move across the main stage, but at a safe distance from spectators, not challenging the sense of wonder too closely by contiguity; it is rarely realised how large the main platform was compared with a modern stage.

The same general conventions may be seen in operation in *Friar Bacon and Friar Bungay*, where the inner stage is possibly used as a kind of subsidiary acting area when the Friar brings before the prince the vision of events remote; in the *Old Wives' Tale* when a story is told; and in Marlowe's later *Jew of Malta* which specifically demands an upper stage.

THE APPROACH TO SET DESIGN

The designer can legitimately call to his service all the usages of later medieval theatre, Renaissance presentation, and the early Elizabethan theatre itself—all its colour, movement, and almost barbaric beauty—so long as he combines these elements in a satisfactory way, and, above all, secures for the producer free and easy movement, and swift flow from scene to scene so that the point and contrast of the existing script shall not be destroyed. Where the producer cares to pause is the producer's business; he should not be forced to pause because the setting has to be changed laboriously or a front curtain dropped in an entirely alien convention.

A basic problem is the entry of the devils. Many stages have no trap sufficiently roomy for the passage of the large group of devils. The designer may revert (as is often done) to a slightly earlier (but still very acceptable) convention of a hell mouth on a floor level. (For suggested construction see page 41). So long as this is to one side of the stage, and within sufficient reach of scatter from f.o.h. lights its purpose will be served. It may, however, be slightly raised above floor level and give access to a ramp up which devils may run on to the main stage. Failing this, the devils may (by modern convention rather than Elizabethan or medieval) descend in two streams from the sides of the stage and then run up onto the stage from floor level. This can be extremely effective—they catch f.o.h. light as they run up, and if different colour filters are in use the total effect may be almost accidentally and fittingly eerie. The reader will note that there is no point in reproducing the exact convention of the original performance unless for some special purpose—what is needed is the total overall dramatic impact and effect—and if two lines of devils from both

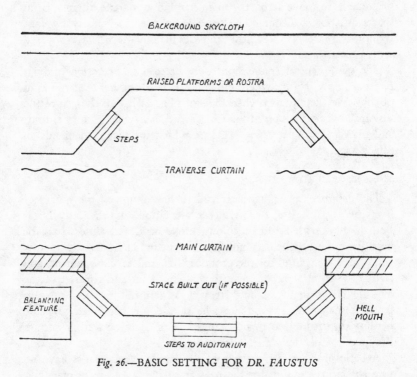

BACKGROUND SKYCLOTH

RAISED PLATFORMS OR ROSTRA

STEPS

TRAVERSE CURTAIN

MAIN CURTAIN

STAGE BUILT OUT (IF POSSIBLE)

BALANCING FEATURE

HELL MOUTH

STEPS TO AUDITORIUM

Fig. 26.—BASIC SETTING FOR DR. FAUSTUS

"right and sinister" accomplishes this, we use this method of entry. Further, many designers will move far away (apparently) from the Elizabethan stage, and yet contrive, imaginatively, to secure the same total effect, and to give the actors all the space and flexibility of action and grouping which they need.

A raised platform across the back of the main acting area, with a traverse curtain in front, will allow the setting of a "study", the ceremonial dais of emperor or pope, or the "tarras" action. Figs 23 and 24 may give some indication of contemporary costume and grouping. The first shown is based on the controversial De Witt sketch of The Swan Theatre, the second from the frontispiece to Alabaster's *Roxana* (1632).

Dance and Decoration

Processions and shows have always been popular. The devices and pageantry similar to the Lord Mayor's Show were repeated many times through the year in earlier times; in Mediterranean countries today religious festivals and carnival have their floats and costumes, their organised and well-trained companies of attendants, and the uniting purposes of theme and celebration. Such festivities originate from the same proto-dramatic forms as the folk-plays and disguisings, or, indeed, as the comedy of ancient Greece. They develop around a particular occasion—a Royal progress, an annual ritual, an important visit, a great event. If a company of citizens wish to show their respect and allegiance, they may repair to the abode of the ruler on his birthday; the whole occasion will be enhanced if they dramatise their offering of respect, going as knights, or Eastern princes, or richly garbed merchants. Then, when they arrive, they must act according to their costume, remaining in character. Thus we have the beginnings of a dramatic form which is to be called the "mask". At the same time, the inevitable human desire to dress up in time of celebration, the particular association of this with carnival, the temporary release from normal social conventions and (by the aid of the mask) from one's own identity, develops a similar theatrical impulse, as all the fancy dress dancers unite in a game of make-believe, sometimes with an actual stated theme. (Consider some "Arts" balls). The dramatic genre repeats itself, redevelops, always hovering on the verge of true theatre, with the implication, however, that the division between actors and audience is very thin. In a sense all who attend (even the dignitary who may be visited or complimented) are potential or actual actors. This participation by all, and its association with dancing, is shown strikingly in contemporary accounts of eighteenth-century "masquerades", less reputable than the "mask" of the sixteenth century. Yet in both there is the demonstration of how people merge easily into a general dramatic activity—when they are habited in garb different from the everyday.

There was no doubt that in essence the form was common enough in England. F. W. Tickner's delightful little book *Earlier English*

Drama (page 34) gives a contemporary account of a visit paid to Prince Richard in 1377 which is exactly in this fashion. The "carnivals" which a few years ago were quite common to celebrate hospital appeals or other worthy causes in our own country, with their set pieces, minstrels, and the performances that were given during or after the procession, show a constant and recurring form of theatre. The "mask" proper was developed further by the elaborate entertainments of Italian nobility and churchmen during the Renaissance, who incidentally did so much to develop the *commedia erudita*, and theatrical technique, especially in scenery and setting. We followed in this country at the homes of such scholars as Sir Thomas More and Cardinal Morton; later Elizabeth I, and, after her, James I and Charles I, encouraged this "fancy dress dance with a theme", if I may be allowed a phrase which sums up some essentials of the "mask". First, there was the basis of disguise, costume, in which all the procession or dancers shared in early days. Second, there was the social occasion—whether a simple "party" or court diversion, or more commonly later a particular visit, marriage, or event. Third, there was the equally important motivation of theme —the selection of some topic round which the dramatic effort could develop, and which (if chosen appropriately) would refer to the particular and contemporary occurrence which the festivity celebrated.

Although the "actors" were originally the "guests" themselves, and although to the end the main performance was given by the wealthy and aristocratic courtiers (Nicoll has called the mask "in its pure form" "a plaything for amateurs, a kind of vast elaborated charade"), naturally enough the assistance of experts was needed as the effects and visual appeal grew more and more elaborate. That the court was never without such professional help we know. The unbroken tradition of drama at royal dwellings or on royal progresses through the country is more than maintained in the reign of Elizabeth the First. Plays of all kinds were given at Court, and the position of Master of the Revels was no sinecure. Professionals were invited to perform there and plays were specially written or adapted for Court presentation (Mr. Leslie Hotson has put forward some theories on this matter which are at least interesting), and for shows which involved Royalty itself—as did the "mask" —even higher standards and greater care would be necessary. The Queen (or the King) required performers to dazzle the eyes and charm the ears of foreign notables—reputation and national pride were involved. Players and nobles from Italy (who represented the most sophisticated and cultured nation in Europe) visited the Court—and must be impressed.

G

Inigo Jones admirably discharged his task as designer of the masks performed during the early sixteenth century. He was a great traveller, visited Italy, studied all the methods of presentation used there, and then gradually evolved his own techniques. The Italians had been fascinated by "perspective" in the early sixteenth century; equally they had tried to revive the classical form of the theatre. Serlio had suggested his own ingenious plans for the theatre which represented a compromise between classical and medieval, with a suitable mixture of the new perspective setting. He published his typical designs for the tragic, the

Fig. 27.—THE COMIC SCENE
After Serlio

comic and the satyric play, following the three main types of ancient drama. Essentially his stage consisted of a platform, with steps to auditorium, backed by "houses" set in perspective along an imaginary road leading upstage from the centre of the platform. The road was necessarily raked, as the buildings diminished to secure perspective as they receded from the audience. So the medieval "house" became reconciled (at least in function) with the "classical" theatre and was set behind the arches in the proscenium which faced in stately architectural grandeur the audience of the later Teatro Olimpico. Italians were concerned greatly with problems of further developing scenic resources. Lighting, spectacular changes, conflagrations—and above all endless elaboration—with a pervading deference to the "classical" (in costume, theme, and atmosphere) occupy their attention through the later sixteenth and seventeenth centuries. When one recalls, however, that the Teatro Olimpico was built at the same time as the first Elizabethan public theatres, and that Inigo Jones' finest work was achieved at the same time as the Italian developments (indeed, the work of Sabbatini on stagecraft was not published until after Jones' career) one realises that our own country was in no way behindhand (at least in the work of its leading exponent of scenic effects).

The ingenuity and beauty of the total "mask" was the test of the designer's success. He had to contrive newer and better ways of presentation each time. Since two settings are better than one, scene change became very important, and not merely scene change, but quick and seemingly miraculous scene change, which would add to the wonder of the whole show. Costume, fanciful as befitted the pleasure and the mood, must necessarily accord in finish, richness, and variety, with the setting. Clearly, the mask had to occupy, because of its detailed and intricate devices, a stage at one end of the hall. To add to the revelation, following preliminary preparation, this was hidden from the rest of the company by the "frontispiece" or decorated curtain, framed by formal and well proportioned pillars and archways. Later the dancers from the stage would mingle with the others in the hall, and in some way, if possible, the royal persons sitting there in state would be brought into the action, for the whole hall was really the place or performance —not merely the raised platform and machinery at the one end.

The mask was linked in this developed form with the Renaissance and its lip-service to renewed classical knowledge. The need for a "theme", mentioned above, afforded opportunity for such interest. Often enough a classical legend furnished the basis for a mask. Later, other stories, or figurative and moral parables, were given a classical flavour by personifications and allusion—and throughout the costume and setting representing an ingenious blend of topical and a fanciful antiquity, of which the costume "à la Romaine" is a pleasant example. Two more or less literary "masks" may serve as example of this development (even if not in themselves typical)—Peele's *Arraignment of Paris*, with its portrayal, using sly humour and delightful wit, of the story of Paris and the apple of discord (the goddesses are appeased by the presentation of the apple to the Queen as fairest of all at the end), and many years later, the young Milton's attempt to use the mask form for edification (again with great beauty and artistry) in *Comus*, with personifications of native English landscape, local reference, introduction of names and figures from the classics, and, of course, specific relation to the marriage at Ludlow Castle.

THE MATERIAL

Can the mask be produced today? In a sense many entertainments of a mask-like nature are still presented—pageants, fancy dress parades, items in revue, certain elements in ballet, and the increasingly popular "dance drama" in the broad sense. Further there are quite a number of modern "masks"—including Robert Bridge's *Demeter*—and even more dramatic pieces which appropriate the term, although it is doubtful whether they can claim it in truth. In general, the overall idea of a fantastically costumed drama with music and dance, poetry, a simple and elemental theme, with or without classical affinities, is still very commonly accepted—modern ballet, dance drama, sequences from musical plays, are often very close, in general style and technical requirements, to the mask. What is lacking is the overall social occasion and the specific pointing and "wit" (in the sense of apt allusion) which were part of the seventeenth-century mask. Audience participation and sense of association with the action—the masquers dancing with these other guests—have now been largely destroyed. The "frontispiece", which hid a world of fantasy in the seventeenth century, held behind it forces of imagination which would flow freely into the whole throng once the barrier was raised. Nowadays the "curtain" marks a permanent boundary between the territories of audience and actors. A further difference is the virtual abolition of the "anti-mask" in modern "mask" presentations. This was a humorous echo plot to the main and serious theme, and was best left to professional actors, the paid comedians. Whether their presence represented the functions of the professional jesters of the court from earlier times, or whether, wisely, the courtly amateurs realised that it takes a professional to play comedy, it was in this part of the entertainment, with its need for crisp timing, coherence, and individual aplomb, that professional actors appeared. Organised pomp, ceremony, group movement, costume elaboration and design—all these things may be successfully and strikingly contrived by a single competent director. This general material may be suitably utilised today, and similarly collected or devised, to prove a pleasing and even exciting presentation. Provided that the director is firm, efficient, and imaginative!

There is delightful opportunity in existing scripts for fresh and (to audiences) original performances. Even the pointing of the mask theme can be achieved, if you select with care. My own students presented Peele's *Arraignment of Paris* for the coronation of Queen Elizabeth II. Without fulsome compliment, it was possible to indicate that the production was a memory of the loyalty and devotion which her predecessor had (rightly or wrongly) inspired in her subjects, and by analogy an expression of contemporary faith and love. Inigo Jones' greatest collaborator was Ben Jonson, who wrote the dialogue and songs for many masks during the reign of James I. The peculiar nature of the mask as a dramatic form and its stress on scenery, show, and decorative organisation, led to the end of the partnership. Ben Jonson could not accept that his script was less important than the work of the great stage technician, quarrelled, and was replaced. D'Avenant wrote the later masks, including the famous *Salmacida Spolia*. In that Jones used the system of scene change which D'Avenant took into the public theatre, and which became the norm for many years in our own country. There are other scripts available, which are listed below.

APPROACH TO PRODUCTION

Flexibility is important. The mask is itself a hybrid form, a synthesis of various dramatic elements and impulses which matured into an impermanent form flourishing for a few decades and then again, without actually dying, taking on a different appearance. Merged with other forms of drama, its spirit lives in their flesh, and can be reincarnated in physical terms more suited to our own time. Clearly the precise occasion, the regal pomp, the lavish technical display, the ritual dignity, cannot be fully revived, unless we can persuade royalty to participate and ourselves become courtiers. But the artistic achievements of the mask—and they were not few—can be suggested to a modern audience. There is pleasing, sometimes superb, poetry, which has to be felt in terms of sound, rhythm, and imagery, and the delights of rhetoric. Look for dramatic intensity of emotion and you will be disappointed. Incidentally you will misunderstand and distort the mask if you do so. Speech must be enjoyed for the sake of speech, as an element in the décor. There are beautiful songs and where the music survives, equally pleasing music. If the music does not survive, songs can be reset. They are a challenge to the musician, who must acquaint himself with the spirit and attitude of the whole production and work with the director throughout. But overall, and enshrining the story, are the décor and the dance movements, the spectacle and colour. All these work together to present a particular allegory or viewpoint. While all these elements form the mask, the emphasis on one or the other may vary, just as the mask form itself varies, fluctuates, and finally passes into spectacular theatre and the "opera" of the Restoration, producing on the way such an academic "masque" as Purcell's *Dido and Aeneas*. The producer has to decide what precisely he can make of the materials to hand. The value of his presentation to the audience must be considered. There is no "take it or leave it" way of avoiding responsibility. Traditionally a mask is designed to appeal visually, verbally, musically. and with some broad "attitude" or "ideal" thought. Thus, Peele's *Arraignment* gave pleasure through the wit and argument of the speeches, the beauty of verbal sound, and the carefully interpreted songs and music—"carefully interpreted" because an overloud accompaniment, a slightly over-emotional rendering, would have shattered the make-believe and lyrical delicacy. On the other hand, the visual appeal through costume and colour, while planned with some thought, was simplified in one modern production to the demands of a small ballroom in what had been a private house. Yet all the mask elements had to be there.

It is fairly clear that a production of D'Avenant's *Platonic Love* would rely far more on the fantastic costumes, dances, and lighting effects. Even its theme cannot be pedantically stressed. Yet its implication—that the mind (or spirit) of man must not be enslaved by material affairs—can be as relevant today as in D'Avenant's time:

Entry

Was of a MODERN DIVEL, a sworn enemy of Poesie, Musick, and all ingenious Arts, but a great friend to murmuring, libelling, and all seeds of discord. . . .

Having settled in his own mind the general trend of the mask, the producer has next the problem: How can this be made sufficiently clear to the audience, so that the dances, costumes, and setting, have unity, relevance, form a coherent experience, and not merely a series of isolated patches of colour, sound, and movement, which is unfortunately the effect on the uninitiated of some ballets? True, he can (and almost certainly will) use the programme note, stressing the elements which he can best present. Here, for example, any attempt to define "platonic love" itself would defeat its purpose. The detailed reference noted by the wits of the time cannot be re-established; but a general note, true so far as it goes, on the importance of mind and spirit, "idealism", and the unceasing conflict between animal nature and human aspirations will be a helpful and sufficient guide for the audience. Next, costume, and setting, and movement, must help positively. How, for example, can the nature of the "modern devil" and his unkind characteristics be demonstrated to the watchers? D'Avenant lays down the golden rule in a further direction. The "divel" is to be attended "by his factious followers; all which" (i.e. the nature of the "divel" quoted above) "was exprest by their Habits and Dance". Further, earlier dialogue by the "magicians" has stated that these shall be "Fine precise Fiends . . . that claim Chambers and Tenements in heaven, as they had purchased them, and all the Angels were their harbingers. . . ." We can envisage puritanical figures, full of their own conceit and importance, thumbing their textbooks, clustering in chattering groups, breaking away with scandalised expressions, shunning the presence of "poesie", mincing through neat pattering movements indicative of their busy little world of nothingness, putting hands before eyes and over ears, and then scampering eagerly to hear a piece of tattle from one of their number —and raising their hats at the end to adore their "boss"—the modern "divel"—revealing as they do so little horns sprouting beneath their very respectable hats. While seventeenth-century "puritan" costume might do well, we might find a modern equivalent—conventionalised Victorian suits, frock-coats, or flannel trousers and sports jackets with whatever head wear is popular at the time of presentation. The modern "divel" himself must be an imposing figure illustrative of all the forces that stifle idealism and the things of the spirit—whether a glorified and horrific pedant, schoolmaster or warder, the possibilities are many. A mixture of costume styles and periods is quite permissible in a fantasy of this kind, save that, overall, the colour scheme and general approach should present some unity. To garb this scene as suggested, above, with the flavour of modernity, and then carefully to use other costume which has the precise period styles of Jacobean/Elizabethan/ pseudo-classical would be absurd—unless the masque involved such contrast of period and fashion. On the other hand fantasy costumes can be quite easily mingled with slightly modified everyday dress— even in such a modern fantasy as Harold Brighouse's *How the Weather is Made*—a play which, with some of the qualities of the anti-mask, will furnish the aspiring mask producer with preliminary practice in his craft. As was said earlier, the director needs skill, imagination, experience, and complete confidence. He must work out from his script his own version, his own interpretation for contemporary performance, plan costumes in relation to this, envisage movement in terms of theme and costume, and then be prepared to drill his actors after several sessions of basic work, along the general lines of his requirements towards the overall effect that he has conceived. He should be able to show those designing the costumes exactly what he wants; he must be able to demonstrate just where costumes will flutter, swirl, or remain rigid. He must be able to state definitely how headgear (see above) will be used and how firm or flexible brims must be. And from the start he must secure the setting he needs and work within its dimensions. Music must be "taped" for rehearsal so that all moves (including entrances and exits) can be practised to it.

ORIGINAL SETTING

Throughout the short history of the mask form (as the term is used in the limited sense) all kinds of presentation were used—from formal houses in the early period to the varied experiments in scene change that Jones sponsored. He tried "houses" which fitted one within the other (two flats joined at the edge, which could be removed quickly to reveal the flats beneath) the *scaena versatilis*—a version of the *periaktos* of the classical Greek theatre, three-sided "wings" which revolved to reveal a new side for a change of set—and finally the *scaena ductilis*, or "draw scene", which D'Avenant was to take, with the aid of John Webb, Jones' assistant, into the professional theatre. In addition, there was the three dimensional "relief" or "set piece" revealed when "shutters" opened. These devices were arranged in perspective along the Serlian centre roadway or space, though since this had to be used for "entries" and dancing it had to be sufficiently large and level. These side pieces, regularly arranged to flank the "stage", were painted as buildings, trees, perspective views, and the set was closed at the point farthest from the audience by a back scene stretching across the entire remaining width of stage, which had been narrowed by the setting in of the side scenes to secure perspective, as well as lowered by their decreasing height. But Jones was concerned not only with scenery at stage level, but also above. Ramps and platforms (sometimes riskily poised) gave access to the "heavens" and cloudland, where gods and goddesses apparently floated on billowing vapours. One of the most simple yet spectacular effects was achieved by the cut sky cloth. From the audience view an actor ascended and vanished into clouds; from his own viewpoint on stage he was simply hoisted through a gap between sky drapings—only the edge of upstage draping was hung higher than that of the downstage draping. From the auditorium the cloud effect appeared continuous. Yet when all is said of such tricks, machinery, and lighting, the essential effort and final achievement of the mask designer was to secure quick changing scenery as background and accompaniment for the movements and events of the allegory.

Thus to show the same landscape at the various seasons of the year was a commendable effect; or, to quote again from *Platonic Love*, to secure that "the whole Scaene changeth into Mist and Clouds, through which some glimpse of a Temple is here and there scarcely discern'd" was another typical task. We may note incidentally that the mask retained the threefold medieval stage scheme, with an underground locality besides the decorative earth and the now classicised heavens, for D'Avenant's next direction orders that "Out of Caves from under ground came forth three MAGICIANS, one more eminent than the

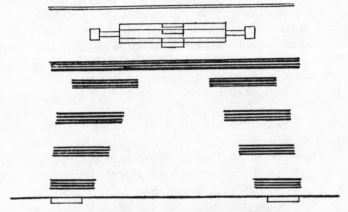

Fig. 28.—PLAN OF WINGS AND SHUTTERS
As used by Inigo Jones *Salmacida Spolia*, 1640

rest, their habits of strange fashions, denoting their qualities, and their persons deformed." The devil himself as we have seen arrives a little later.

APPROACH TO MODERN SETTING

The first requisite is enough space for free movements of dancers and large groups of actors. If this cannot be achieved on the "stage" itself, part of the floor space in your hall or theatre will have to be used, with steps provided leading down from platform into auditorium, or an additional platform built out from the main stage. For dancing and movement the solid basis of the floor is preferable. Rostra, however securely bolted together, tend to move under the rhythmic stress of a dance. In any case, movement out into the audience is quite in keeping with the nature of the mask. We may note here that *full* arena presentation is completely opposed to the basic mask idea—the procession out of a world of fantasy into the present space and time of which the "audience" are part. There must be a background of setting which accords with the costume and theme. Actors may well leave this and come into a large "open stage"—almost arena—but the background must be retained as part of the essential mask. Scenic detail may be introduced into an arena, but on the scale demanded by the mask, would make vision and sightlines very difficult, while the quick change demanded would be almost impossible.

If the stage is large enough to accommodate scenic effects *with* all necessary action and movement, you are fortunate. Most producers and set designers find they have to compromise. Either the setting has to be underplayed (which is the appropriate term when one considers its active function in the mask), or the action has to be moved out as suggested above, leaving the setting as a Serlian background, whether in perspective or not, from which actors move forward. The cloudland of the gods must, of course, be arranged within the setting area, and the provision of a high platform, suitably draped, and access, with a means of curtaining the whole from sight, will still further lessen the acting area, though not necessarily excessively.

As a basis for elaborate and traditional scenery, the same plan and techniques as Jones used may be employed—the three-sided *periaktos*, the wing flats (or curtains) drawn off or on, and the booked flats. In the case of the first and last, efficient stage hands must know precisely what alterations are necessary. Back scenes and lighting, music, performers, and costume changes have all to be organised into synchronised efficiency. The set designer, may, therefore, have to simplify his wish to emulate the full apparatus of the Court mask. Two simplifications are obvious—you may rely simply on wings and backing, using, say two wings in place of the original four, on a small stage. Even then you may need four or five sets of curtain wings to cope with changes, and temporary wires may have to be slung across the stage to accommodate these which are pulled out or drawn back as needed. Some drapes can be made to extend right across the stage to hide any changes needed upstage of them. A study of the script will determine the exact planning—the basic principle remains. Wings occupy little space, and entrances are possible for dancers from the sides, and even if, through lack of space, there is contact with the "scenery", no harm is done. So today for musical shows and pantomimes the wing curtain is still part of normal practice. A possible alternative is to use a form of *décor simultané*, placing in your set all things necessary for the entire performance, without attempting to extend change to the whole of the acting area. Temporary curtains may be fixed to mask in parts not needed—these hangings should themselves be decorated with device and colour in keeping with the overall costume and design of the mask. Thus, in *The Arraignment of Paris* one end of a hall was used for the presentation. A large and rich curtain took the place of the "frontis-piece". This was drawn so as to leave sufficient concealment on each side for performers and a small orchestra. Screens were placed upstage and at the sides. Along the sides was a formal platform for the gods draped with cloud folds. A platform and throne were set upstage. A flowery bank was used for Paris and Oenone, and the temporary concealment curtains in front of the extra apparatus, as well as a complete traverse, were decorated with formal "Mount Ida" trees, shrubs, and flowers. Costumed attendants drew on any part of the setting needed. The large windows of the hall were also utilised for setting; "devices" and decorations were hung within, and revealed by drawing back curtains hung in front. Lighting can be used effectively to help such a setting, which is really a reversion to the medieval house "platea", with the unifying effect of decorated curtains which blend or cover the various parts. On too large a stage such a method of presentation would become "bitty" unless the various "houses" were made sufficiently impressive. But since the method is an attempt to make the best use of a small acting space on to which the actors emerge from various localities, the danger should not arise. Even here, of course, the heavy front curtain and the repeated pattern of decoration on side curtains and traverse must be retained in order to give unity.

As to the general style—classical, romantic, Gothic, or modern—the producer and set designer have only to decide in consultation. The mask (as I have stressed) is a flexible and imaginative form. Each direc-tor will have his own particular ideas and thematic emphasis and will work with his set designer to achieve this. Crowd movement, grouping and points of entry and exit must be determined from the start. After preliminary sketches of setting, there should be further consultation, and here, if not before, the costume designer must be called in. The setting can be established in more detail, once the mechanics are settled. Costume and décor can be correlated, with reference back to the director's needs in regard to costume and movement, costume and character. When all problems have been solved—at least for the time being—rehearsal may start with the cast. It is this careful preliminary planning and overall organisation which is essential to the mask, even though some further adjustments may have to be made to help actors and to facilitate dance movement.

Much of the technique of scene arrangement used today, especially in musical plays, "spectacular" shows, and variety, is based on the methods used or developed by Inigo Jones. In straight plays with formalised settings, the *periaktos* small or large (it can be used as a main scene backing or filling), and various kinds of angle or booked flat are common devices. They are specially useful in Shakespearian production. Reference should be made to books listed in the Appendix. (See also Figs. 28 and 39.)

Shakespeare

Tнᴇ work of Shakespeare is part of, and emerges from, the drama and theatre of his period. It is not something separate and distinct in kind. It must be approached in the same way as other dramatic work—as something essentially theatrical, not as literature, except incidentally. Early plays reflect the style, influence, and theatrical concepts of other dramatists; later plays the changing atmosphere and the taste of audiences, as well as the professional and skilful use of developing theatrical forms. The whole range of theatre in his time is found in Shakespeare's dramatic work. Successful in theatre business, successful in his professional duties, a leading member of his company, he was admired and celebrated by his fellows and co-workers; so persistent were his plays in holding the stage that these were collected after his death in the volume known as the First Folio.

The plays themselves are, of course, so much part of the theatrical enterprise of the period that one realises that others had some share in their composition. Indeed, as other dramatists, Shakespeare in his youth must have taken his turn in revising and preparing new acting versions of already existing plays. Sometimes he seems consciously to imitate in his original work an established success. Several plays are ascribed to him which may or may not have received some revision or addition, but which, clearly, as they stand (such as *Arden of Feversham*) cannot be said to be his with any real probability. Again, towards the end of his work as a professional theatre worker, he may according to custom have collaborated with others, perhaps, for example, with Fletcher in *The Two Noble Kinsmen*, when Fletcher had lost the substantial help of Beaumont. All this we recall to establish that Shakespeare's work is very much part of general theatrical activity; his scripts were the working equipment of professional companies, and not the rarefied and minutely plotted literary exercises of some remote genius. So much so, that accepted texts clearly contain additional material added by later playhouse scribes—such as Middleton's expansion of the witch scenes in *Macbeth*. Yet, by and large, the texts as we have them are those which stood the test of theatre conditions —too much tampering with the essential wording, the speeches, and the characters, which had achieved the popularity and accepted greatness of the play, would destroy the appeal that revision, in lesser dramas, was intended to secure. It was this common acceptance of the greatness of his work that allowed his plays to survive, to be published by his fellows, and to be transmitted to us today—the acceptance of their greatness, that is, as theatre. Other dramatists, we know, had a far greater output, yet, unless they themselves sponsored publication, only those plays which achieved some equal measure of popularity have been preserved for us. The text of Shakespeare is, therefore, to be regarded, on first consideration, as likely to have considerable authority. Because of the need to retain the appeal of his plays, alteration and addition would not be made without serious purpose. There has been much research on textual problems, and the producer is advised to examine one of the recognised authorities before starting work on any text itself.

The range of his work, as befits a dramatist whose career straddles the most formative years of theatre in this country, is immense. The producer, again, must recognise this. The question is not simply one of division into comedies, histories, and tragedies; it involves a great variety of theatrical approach: chronicle histories of a somewhat elementary kind (although with emerging character interest and subtlety), studies in Renaissance thought and argument, comedies of contemporary foible and affectation, romantic stories with satiric point, man shown in his universal relationships in (perhaps) the final and fullest tragic statement of Western theatre, plays of cynical social comment, poetic dramas in which the giant figures of morality drama engage in a patterned action which somehow presents in its totality the whole human situation—with all that Renaissance hopes and Shakespeare's own times would bring to interpret that human situation—one could extend the list. Yet through this universality there is always the awareness of the demands of theatre. All his sensitive experience of life is used in the art form which is his everyday task—this theatre, with its setting, sounds, actors, and audiences. And through it all one can glimpse the events by which he was surrounded, illusions, discussions, arguments, politics, and in order fully to appreciate his greatness one must know something of that world. His comment upon this, in terms of human action and character, constitutes his universality; it is in specific human situation that the common tragedy and comedy is revealed.

The producer will be helped in his task if he knows also a little of the stage history of the plays. In the case of the greater tragedies there is, for example, a virtually unbroken tradition of interpretation from Shakespeare's own day; the romantic comedies were for a long period "non-acting" plays, and when they were revived it was with a certain sentimental bias and "feminine" appeal which was probably not there in Shakespeare's own time. Undoubtedly each great work of art, just because it is universal, has a differing impact on each succeeding generation. The vital reality presents differing aspects to the differing life of the community as the years pass—but it will prevent actual distortion and loss of the total experience if the producer can assess something of the original dramatic theme and its impact, instead of improvising too cleverly on barely understood lines and situations. This will forbid on the one side, a too ready acceptance of popular interpretations of the play, and on the other the arbitrary and unbased originality which will serve in the end no useful purpose. The true objective is to realise the play itself, unsentimentalised and yet emotionally complete, even, if it is so, stark and brutal. No one can dogmatise on the correct interpretation of a play; but each would-be producer should be in a position from which he can make judgment; the set designer should have a basic understanding of the needs of each play so that he, too, is ready to approach his task.

The first way in which producers may widen their theatrical view is by considering all the plays in the Shakespearean group. Too many accept only the plays commonly performed. There are certain great dramas which have held the stage through the centuries, and others the greatness of which has been freshly perceived and which have now attained the unfailing theatrical appeal of *Hamlet*, *Macbeth*, and *Othello*. *King Lear* has gained in appeal; its tragic grandeur became more apparent as the exploring human mind returned to deeper, ultimate, problems in the later eighteenth century; this suggests that other plays less acted at present may be ready for more frequent revival, if approached with the sincerity and care of the good producer. One would welcome more revivals of the apparently gloomy plays— *Timon*, *Measure for Measure*, *All's Well That Ends Well*—of the Renaissance romanticism of *Two Gentlemen*, the pseudo-romanticism of *Cymbeline*, or the satiric comment of *Troilus and Cressida*. One would also welcome (even more) an honest approach to such a play as *As You Like It*, instead of a constant rehash of woodland appeal and optimistic escapism, which may have suited an eighteenth-century

revival but hardly fit robust Elisabethan attitudes or the careless
inconsequence of the title.

For the greater part of Shakespeare's career his plays were presented
in the large and splendid later Elizabethan theatre, although we must
remember that his company used an indoor house of small dimensions
as well. Again, we are not concerned with scholarly details of production—interesting as these may be and often relevant to the correct
interpretation of some scripts—but rather with the overall emphasis
and general conventions of presentation. Particular editions (which
the producer will study) indicate points of special interest.

The main acting areas were developments from those existing in the
earlier theatres. Thus we have the large platform, the curtained
inner stage, the main doors of entrance, the "tarras" above the inner
stage, the side balconies above the doors of entrance, the still higher
"musicians" gallery above the "tarras", and the large trap. The dominant factor in this was (if one studies the existing dimensions of, for
example, The Fortune playhouse, built to parallel Shakespeare's own
Globe Theatre) the vast area of the main stage. It was all the larger because
(and this is often overlooked) unbounded by wings or side scenes. An
actor could advance, if necessary, right to its front or side, with an
unobstructed view of the audience and close proximity (wherever he
went) to some of his hearers. Actors actually did "travel" about
this area; it took some appreciable time to advance from the
entrance doors full on the acting area. Similarly, when an Elizabethan script indicates that a character says "Let us go" and then
gives him his two or three more lines of dialogue, this is not bad
writing; it simply calls attention to the fact that it took him
(and his colleagues) some time to return to the tiring house and
to enter it by one of the great doors. Note also that entry is not the
quick appearance from a side scene or a door in the wall of a set, but
a long progress out into the body of the theatre and back again for
exit. Further, it is quite possible for groups of actors to stand on the
stage in such a way that one group is (feasibly) unseen or inaudible so far
as the other is concerned. Again, grouping is three-dimensional;
actors are seen perhaps from the front, but also from the sides, from
above and from behind. They do indeed "walk the stage". The re-
strictive and fussy rules of the picture-frame are hardly applicable. An
additional technique and an awareness of position are needed—the
avoidance of over-tight clustering, a certain ritual conditioning of

movement which demands that (as in a church) the officiants stand and move with due consideration and good mannered adjustment of distance and position. Granted this, the ceremonial, procession, and court dignity required in Elizabethan drama are made possible. Study for example, the procession in *Henry VIII* with its meticulous demands. Further, this same use of spacious movement can be sensed in the more domestic scenes—the dance in *Romeo and Juliet*, the choice of the caskets in *The Merchant of Venice*, or the group of disaffected insurgents in *I Henry IV*. Again, consider the ease with which the garden or the open space could be accepted as a place of action—the formal garden at Olivia's, the Duke moving with his courtiers about his grounds, the orchard below Juliet's balcony. So, too, with the larger areas of woodland or battlefield; there was ample room for movement and at least the suggestion of two massed armies as they entered on opposite sides. The hurly-burly and swirl of fighters, advancing now from this side, now from that, could aptly catch and communicate the hubbub and confusion of battle—a battle into which the audience were almost drawn by proximity and three-dimensional reality—so different in quality from the moving picture behind the footlights which was the aim of many Victorian producers. The nearness of the audience was not unnatural. In the courts and audience halls of nobles, in open streets and market-places, the Elizabethans recognised and moved with the great ones, and shared in their pageantry. This pageantry transferred to the theatre involved them with the same familiar sights; they became actors themselves in the scene to which they were so conveniently and closely admitted. This three-dimensional quality of the action must be recognised, and we must recall, too, that this was only at ground level; from the platform the actors could speak up to the "tarras" and balconies. The action was on two levels—the emotional pull of gesture and voice exerting itself upwards and through the great "volume" (if one may use the term), the actual air, of the auditorium.

But with this grandeur there was too a tremendous intimacy, a fact not recognised by those who think of the Elizabethan actor as ranting his way through over-dramatic speeches. The intimacy consisted in this—the acting area ran into the actual centre of the auditorium. An actor stationed forward was no farther from the auditorium wall in front of him than he was from the tiring house behind. Large as the theatre was he was close to even the furthest spectators. All round him rose the wooden galleries and retaining walls, to throw back his voice, if need be. But—and the fact can be easily tested—he could stand near the front stage, speak barely above a whisper, and still be heard perfectly—provided the audience were hushed by the drama of situation. The Elizabethan soliloquy is no false situation where an actor jerks words behind a half-raised hand to the audience across the footlights—it is a human speaking aloud, much as many people do in moments of stress, overheard, almost by chance, through their fortunate contiguity, by those who stand or sit round him. Every shade of expression, every slight alteration of facial muscle, every tremor in the voice, is apparent. Much later Cibber was to say the same of the advantages of the apron stage, the lessening size of which he deplored. How much more was this the case with the Elizabethan platform. This is not a "projection" forward from a separated acting area; it is a sharing, a spreading around, of one's hopes and fears to intimates or eavesdroppers. The producer must note this convention and use of soliloquy as something natural and easy in Shakespeare's theatre and plays.

Once this importance of the main stage is realised, the use of the other acting areas in relation to it seems to become apparent. The "inner stage" becomes a study, a tomb, perhaps an arbour in a garden, or a stage within a stage (for the mask knew the convention of the curtain); the main doors are the entrances to houses in a street, the "tarras" is a castle wall, a city defence, a lady's bedroom, while the side balconies above the doors may be the upper stories of a citizen's home. Again, all these places may symbolise rather than represent; above may dwell spirits of the air and angels, just as from the trap may still emerge the ghosts and devils of the lower regions. With this knowledge the producer may construct his own imagined plan of action as it took place in the Elizabethan theatre; he can consider himself as working at that time, and place his actors so as to gain the greatest clarity of presentation. Crowds, he knows, must almost certainly use the main space, unless they are defending a beleaguered city; studies, tombs, and arbours, or "behind the arras", will be probably on the inner stage. And so on. It is this general visualisation of the emphasis and possibility of Shakespearian presentation that will shape in his mind the original play, and prepare him for his own task of presenting it today.

There are other relevant considerations. One was the Elizabethan habit of placing quite elaborate properties on the main stage, as well as tables and chairs, transported there by servants. He will observe, too, the "heavens" or canopy which ran over much of the main stage, decorated with the stars and "heavenly bodies" liked by Elizabethan and later medieval artists. He will recall that this canopy was supported by two heavy pillars which rose from the main stage, and which served the obvious (if accidental) use of delimiting and dividing the great acting area if necessary. These could be trees, a hiding place, a suitable leaning post for a reflective gallant, or might jointly suggest the entrance to a formal temple or a church, to which the heavens became the roof. He would specially bear in mind the position of the music—high away just below the "heavens" in an additional gallery over the "tarras". . . .

> And those musicians that shall play to you
> Hang i' the air a thousand leagues from hence. . . .

It was easy too for the "isle" to be "full of noises"—the plaintive notes echoed down from the "heavens" high above the spectators, from unseen musicians, wistful, blending subtly with action and movement below. To balance this he would recall that it was also possible to bring musicians on stage for dance, festival, or jig.

Over all is the impression of "blending"—blending of audience with actors, blending of acting areas, the functioning of the whole "theatre" as a unity, in which all accepted the means of communication because they were familiar with such spectacle, action, colour, dance, wrestling, procession, in daily life and custom.

Mr. Hotson's scholarship has enabled him to put up a plausible case (in *Shakespeare's Wooden O*) for a stage plan different from those more or less generally accepted. Admittedly the Elizabethan theatre used varying methods of presentation, but his interpretation of references and localities seems to establish a rather unlikely convention for normal theatre practice. Apart from other references which (on face value) contradict his assumptions (as for example the reference to "tedious sieges to the tiring house" as being common) the theatrical inconvenience of his scheme (however ingenious the scholarly evidence) seems to me almost an insuperable obstacle to its general use. All preceding forms of staging have been tested in modern practice, from the ritual plays onwards. All have clearly their own especial dramatic value and technical advantages. So have the more generally accepted Elizabethan stages. Their relevance to the performance of Shakespeare's plays can be shown. Moves demanded by the script are immediately possible; groupings (and separation of groups) on stage follow easily. Dressing, equipment, and entry of actors, clearly present no problem. So also ceremonial processions, banquets, dances of devils, are suited to the overall plan. Mr. Hotson's stage, while not actually in opposition to, seems to demand rather different scripts from, those in existence, and a completely different attitude to the acting area and the actor's task from those obtaining immediately before and after the Elizabethan period. The threefold concept of hell, earth, and heaven, which motivates such Elizabethan staging, would seem to be rudely broken, only to be resumed (tacitly) in Restoration theatre. Lastly, the medieval staging with which Mr. Hotson's reconstruction seems to have affinities was probably not in the form suggested common in this country. The question of "the Lords' room" and its locality over the "recess", to which the actors were supposed by Mr. Hotson to turn, can be paralleled by the similar "back-stage" position of aristocracy in the eighteenth century, when they were, on occasion, accommodated "within the scenes". There was presumably no question of the actors on the "apron" turning their backs monotonously on the audience to please their noble patrons. Nevertheless, Mr. Hotson's book contains so much valuable material that no student can neglect its contribution to our knowledge, whatever view he may take of its conclusions.

Costume was, broadly, symbolic. That is to say it communicated the general rank, style, and import, of the character. A nobleman was dressed richly in the fashion of the day, no matter what his country or period; a king even more regally; a Puritan in sober guise, a wanton in garish colour. Costume was, at least, basically theatrical; it was exaggerated from the fashions of daily life. On the one hand, actual symbolic and fantastic costumes might be used on occasion; and there were the throngs of fays, elves, witches, devils, and spirits to be presented, too; on the other, some costumes attempted to represent—thus a kind of mask costume "a la Romaine" might be used for characters from classical times, Henry VIII might well repeat the Holbein portrait, and some characters had a kind of traditional garb which showed that their original portrayal had been the subject of conscious consideration —Falstaff, for example. Such characters are either leads, or comics who have exaggerated styles for ever associated with the clowns and buffoons. Sometimes, one is tempted to compare the stylised plumes of tragic heroes and the over-elaborate signs of rank and authority (to be perpetuated in theatre at least until the nineteenth century) with the traditional costume and alarming head-dresses of actors in the Chinese theatre, symbolic theatrical dignities and adornments. The rich colour and massed brilliance of an Elizabethan court scene, too, would have conveyed something of the same impression.

This essentially theatrical use of costume is not without relevance when one comes to consider modern experiments in costuming. For example, to secure some greater emphasis a producer garbs a comedy of Shakespeare's in eighteenth-century dress. There is the same "theatrical" approach, whatever one may feel about the suitability in this or that instance. The fussy attention to period detail beloved of the Victorians is not really natural to Shakespearian drama or even suitable for his action, character concept, diction, imagery or dramatic range.

THE PRODUCER'S APPROACH

Having related his script to its possible presentation and having attempted to gain some idea of the movement, pageantry, and visual appeal, of the original play, the producer now considers its actual "running" and movement from scene to scene. He notes again that there is no "front curtain" to interrupt. Action is continuous—if need be—conditioned only by the need for a break to relieve tension and stabilise the flux of action for a few minutes. He realises, of course, that the so-called "scenes" are only an indication that the action has moved to another place—sufficiently indicated in Shakespeare's theatre by the going off of one group and the entry from another door of another. There is no "break". He looks at *Antony and Cleopatra* and admires the quick sequence of short scenes as we move about the battlefield on the platform. He is aware that the conventional scene directions are often the work of editors, as are divisions into acts and scenes, though a glance at a First Folio reprint shows that some of these have a long ancestry. Still, he is fairly confident that if it comes to an issue the existing script (not its directions in every case) is his working basis, and he may well query traditional and accepted scene division and acting locality. Thus, when Lear lies sick and ill, the obvious place for his reception is the inner stage; Kent and Cordelia enter by the main door, walk forward and are met by the doctor as they seek to look into the "recess". He then sees that some stage directions stipulate that Lear enters in a litter. Although this direction dates from an early edition, he still feels disquiet, and finds, on looking into a further authority that the litter "business" (so unnecessary and laborious) may well have been added for performance in a theatre which had no practicable inner stage. Which reminds him again of the variability of Elizabethan stage conditions. Our producer does not take this as a suggestion that he can do exactly as he pleases, but as an indication that careful thought and critical judgment may help him to recreate the emphasis of the original play. His basic consideration is to secure the smooth running of the play, to build its mounting action, to secure his crowd effects and crises, to give his leading characters their due prominence and facilities for movement and gesture; and these needs he passes on to the set designer, showing his own minimum demands.

Having charted the action, he now weighs carefully its motivation and balance. Where does the real climax come? What precisely are the contending forces, the dramatic tensions? Each producer will decide for himself and will interpret a great play in his own way. And each will be in a sense correct for his own time, theatre, actors, and audience. Next, who are the people who constitute the agents of the action? He considers his humans, supernaturals, spirits, officials, crowds, and, again, sees the kind of pattern which they form. In the case of the humans, he must examine character motives carefully—but he always remembers that whatever concept he forms of characters, they are characters who act *in the way demanded by the play*. Action and event, clash and struggle, these are the basis of drama; character is involved. He begins, too, to perceive an aspect of living experience emerging, a theme which somehow binds, or pervades and unifies, the whole play. Such a theme may manifest itself differently to different people; the great play mediates life, and at various times the life it mediates seems to meet humanity at various points; to one age, this is obvious, that is not so obvious; prophetic enlightenment comes when the "not so obvious" is revealed.

If we examine one or two popular plays we may see what form our approach to the action may take. We might consider that the theme of *A Midsummer Night's Dream*, remembering that its original performance was possibly linked with a wedding celebration, is "Love and Marriage" the two regarded as a single and inevitable progression. We have the marriage of the ruler, Duke Theseus, to Hippolyta, pomp and circumstance and classical dignity, scholarly association and reference; then there is the idealised poetic love (almost unreal and child-like in innocence and directness) of Lysander, Hermia, Helena, Demetrius; again, there is the broken marriage of the supernaturals—the fairies—Oberon and Titania have quarrelled; and, finally, the comic burlesque and frustrated efforts of Pyramus and Thisbe. We note that in each of these there is the suggestion of cross purposes and strife. Theseus had won Hippolyta, "doing her injuries"; Lysander and Hermia in a kind of thematic statement talk ritually of love's inevitable disasters; Oberon and Titania have so quarrelled that the whole world is upset—storms, floods, disasters, follow love's own troubles; and the country players in their "anti-mask" sum up the struggles of futile humanity by revealing the comic aspects of the whole business; walls and lions remind men of their limitations, just as earlier the unknown forces that sport with us had misled the helpless lovers in the wood. We cannot help noticing, too, that the varying conventions of Elizabethan drama are all represented—the erudite and classical, the romantic youthful love (so innocent and unworldly that the curious revelation to Helena of the intended flight and the equally stupid and impulsive infatuation which leads her to tell Demetrius of the elopement are all in keeping with the nature of things); the nature drama of woodland deities; and the native farce of the workmen, which satirises the curious mixed dramatic styles which had held the stage in mid-century—tedious, brief, tragic, and comical—the departing semi-professionals, who still look for a pension from the lord in whose house they play.

Unless these varying approaches to the theme are sufficiently balanced the real impact of the play will fail. As a recent writer has said, the essence of *The Dream* is hierarchy. Love and marriage are seen in various contexts—and the contrast of these constitutes the dramatic pattern. The dignity, the pomp, of the Elizabethan theatre must be retained for the ceremonial scenes at Court which open and close the action; the freshness and impulsiveness of the youthful lovers must be set against this; the wayward powers of earth and the spiteful or wilful sport of the fairies must have their due emphasis; there is probably little need to worry about the due prominence of the "academicals" in the play. Yet production after production casts aside one or the other of these, and seems to give us only part of the play. Perhaps, of course, the producer may consciously decide to play for the appeal of only one group—I can remember one uproarious professional production which enlivened wartime years in which the play of Bottom and his fellows at the end occupied quite a third of the total acting time. But what he does must be done *consciously*, with realisation of the actual task involved. In the course of production, many further constructive ideas will occur to him provided he has this serious purpose—lines will take on a new significance. He has found a way into the drama; he and his actors are alerted to character, situation, dialogue, which patterns themselves around the considered theme.

Examine a history play that is familiar to all, one that has held the stage ever since its first performance, *I Henry IV*. Let us try to free our minds of an overwhelming sense of Falstaff's presence; read the script to reassess the theme and the pattern of action. You find that this is the story of a revolt, not just isolated incidents from a chronicle in which the same people happen to recur—a revolt in which quite estimable men are opposing their monarch, men with whose bravery and sense of injustice it is possible to sympathise. Yet the revolt must be subdued—for whether the king is monarch by rights or not he represents and cares for the whole community—he loves his people—while the rebels would break the country up for selfish consideration and even argue childishly about its division. Blunt answers them briefly; he is not concerned with finer issues; he must, in God's name, oppose them "so long as out of limit and true rule" they "stand against anointed majesty". The welfare, the life of England, is involved—human and communal survival, The producer may consider how far in Shakespeare's day the monarch was the "life giver", the Divine figure, upon whom the vitality of his people depends. Contemporary attitude does not affect dramatic truth; when appreciated it reveals it. As he reads again, it may occur to him that the king is not really the central figure in this strife—it is his son, Prince Hal, who represents the hopes of England. He will see that Shakespeare has changed the "facts" in the interest of dramatic truth, that experience of life which he is sharing with us. The king is made older, and reliant on his son; deploring the boy's faithlessness; complaining that he must "crush our old limbs in ungentle steel". This is the drama of Hal, later to be Henry V; the theme is even now "Henry and England"—for Hal will inherit, even as he now supports, his father's throne and position as the anointed embodiment of the nation.

The situation and theme is then further enforced by singling one rebel and opposing him directly to the price—by word and emulation as warrior and man, the rivalry and the opposition is built up, until on the field the prince, having saved his father, the king, kills Hotspur in single combat—the theme of "revolt" is fulfilled as the contest between these two ends. Again history is perverted to fit the dramatic pattern; Hotspur is made younger so that he may become the fitting rival with the Prince for England's future.

What, then, of Falstaff? Here history has helped Shakespeare, though he develops and balances the action in his own way. Hal represents us all. It was the appeal of his robust personality in old scandals that fitted him so eminently to be the "ideal" embodiment of his people. Theatrically, Falstaff and his friends can show us the lighter side. It is no longer necessary (as in *Dr. Faustus*) to insert unrelated comedy to keep the groundlings entertained. Farce, history, and tragedy, differing dramatic conventions, are all united by Shakespeare in one pattern of action. This prince is high born, but "sworn brother to a leash of drawers". His warm humanity and sense of amusement, his almost cynical observation of life, these must be overruled by his sense of duty and authority. Humanity must be subordinate to kingship and future responsibility:

> I know you all and will a while uphold
> The unyok'd humour of your idleness. . . .

All is part of his "policy", his concern for his future situation as leader of his people. Whether such a character is attractive or not is really beside the point. His rejection of Falstaff in a later play is his own testimony to his kingship. Only an over-emphasis on the "character" aspect of drama can make us carp. Shakespeare is not concerned to embody pleasant men and women; he is showing the actions, the strife, the clashes, of human life, in individual and community, and through all the theme is of ultimate well-being and social fruition.

Note, again, that this play is a unity within itself—a phase of history, a sequence of action, perfectly accomplished. Scene I (a magnificent expository opening) shows the king at furthest remove from his son; scene II presents the son with his companions—at furthest remove from the king—planning highway robbery. Through the play they gradually move closer until there is union in thought and trust between them in this play. Similarly the sub-plot moves into the main plot, and at the end, Falstaff, too, is brought into this, pretending that he has killed Hotspur, acting a kind of comic anti-mask of his own to the serious theme.

Hal, therefore, is central. Round him are ranged his triangle of interests—the king, Falstaff, and Hotspur. From their interplay comes the pattern of action; a pattern, let us say once again, which does not primarily exist to show the interests of character, but to present dramatically the clash of order and disorder, fertility and destruction, life force and death.

Because it is reputed to be an unlucky play, and because there are so many conflicting opinions on its problems, we may well examine the script of *Macbeth*.

Many producers seem to be worried by such questions as "Are the witches meant to be real people? Or are they subjective—the product of Macbeth's mind?" Only a misunderstanding of the dramatic tradition and convention of which *Macbeth* forms a part, can cause over-concern. Familiarity with the naturalistic approach to performance and to theatre in general has led some to treat a play as a kind of "documentary" in which we look for a lifelike and "natural" moving picture of daily life and events. So we are worried by anything that cannot fit easily into a "tea-cup and saucer" world, or spend an endless amount of anxiety over exact period replicas of costumes and properties which are often essentially untheatrical. We should be trying to communicate living realities, not necessarily surface appearances and outward trivialities. True, the apparently trivial may become dramatic when it has real significance; but then it ceases to be trivial. We have to select and to communicate according to the resources of theatre. Were the witches real women? One might as well ask whether Lady Macbeth is historically "accurate" (with the implication that if she is not something is wrong), or whether the porter is a real man— and not an actor "representing". The Elizabethan drama adopted and used the full scope of theatre, including the morality convention. Are the qualities presented in *Everyman* real people? Yet the overall action and interplay of actors within it presented the reality of human life and death. So with such a play as *Macbeth*—the means used are to be accepted as such. Your particular interpretation of the witches will be determined by your decision on the best way to communicate the theme and implications of the play—movement, décor, and lighting all being involved—and not ultimately on some scholarly discussion as to the nature of such entities if this were a real life report and not a script for theatrical performance. The same trend of anxiety led actors in the twenties, frightened by blank verse far removed from the naturalistic chatter of modern comedy, to endeavour as nearly as possible to speak the verse as prose, instead of realising that the poetic form is again a vital means of communication, telling in its imagery, its rhythms, its grandeur, of the essential struggles of humanity, a part of the total means of theatrical communication, part of the décor, the lighting, the movement, and, if you insist, the characters themselves. Curiously, when one comes to the later plays such as *The Tempest*, although the problem is clearly more acute if one persists in this naturalistic obsession, the utter impossibility of interpreting Ariel and such creatures as normal human beings prevents the issue. One then tends to assimiliate the whole action to some kind of "fairy story"—and to accept, rightly or wrongly, on that basis. Yet the dramatic pattern is similar; there are forces, powers, intuitions, elementals, of earth and nature maybe, which are powerful in human struggle, and these, whether witches, sprites, or Calibans, are presented in theatrical terms for dramatic purposes—whether in morality or Shakespeare, *The Old Wives Tale*, or the expressionist drama of the twenties. *Macbeth* is the story of usurpation through murder. While in *The Dream* hierarchy is established as a framework, and while in *I Henry IV* hierarchy is challenged, here the due order is for a time almost completely broken. A rift is achieved through which the force of evil may enter to poison and corrupt. The nature of things is superseded by the unnatural, the healthy by the unhealthy, the fruitful by the deadly. And again it is the whole community that is threatened; although this is Scotland in particular, we feel that such a catastrophe may overwhelm all humanity—the theme is universal, it is essential tragedy when the potentially good is destroyed and lost. That is humanity's plight—so much power, promise, and the superb lordship of creation, wrecked by the entry of destructive and corroding forces, an entry that humanity itself makes possible through some initially disregarded weakness.

The story develops around the actions of Macbeth. A man of excellent promise, universally praised, he is tempted by the ambiguous promises of three "witches"—or fates, if one attends to another implication of their title, "the weird sisters". The temptation emerges into more positive form after his conversation with his wife to whom he has told the prophecy. Between them they plot and achieve the death of Duncan. Macbeth at first still flinches from the consequences of his guilt, but then realises that there is no turning back; he must go on.

> Returning were as tedious as go o'er.

Now the end is inevitable. His wife, at first apparently stronger, is left behind in evil. She has screwed her courage "to the sticking-place" while she derides her husband as "infirm of purpose"; but having made the effort, and forced a breach by which evil enters, she fades into remorse and dies persecuted by conscience and the evil which has entered her own life. The dominating power of such inhumanity is terrifyingly presented; she said quite confidently "A little water clears us of this deed"—but at the end in her delirium knows that she can never cleanse herself. Not "all the perfumes of Arabia" will sweeten her soiled hands. Her own humanity is destroyed through her inhumanity to Duncan. Once such "anti-life" processes start they have to work themselves out.

In Macbeth the evil corrupts until his own existence is totally destroyed, first, while he still lives. Life becomes "a tale told by an idiot . . .", "signifying nothing". It is perhaps this removal of all value or purpose from his being which is the more terrifying. His subsequent physical death is a relief—a recognition of the inevitable. He had become indeed a "rarer monster", all humanity defaced. Death physically (and bravely) in some sense restores his status; he no longer exists as a "monster"; he has at least died as a man.

Again, the approach solely in terms of character will mislead. The action is between good and evil, light and darkness, even though these are objectified in the lives of individuals. The essential theme is presented not only in events, but in the total power of theatre—words, rhythms, imagery, the implied décor, and symbolic comment. Thus the "natural" state of health while Duncan reigns is conveyed in his own speeches, full of suggestions of growth and fertility. "I have begun to plant thee", he tells Macbeth. He notes the "pleasant seat" of Macbeth's house (where Banquo points out the "procreant cradle" of the martlet) and purposes to continue his "graces towards him". But Macbeth breaks in with images of death and darkness.

> Nature seems dead, and wicked dreams abuse
> The curtain'd sleep; witchcraft celebrates
> Pale Hecate's offerings.

The play moves on through ever-widening destruction and loss of human life. Scotland "cannot be called our mother but our grave. . . . Good men's lives expire before the flowers in their caps".

Malcolm can restore the natural life and healthy vitality. The long scene with Macduff has seemed to many (working from a naturalistic viewpoint) to be almost redundant. Why this long pother? Because Malcolm must know that he is moving forward with the restorative forces, which will bring health to the commonweal, and not merely sponsoring another destructive and selfish irruption upon his people. Hence he must test Macduff to the full; hence also the suggestion that he will move forward from a country sanctified and blessed by a royal saint. The producer can study for himself in detail—there are many books now available—the working out of the theme, not only in this play, but also in the other tragedies. Imagery is constantly relevant, though how far consciously planned is another matter; it is part of the dramatist's instinctive concern to communicate; we, at least, must not fail him by deliberate insensitivity.

The theme might be summarised as "inversion"—the supplanting of right by wrong, true by false, and (at a much higher level) of the natural by the unnatural, of the life forces by the death urge. Notice how everything sustains and enforces this pattern. It is established by the entry of the "witches". . . . "Fair is foul and foul is fair. . . ." They indicate complete "reversal" by their chant. They "hover through the fog and filthy air", and seek the unclean and the murky by choice, for that is their "good". That there is an irruption of destructive force is indicated by the evil weather, and by the conversation of Ross with

the old man; day has become night, steeds eat each other—The
falcon is killed by the owl. All is

> unnatural
> Even like the deed that's done.

An interesting study might be made of the significance of the apparently
gratuitous "old men" who appear in serious Elizabethan drama to
present simple human wisdom, a symbol of kindly human experience
learnt through the years. More striking still is the symbolism of hell
in the porter scene. Before the murder Macbeth's castle had been
regarded as an emblem of peace, hospitality, and fruitfulness. After the
murder, the drunken porter imagines he is letting people into hell—
as indeed he is. Macbeth's home has become hell, not least for Macbeth
and his wife. Shakespeare's perception of hell agrees with Marlowe's
Mephostophilis. . . .

> For where we are is hell.

It has been suggested that the porter may have entered by the trap-
door, actually emerging from the "hell level" of the mystery plays.
Possibly, but the dramatic effect is clear enough without this. How
far the eighteenth century overlooked the essential drama, attempting
to read it almost solely in terms of character study, may be gauged by
Garrick's triumphant statement that he had purged the play of the
nonsense of the porter scene. From the eighteenth-century attitude
we progress logically to the anxious discussion of the question: "How
many children had Lady Macbeth?" But the real issue is the loss of
her own nature; she would unsex herself, dash the babe from her
breast, in order to achieve her purposes; this is the import of her words.
(To reduce this to an inquiry into the events of her past private life is
unhelpful, however interesting such speculations might be.) Here again
is inversion, even sexual inversion. She becomes the man, while
Macbeth is too full "o' the milk of human kindness".

How far then should the producer consider character? Undoubtedly
these are human beings, and must be presented as such. There are many
helps towards this—Macbeth's own confession of his inner ambitions,
the interplay of speech, his arguments, and emotions. But whatever is
created from such suggestions in the play must clearly be within the
context of the overall action and theme. Similarly, the events of
Shakespeare's own day, the interest in witchcraft, the implied compliments to James, King and descendent of Banquo, stories current at the
time and the earlier use of these, are material available for the playwright, arresting attention, using current allusions and ideas to enforce

the theme and alert the audience; but they are not the play itself. The producer, while knowing the vocabulary of the time, must not mistake this vocabulary for the actual statement made with its assistance. He will note, incidentally, that the Hecate scenes, which reduce the witches to more conventional members of the local coven, were perhaps by Middleton, the playhouse scribe.

APPROACH TO SET DESIGN

The three plays outlined above all demonstrate the fairly constant needs of a Shakespearian production—a large space on which to

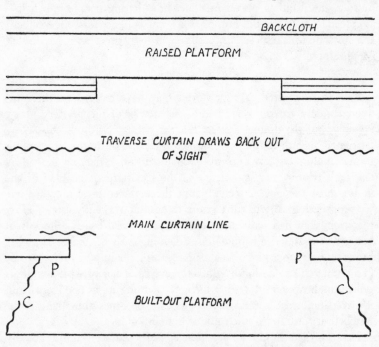

Fig. 29.—PLAN OF BASIC SETTING FOR SHAKESPERIAN DRAMA
PP Existing proscenium
CC Additional curtained entrances on to front stage

marshal court scenes, battles, the flittings of fairies, or the skulkings of robbers. In all there is demand for ceremonial and significant entrances, doors of access to castle, or of egress for opposing armies; again, the bower of Titania, or retreat "behind the arras" for Falstaff, postulate more localised and detailed use of the acting area; while a certain amount of setting may be needed for providing seating in inn, court, or "the Archdeacon's house at Bangor".

The producer will bring to the designer's notice the need to move and group actors—often in large numbers—and to be able to distinguish opposing parties. As against this, his actors require at times an intimate relationship with the audience. To achieve both these requirements is difficult within the conventions of the picture-frame; nothing is impossible, but the three-dimensional grouping and movement needed become merged and muddled unless there are exaggerated differences of level within the proscenium; and the speaking of asides and re-flective comment is difficult across footlights. One solution is to leave the stage as it is (without building out apron or platform) but to remove the existing proscenium frame and front curtain, at the same time reducing the wings space to the minimum. Alternatively, actors may enter from the sides of the auditorium near the stage and walk up on to it by stairways. This device has received professional blessing during the last decade. Lighting will aid immeasurably in emphasising grouping and dramatic relationship, and will add three-dimensional solidity to the actors and their movements. Yet, in the end, one feels that some measure of forestage beyond the proscenium is a natural requirement. Whether (proceeding further) one might stage Shake-speare satisfactorily in the arena is another matter; this is to go deliber-ately counter to his own script. It is one thing, when action has been relegated to a naturalistic drawing-room, within the picture frame, to take this bodily out and to allow the audience to sit (as it were) in the drawing-room for "theatre in the round". It is quite another deliber-ately to pervert an art form carefully related to platform stage and solid architectural backing. In plain experience, although one may go *almost* into full arena, common sense and the script] requirements suggest some kind of established physical structure on one side. In other words, one may go from one possible extreme of Elizabethan theatre to another extreme of Elizabethan theatre, but the components should still be there. Complete picture-frame, on the one hand, or complete arena, on the other, do not seem to have (potentially) much to commend them.

Such physical requirements should be considered carefully. The designer will almost inevitably be led to the use of rostra, either functionally, or with some attempt to justify them as part of a "scene", to create differentiation of level and possibilities for movement and grouping. He may enlist that time-honoured device, the traverse curtain, to enable main scenes to be reset behind while a less exacting

episode is played front stage. If so, he may well use the existing front
curtain as his traverse, building out a forestage in front of it. Action
must be as continuous and swift as in Shakespeare's own day. Whatever
kind of setting be devised this physical ease of manipulation is essential.

Again, he may relate the equipment of his Elizabethan predecessor
to his own running of the play. His whole acting area, with forestage
included, represents the big platform; perhaps he may decide to place
a raised platform across the back of this to represent the "tarras", and to
function as a low gallery. Often in the professional theatre (I call to
mind the Michel St. Denis production of *Twelfth Night*) this is an actual
balcony with a stairway leading to stage level. At once there are varied
possibilities for dramatic grouping; and in any case such a raised area
is rarely out of place. Retaining this platform, he may stage fairly
easily a throne room, a banquet, or a retired bower in woods. The
side doors of entrance in the Elizabethan theatre helped to emphasise
formal distinction of party or army. The designer may go back to
a slightly earlier convention with which these link—one more suitable
for modern theatre than the formal doorway—the pavilion or tent.
On each side of the stage, then, hangings or curtains may represent the
formal entrance. Sometimes these are placed nearer the front (in the
position of proscenium doors of the eighteenth century), sometimes
angled across the upstage corners so that actors can emerge diagonally
on to the main acting area. For pavilions on battlefields the use of such
curtains is obvious. A downstage hanging can be looped back to
indicate that we are looking into a tent; or both can be draped to
represent ornamental hangings merely, without particular place
reference. Fuller pavilions may be made with hanging hoops as
suggested above. Add a small flight of steps each side of the back
platform; back this with a plain skycloth, which can be lit if and as
desired, and, with forestage and front curtain, you have a simple and
flexible setting which will enable you to stage quickly and simply
most of the scenes in a Shakespearian drama. The "pavilions" may
revert to the front stage position suggested in settings for the ritual
plays. An additional mid-stage traverse will give extra possibility for
setting.

When we move on to asymmetrical setting, we engage at once in
a more exacting enterprise. Suppose our raised platform, or balcony,
is set to one side. One pavilion is placed upstage opposite to it. Another
curtain is allowed to fall across the balcony. Scenes produced with relation to this physical basis are now carefully lit to enhance grouping. We
have found a way into the fascination of set design, as intricate and

exciting as can be desired. But we have done this from a primary consideration of the needs of the play, not as an exercise in picture-making. Much more remains—to consider the texture and colour of hangings, and to relate these to the costumes to be used, just as the costumes must be related to the overall intent and atmosphere of the production.

Now let us start again. The Elizabethan setting—using this term to mean the backing of the stage—was architectural, not pictorial. It was an impressive building, suggesting castles, walls, houses, both externally and internally, for the "tarras" and the curtained stage could be regarded as shop and upper projecting storey, or study and over-hanging interior gallery. Suppose we concentrate our design on this aspect. Let us make the raised platform across the back of the stage to represent stonework; let our "tents" become canvas bookflats, painted as stone, our entrances as solid and practicable doors. Now, with backcloth lit, we have ramparts and exterior scenes. With hangings dropped in front of the platform, we have an interior, a castle hall. The Elizabethan doors have become part of a setting acceptable to modern audiences, and the flexibility has been retained. The architectural setting has many developments—from our simple efforts to the gigantic mass effects of Gordon Craig, dwarfing actors beneath symbolic menace; or to the easily portable and variable devices suggested as typical for a slightly impoverished (yet would-be artistic) presentation in Terence Rattigan's *Harlequinade*.

Fig. 29 shows a basic setting. To this may be added further wing curtains or "hoop" pavilions.

I

The Later Elizabethans

THE MATERIAL

THE term "Elizabethan" has been retained; although a more accurate title would be Jacobean and Caroline drama. The period is a long one; it includes several important developments in play styles and theatrical presentation. Again, if one terms Webster and Beaumont and Fletcher "later Elizabethans", Shakespeare should also be included under this heading. He was writing after Beaumont's death, and Webster's best work (commonly considered as later and "decadent") was written in Shakespeare's lifetime.

In comedy, the period is notable for the establishment of the "satiric" or "humours" play, which we associate especially with the name of Ben Jonson—from *Every Man in His Humour* to *Bartholemew Fair*. This involves, in its conscious approach to classical theory and models, a different attitude in professional theatre towards play script. Jonson was laughed at for calling his plays "works", and for his careful publication, laborious comment, and scholarly pride. Although, to the end of the period, the playhouse scribe still adapted and arranged the company's scripts as occasion demanded, the playwright had, in Ben Jonson, demanded and in some measure obtained a higher status. Whether this was desirable or not may be argued; the substitution of theory for practice and theatrical disciplines perhaps helped the development of the literary attitude towards script, and looked forward to the classroom "reading" or annotation of plays meant to be acted. On the other hand, immediacy of appeal and relation to the life of the age, its types, follies, and special pattern, restored the original function of comedy—assuming that this is represented by the work of Aristophanes.

Towards the end of the period, there are signs that the comedy of manners is to supersede the rougher and more strident appeal of the "humours" play. Historians of drama have so stressed the influence of France after the Restoration, admiration of Molière, and the contempt of the Pepysian playgoer for the crudity of the Elizabethans, that we sometimes forget that there was no complete break in dramatic fashion and development, or, indeed, in theatre as a whole. The Commonwealth period intervened, but much that was to be popular after the Restoration was already known in the later years of King Charles I. The works of Shirley, who lived on into the Restoration years, were highly successful on the stage both before and after the Commonwealth period. The emergence of a polished and more or less self-contained social group around the Court, with its own conventions, culture, and code of behaviour, gives the necessary basis for this type of play—so very different in substance and approach from the townspeople, tradesmen, and rogues, who strut across Jonson's stage. Even the title of Shirley's *Hide Park* indicates new material and interest.

Perhaps the period is best typified by the plays rather vaguely termed "romances". Although these may vary from the superb poetry of *The Winter's Tale* (a title again which sufficiently suggests an attitude) to the rumbustious action of Fletcher's *Wild Goose Chase*, there is still a persistent similarity through all, the thrill of action and event within a "never-never land" of the imagination. Critics have called this "escapism"; but Shakespeare is able to present some of the greatest and most moving human experiences through symbol, language, and situation in *The Winter's Tale;* for others the far-away country is perhaps merely a convenient device to involve their audience immediately in the world of make-believe, to detach them from everyday life. Shakespeare himself, in his "romantic comedies", used such remoteness. "This is Illyria, lady". Anything can happen there, just as in later Ruritania. The important thing is to approach these plays for what they are, and not (as some misguided Victorians) as naturalistic drama related to historically accurate backgrounds. Charles Kean's laborious efforts with *The Winter's Tale* are notorious. Perhaps the romantic play was a means of escape in times of disillusion, but the theatre still, using the means of expression available, dealt with life, or could do so. Many of the plays printed as "Beaumont and Fletcher" belong to this style—but there is infinite variety and the "romance" merges into other forms.

Intrigue, bustle, and gentlemanly amusement, are found in some plays, involving the wandering cavalier and his servant (perpetuated in eighteenth-century theatre, when many of these same later Elizabethan plays still held the stage). Such was Fletcher's *Rule a Wife and Have a Wife*. Again, one feels the influence from abroad—Lope de Vega's ingenious entertainments, bright, diverting, but "romantically" detached from ordinary life were known to the Jacobean playwrights.

The attempt to bring to the English theatre something of the interests and tastes of the travelled courtier—and the expression of his attitudes —was inevitable. The theatre catered for "upper" and "lower". The middle classes were satirised—but were not so important, perhaps, as potential audience. Beaumont, Fletcher, and Shirley were themselves in the circle of the "genteel". Shakespeare had aspired to, and had gained, "gentility". "Love and honour", "gallantry" in both the old and the modern senses of the word, was, to be a persisting dramatic theme for many years. From the slower moving, heavier garbed, Elizabethans we come to agile and witty gentlemen of fortune.

Yet at the same time, there were dramatists whose serious purpose and anxiety was reflected in their drama. Massinger in *A New Way to Pay Old Debts* established his action round the social injustice which allowed the grasping money-grubber to flourish. But even more typical was the dramatic use of moral arguments and dispute. Social justice or injustice one had to accept, to circumvent, or to use. But man's moral responsibility, man's duty and faith, these matters were still important to each individual who cared to order his life aright. The thinkers of the Renaissance, the theologians of the Reformation, had raised doubts, everywhere, in the minds of men. Old landmarks had vanished. By what did one direct one's course, judge one's actions? Here theatre, by "trying out" (as it were) situations, by presenting experimentally the crisis of life, enters into one of its most important artistic and creative functions. Ford, in such a play as *'Tis Pity She's a Whore* pushes the demands of sexual love to the uttermost; earlier, the social question had been whether father or mother should interfere with the course of passion, and the issue is by no means clear, even in *Romeo and Juliet*. Now, apparently, no barriers are to be admitted. Adultery, incest, nothing can be really bad so long as passion is obeyed; the sympathy of the audience is invoked for the lovers.

Who would not say, "'Tis pity she's a whore"? In an age when temporarily (despite all efforts by rulers and church dignitaries) mental chaos had come, theatre explored (quite effectively) some potential arguments and positions. Ford has been called our first "problem" playwright. The definition is one of emphasis. Every play contains its problem if it reflects and interprets life; Ford is using contemporary situation and thought to create an effective piece of theatre—not primarily to preach; if he did so he would cease to be an artist; and he never does.

Further interest in life at the social rather than the metaphysical and religious level is reflected in the tragedies of the later period. Again there is the link with Continental travel, thought, and story, the recording of events in corrupt Italian princedoms. God's name may be invoked; we are not dealing however, with essential tragic themes, but with intrigue, waste, frustration, and sheer brutality, as typified in the selfish strivings of man with man. There is no compelling fate, other than man's own inherent corruption. Which is indeed a tragic theme, but ceases to be so when taken for granted as a basis for all action. There is no clash, no suspense, as a hero or heroine strives unavailingly with the nature of things   but simply the contest of gang against gang, horror against horror. Accepting this, we still find in the nightmare world of Webster or Tourneur beauty, and significance for our own age. There is human achievement and human values even alongside the most sordid murders. That is the significance, surely, of the famous and not overpraised line

> Cover her face; mine eyes dazzle; she died young.

It is theatrically powerful.

For the more ambitious producer and his company there is varied and exciting theatrical material in this period, provided, as always, he (and they) can find a way into its life and experience. It must be accepted on its own terms, approached seriously, and not with the intent to exploit solely the shock and horror of the action.

THE STAGING OF THE TIME.

The existing features of the Elizabethan theatre remained until and during the period of the Civil War. One Elizabethan theatre at least, the Red Bull, was reopened and used after the Restoration. There was, however, some change in the emphasis of presentation. The influence of the Court mask, with its beautiful and fantastic costumes, dances, music and symbolic settings, was undoubtedly felt on the public stage. The insertion of masks into play script (as in *The Tempest*, or even the short Hymen procession in *As You Like It*) shows that dramatists considered and used this elaboration and embellishment. Clearly, too, the possibility of "scenery" was not forgotten, whether in "private" or "public" theatre. There are, however, two contemporary trends in "scenery". There is the set piece (comparable with the "houses" of medieval times) adorned and beautified as desired; hangings, curtains, decorated devices, would all be part of this; and there is changeable scenery, which could be altered (as in the mask) from time to time as locality changed. As we have seen, even if adorned only by its ordinary architectural features, the Elizabethan playhouse furnished an elegant "setting"; this could be further enhanced by suitable hangings, devices, or properties—thrones, canopies, or (realistic horror) a heap of waste soil. In the private theatre the more formal "house" system was still appropriate, and probably survived with the "labelled' entrance. There is nothing really surprising in further "decoration" of the scene, especially when one considers the luxurious corruption of localities presented in later plays of the period. When a play *The Royal Slave* had been performed at Christ Church, Oxford, in 1636, the Chancellor, at the Queen's request, sent the "Cloathes and Perspectives of the Stage" to Hampton Court, but asked that neither the play, nor clothes, nor "stage" should come into the "hands and use of the common Players". The desire of the professionals to secure such effects and to use them is apparent. Indoor theatre—specifically the Blackfriars—did produce plays with scenery towards the end of the period. Sir John Suckling's *Aglaura* (1637), Habington's *The Queen of Arragon*, were given there with "scenes". More significantly, the latter play was first shown at Court. Court dramatic décor could, apparently, be used in the indoor public theatre (the so-called "private" house). Further, at Court plays were now presented with scenery in addition to the masks embellished in this way. Fletcher's *The Faithful Shepherdess* was acted at Denmark House with scenery as early as 1634. The interchange between public playhouse—anyway of the indoor type—and the Court was at least a constant possibility. That for a worker in theatre scenery meant "changeable scenery"—and not the simple embellishment of the architectural setting—again seems fairly clear. That it was indeed not usual is indicated by the notice taken of it; the prologue to Nabbes' *Hannibal and Scipio*, (at the Phoenix in Drury Lane, 1635) states that "the places sometimes chang'd too for the Scene". Brome's *Antipodes*, has a prologue (1638) which seems to mock the "Scene magnificent". Finally, that the theatres of the day had not yet normally adopted "scenery" of the changeable type—indeed, how could they?—is indicated by D'Avenant's application in 1639 to be allowed to build a theatre with scenes. He had to wait through the turmoil of the Civil War before his ambition could be achieved. He, again, in his own career illustrates the continuity of effort and development which the Civil War failed to break permanently. The Restoration theatre and its practice emerge from the trends and styles of pre-Commonwealth work.

The more elaborate indoor setting moved along lines established by Italian theatre builders. It is, indeed, the combination of the medieval house convention with a classical and unified plan, architecturally observing accepted Renaissance models. At the Cockpit in Court (probably) the stage was backed by a semicircle of entrances contained in an elaborate architectural façade. Later, another design shows such entrances reduced (apparently) to a single large semicircular arch, behind which scenes may be placed in perspective. Although this was probably only a project, the blend of conventions may be perceived—the formal places of entry with scene change for pictorial effect, the medieval and pseudo-classical on the one side, and the newer "changeable" scenery on the other.

What, then, can we imagine as normal setting for our plays of this period? In the main, probably, the usual Elizabethan "open-air" conventions, but with increasing interest in costume, mask, and at times almost grotesque and vivid elaboration, implied by stage directions and the general desire to emulate court lavishness and spectacle. When plays were produced in "private" houses, contained by firm side walls, free from gallery seating, there were two possibilities; first, to establish a more imposing fixed setting which related to the "house" tradition of presentation; second, on occasion to import and to set up the "sliding" scene changes (or other technique) of Court theatre. The earlier linking of the Blackfriar's Theatre with the Court and academic drama may be recalled; Lyly's plays used the "house" conventions, which could easily be construed as demanding the "magnifica palatia aedesque apparatissimae" used at Oxford as early as 1566, and continued into the sixteenth century in such a play as Percy's *Fairy Pastoral* with its numerous "houses" and localities, and signboards (or labelled entrances) where these were not possible. Scenic enlargement and embellishment would be natural in such a theatre, and its varying usages would be combined to meet the public interest in scenery, and to its "house" or "architectural" décor, the changing setting adopted from the Court masks could be added.

APPROACH TO SET DESIGN

The designer may well start from the later Elizabethan theatre, its levels and areas of acting; to this, if the play seems to suit, he may add further architectural dignity; on the other hand, he may secure his effect by imaginative use of hangings, lighting, and richer decoration; even, perhaps, by painted scenery, which could have been used by the theatre of the time, though with some sense of its "modernity". This is his starting point, the kind of assumptions he may legitimately make about the presentation of plays in the period. From them he will see how he can best interpret the play, as his producer desires, to the modern audience.

With this developing richness in presentation, there is scope for a very varied approach. The increasing emphasis on scenic awareness subtly changes the style and pattern of play scripts designed for the public theatre. It would, of course, be easy to select examples to the contrary, but overall there is a move from the architectural stage to a decorated setting, decorated perhaps through words, subject, and implication, rather than by definite instructions, despite the indications of careful background noted above. Thus a rapid succession of "scenes" on the platform is rare in later plays of the period. The "classical" division into five acts becomes more normal, in place of the looser groupings of early scripts; dramatists work to a definite form, which encourages longer "episodes" and sequences of action, with an attempt to observe (in some cases) the classical unities of place, time, and subject. So it has been found possible (if not actually completely satisfactory) to stage the more developed plays of Ben Jonson within the picture-frame, almost without modification of normal modern practice. *The Alchemist* with its insistence on the apparatus and "scientific" devices of the charlatan comes to mind. The locality persists. Even here, however, before he diverges too abruptly from Elizabethan theatrical convention, the scene designer may do well to examine the action of the play carefully. He will find that doorways have a significance and a dramatic import which at once indicates Jonson's use of the typical entrances of his time; further, the disguisings and emergences of Doll are planned from the position of these doorways. He will find, too, the convenience of the large curtained inner stage—and the value of the "tarras" for flexibility of grouping and pointing of incident. Again, before he deviates into some over-cosy and villa-like interior, he will recall that the setting is the house of a wealthy man—which might well have its musicians' gallery, its due dignity and opulence. Indeed, it is this very authority of setting which enables the rogues to impress their dupes. Jonson has his own stage in mind when he writes his script. Heavy and impressive doorways, two levels of acting, rich curtains, may well be incorporated into the presentation after the producer has indicated the movements and entrances desired.

On the other hand, the same writer's *Bartholemew Fair* suggests (even in its title) the use of "houses", booths, and the open space. Light, sunshine, the movement of crowds, replace the interior, hushed and impressive, of *The Alchemist*. We have to establish the intent of the dramatist; had he written today, he would not have spurned the extra aids that we have in production, in lighting and varied stage pattern; his intent we may realise fully for him, provided we establish, first of all, how far he could fulfil it with his own stage.

The use of the traverse curtain—or curtains—is valuable today in the tragedies of intrigue and hate. Nor need the curtain be hung parallel to the front of the stage; angled slightly it will give a more dynamic pattern for grouping and entrances. Its colour and texture may well reflect the mood of the play; its draping gives varied possibilities—the half open, looped folds of a hanging before a lady's bedroom; the wider opening which gives access to a state chamber; or the straight formal line which may unobtrusively mask in the stage sides and blend into wings set behind it during the previous scene when the traverse was closed. Further, two or three such curtains may be placed immediately behind one another, so that, although the pattern of stage space is almost identical, varying moods and localities can be quickly suggested. *The Revenger's Tragedy, The White Devil, The Malcontent, The Cardinal,* suggest the skulker behind the arras, violent action emerging from the heavy draperies of outward luxury in which corruption lurks. The creation of atmosphere by such means is the achievement of the set designer, and satisfactory scope is afforded by these plays. Lighting will help him; costume will (by its rich decadence, perhaps) assist the general communication of mood and situation to his audience. This period of our drama can (in this respect) be a valuable training ground; but at the same time the designer must not neglect the physical requirements of the presentation. However he attempts to convey corruption, whatever symbolic device he may choose, the grinning skull or the voluptuous Venus on the tapestry, he has still to provide for the trial scene and its formality in, say, *The White Devil.* In short, he must consider the total resources available to the original company and must provide equivalents in his own design.

Later comedies, such as Shirley's *The Lady of Pleasure,* begin to suggest the more elegant interior setting. This was to merge into the "private house" convention of the Restoration theatre, a place where a gentleman met his friends, and where the people upon the stage were known almost as intimately as his acquaintances in the audience. We are witnessing the emergence of a "class" theatre, in which actors and audience belong to the same "set", and accept certain fashions, behaviour, and ideals; and, equally, regard certain other attitudes with disgust; all are united by common assumptions. Our setting may indicate the more delicate furniture, the less ponderous hangings, the fripperies of the Cavalier. In such accessories intent and atmosphere

will emerge; the acting space should be uncluttered, and freely available for the sweep of the hat, the elegant bow, the movement of the swordsman. Exteriors, too, may be simple, but with a suggestion of open space, parterres, parkland, and gaiety, the heavier hedges of the Elizabethans opening to admit air—and colour.

As for romantic plays of intrigue and swashbuckling, their locality is an imaginary land for which any style suggested by events may be adopted. Costume may be pseudo-Spanish or Italian based on styles of the Renaissance period; but always, I think, with suggestions of gay exaggeration, the slightly exotic and bizarre, not the "fantastic" of the poetic romances. These plays are part of the "fripperies" of ladies and gentlemen, light, inconsequential, bustling, and fanciful. In them, the period is "romanticised". Again, physical requirements are not to be forgotten, the important doorway to the inner room, the lady's mansion, the inn-yard and its upper window, were basically provided by the original setting.

Restoration Theatre

THERE was no abrupt break, between the so-called "Elizabethan" and "Restoration" drama and theatre. During the Commonwealth drama had persisted; some kind of tradition had been maintained. An apparent difference is accentuated because the Restoration period maintained only one kind of existing theatre, one aspect of theatre practice—the "private house". True, the Red Bull survived for a few years—unfrequented. The smaller indoor playhouse became the norm. The vast theatre-going public of the period before the Civil War had dwindled to the court party, the fashionable and loyal. Puritan opposition had successfully broken the "popular" appeal of dramatic performances. A glance at Pepys' *Diary* will show how, for a man of the middle classes, even one associated with the Court, theatre-going was a rather shameful indulgence. Wealthy middle-class merchants and citizens had opposed theatre; the common people and the lower middle-class had filled the Elizabethan playhouse; it was not entirely the disreputable elements (noted by the preachers) who, with the court gallants and wits, made up the audience. The ordinary citizen and his wife—as *The Knight of the Burning Pestle* may suggest—still took their customary and traditional interest in drama. Yet after the Restoration, despite renewed opportunities for playgoing, it was the smaller, more "select", private house that survived. Further, since the reopening of theatres was achieved by the Restoration of the Monarch—the Commonwealth had done all it could to shut theatres permanently—it was only natural that these new playhouses should associate themselves with their patrons, and acquire in the eyes of respectability something of the suspicion that attached to Court behaviour and morality.

Here, again, Restoration practice continues the trend established before the Civil War, the attempt to transport into the public playhouse the styles and scenic device of Court plays. Even more remarkable, the brooding presence of persistent D'Avenant is felt before, during, and after, the Commonwealth period, striving towards the theatre with "scenes", for which he had secured a patent in 1639. Thrones may fall, revolution and conflict tear a kingdom asunder, but the true man

of theatre goes steadily on his way, waiting and preparing for his public. With considerable skill he managed for a time to evade the government prohibition of dramatic performances by putting as it were "oratorios" in costume, with scenery designed by John Webb, during the Commonwealth. Again, the significant pattern (from Court to private house theatre) emerges. John Webb had been Inigo Jones' assistant in the Court masques. After the Restoration, D'Avenant was

Fig. 30.—CROSS SECTION THROUGH ACTING AREA
OF A RESTORATION THEATRE. *c.* 1680

at once ready to open a theatre "with scenes"—which meant changeable scenery on the model of that finally achieved in the masks—sliding wings and backing, or "shutters", as the wings became when they moved right across the stage to meet in the centre. Killigrew, his rival director, who had secured a patent (still possessed by Drury Lane) from the King for theatrical presentation, took much longer to establish the use of "scenery" in his own Theatre Royal. Not until 1663 was he able to open a theatre thus equipped.

When drama became "legal" once more, we have then three

forms of theatre: (a) One or two old private houses, such as the Salisbury Court, (b) One at least of the old "public" playhouses—several had been destroyed or pulled down, (c) the use of further "private house" theatres, notably the alteration of tennis courts, Gibbon's (Vere Street) and Lisle's (Lincoln's Inn Fields), into auditorium and stage, This device was repeated on other occasions; there is no special significance in the operation, merely convenience, as in the earlier use of an inn-yard. The covered court used for "real" tennis was clearly "private"—it gave a suitable acting area and auditorium; few private houses available were so convenient. Further, the covered gallery along one side was all ready for spectators. The height of the building, again, afforded the amplitude and magnified effect the actors were accustomed to demand. By digging out the floor of the "court", a raked auditorium could be contrived, sloping down towards the now elevated stage. So, we are told by some, the term "pit" came into use, and indeed the "pit" is often well below existing ground level. By a process of development and elimination, the large public theatres were disused, while the smaller private theatres continued, but added changeable setting, and accorded with court fashion and taste. It is important, however, for producer and actor to realise that Restoration drama and theatre had evolved and survived from total "Elizabethan" stage activity; there is no abrupt break, only a confirmation of tendencies already established. Thus any rather artificial and precious approach to Restoration drama will be avoided. It has the same vitality and sincerity as the earlier drama, but it is the theatre, rightly or wrongly, for better or worse, of a minority, a drama of class and party. Their assumptions and ideals, codes of behaviour and intentions, must be accepted, both in the study of the script and the methods of presentation. In addition, there was one very significant change—the advent of the actress. This, indeed, unlike so many of the changes which were more apparent than real, was of fundamental importance. Even here, however, women were not used immediately and always; but when the actress was established as the normal portrayer of the heroine, dramatists wrote with the actress in mind, audiences came to see the actress; the connection with the social life and amours of the court became even closer, and the theatre even less respectable in the eyes of some.

THE MATERIAL

At first theatres competed to use existing play scripts. Thus the dramas of Shakespeare were divided between them; Betterton was kept for many years from essaying some of the chief Shakespearian parts. Although in tragedy Shakespeare still held the stage—and would continue to do so—in comedy (apart from *Much Ado*—a study of courtly wit much in keeping with the new taste of the time) his work often seemed childish and upsophisticated to people who had lost the clue, as it were, to its significance. *The Dream* seemed "silly" to Pepys, who noted that these old plays began to "disgust" his more polished times. Again, as one might expect, the plays of Beaumont and Fletcher and the comedies of Shirley were popular, just as in the later years of the preceding period these had represented the trend of taste. And this trend was further emphasised by the fact that the theatre was the theatre of a class; thus a true "comedy of manners" was possible, comedy in which the slight deviation from the norm expected could be held to ridicule, or various interpretations of accepted patterns of behaviour could be exploited, and attempts to conform to fashionable practice could be examined and lightly satirised. The king had become accustomed to this dramatic form in France, where Molière could, with Royal support, expose the follies of those who marred and spoilt the accepted order, who erred from the behaviour and taste expected of lady and gentleman. It is this accepted code (or its existence) which must be perceived to secure any rightly directed production. The comedy of manners is a delicate thing; it is by no means a rumbustious immoral romp; it has its standards and its codes, varying as the years pass. Nor are exaggerated affectation and satiric heaviness the way to exploit its true flavour, however hard it may be to find a way to the heart of a modern audience, who do not share for one moment either the culture or the moral attitude of those who witnessed its first performance and caught every innuendo and passing reference to fashion and fad. Cynthia in Wycherley's *The Double Dealer* asks what a "manner" is. Lady Froth tells her: "Some distinguishing Quality, as, for example, the *Bel-air* or Brilliant of Mr. *Brisk* . . . or some thing of his own, that should look a little Jene-scay-quoysh", indicating what Nicoll has so well termed "a grace or a habit of refined culture".

The material available for the producer in this period is varied, unusual, and has never been fully exploited, or only sporadically revived. Again, like the so-called Elizabethan period, the term "Restoration" is used carelessly to cover fifty years of theatrical activity during which there were important changes and developments. Even the dramatists who are thought of as typically "Restoration"— for example, Congreve and Vanbrugh—actually worked in succeeding reigns, Vanbrugh into the early eighteenth century, and the clothes and manners associated with their work are very different (*pace* some producers and designers) from that fashionable in the true Restoration period of, say, 1660–67.

During the years 1660–80 we have the early comedy of manners, co-existent with the revival of Court life and the growing French influence, the work of Etherege with his dandified Sir Fopling Flutter, the frequent adaptations and imitations of Molière, known to exiles during their life in France. The comedy of manners develops into the more savage work of Wycherley, and culminates in the work of Congreve during the reign of William and Mary. The passing of the Court society of the Restoration, the more puritanical and philistine attitudes of William and Mary's reign, virtual withdrawal of active Court patronage, make the continuance of the true "manners" comedy difficult. The society which it celebrates, and the audience which appreciated it, have both passed. Congreve's last comedy *The Way of the World* was noticed by a fashionable correspondent; her brief verdict was "it doth not please".

The serious ideals of the gentleman and courtier, and the imitation of the "classical" drama which he found to his taste, produced the "heroic" plays. Charles II considered that serious tragedy should be written in rime, as were the stately plays of Corneille and Racine. Dryden's *Essay on Dramatic Poesy* is the work not merely of a skilled and sensitive critic but also of a practising dramatist; the various controversies, the conscious artistry of the age, may be studied there. To know the aims behind the play scripts of the period, the producer should examine Dryden's arguments. The heroic plays, far-fetched and rhetorical as they seem at first reading, have their own appeal. Once, again, the existence of a separate dramatic genre should be acknowledged; and they must be judged by their aims and for what they are, and not by reference to Shakespearian tragedy on the one side or modern naturalistic drama on the other. Played, again, with sincerity, and with careful attention to the subtle rhythms of their diction, the studied classical dignity which they tried to emulate, they might well be revived with some success—even though the neo-classical theories, mediated through France and French theatre, which led rather self-consciously to their production, are felt to be dubious and invalid. So, too, one must accept, as a basis of presentation, the conflict between love and honour which occupied so much of the serious thought of the Restoration gentleman. His integrity as a subject, his loyalty to the ideals of chivalric love, are not to be scoffed at—however his behaviour

in more mundane affairs seems incompatible with such lofty protestations. Even today love and honour are not entirely outmoded forces
in human life. The first phase of heroic tragedy developed with the
comedy of manners; gradually writers returned (Dryden included) to
blank verse. Again, with the increasing moral earnestness of the con-
cluding years of the century, heroic tragedy revived for a while.

Alongside these two typical styles, we find dramas of satiric humours
—Shadwell wrote several which held the stage, and could again be
revived successfully, such as *Epsom Wells* (1672). Perhaps alongside
this drama of "types" one might mention the influence of the *commedia
dell'arte*. Admittedly Molière's plays, which inspired the comedy of
manners, had originated from work in the *commedia* tradition, but once
he applied his mind to the dramatic examination of his own society the
theatrical work of his company became more subtle, refined, and
pointed; the improvisation and repetitive business of the stock professional company developed into the comedy of manners. Nevertheless
in the English Restoration comedy, its themes, characters, there is, often
enough, the "feel" and "style" of the professional *commedia*—the old
dotard, the faithless wife, the intriguing servant, the "poetic"
heroine (so strongly contrasted with less moral ladies in the drama),
all recall the masks and movements of the *commedia*. Yet, essentially,
in the comedy of manners we move into another theatrical style.
That was why it was possible for genuine *commedia* characters to be
introduced, for example, by Mrs. Aphra Behn into *The Emperor of the
Moon*. These characters were to emerge in the specialised English
theatrical style termed "pantomime" in the eighteenth century. The
native satiric comedy of types, however, stayed with us. It became an
ingredient in nearly all dramatic writing, an accepted convention,
especially in the rather repetitive plays of the early nineteenth century
But original satiric impact and relevance was lost; the dramatists used
types simply as useful puppets, a short cut to an acceptable play,
rather than with intent to enlarge the vision of the audience. There is
no venom, no sense of urgency. Types remained; their real theatrical
function was lost.

A further development and one that has proved relevant to modern
theatre was that of the so-called "opera". When one recalls that
Downes, prompter and book-keeper (earlier playhouse scribe) for
D'Avenant and Betterton, defined, in his *Roscius Anglicanus*, an opera
as a play with "machines", it is immediately plain that the term is
used with reference to elaborate effect rather than musical elegance. And
yet the two went together. D'Avenant, the writer of masks and lover

of scenery, was the man who went furthest in his efforts—expensive ones—to attract audiences through this style of play. Basically, he relied on extravagant setting, ingenious scene changes, puzzling and dazzling effects, associated dances (involving delightful and fantastic costumes), and the music and song which naturally formed a part of such stage spectacle. The link with the mask was clear. Here, too, dance and music—as well as sumptuous dress and setting—were important. Normal scene change, standardised from the later masks, and close to his productions at Rutland House, were insufficient for "opera". Settings were "built up" on stage, all kinds of extra effects and magical transformations took place; such methods were associated only with the "operas". Hence, Downes' remark is not altogether irrelevant. When the music of Purcell accompanied such productions, the total theatrical effect must have been very great. Shakespeare's plays—perhaps because of their imaginative scope—were sometimes used as material for these entertainments. Naturally, wherever supernatural effects and magical powers were needed, there was potentially a basis for operatic presentation. Thus, *Macbeth* became an opera with magical flyings and additional wizardry; while *The Dream* became *The Fairy Queen*; the entire last act was concerned with the visit of Oberon to the Court of Theseus, during which he put on a show of his magical power—really a demonstration of stage techniques then available. Scenes change, objects fade and disappear. . . . Similarly in Dryden's *Albion and Albanius* (1685)

The Clouds divide, and Juno appears in a Machine drawn by Peacocks; while a Simphony is playing, it moves gently forward, and as it descends, it opens and discovers the Tail of the Peacock, which is so large that it almost fills the opening of the Stage between Scene and Scene.

In stage directions to *The Prophetess* (an "operatic" adaptation from Beaumont and Fletcher) "Figures come out of the Hangings and Dance; And Figures exactly the same appear in their Places. When they have danc'd for a while they go to sit on the Chairs, they slip from 'em, and after joyn in the Dance with 'em".

Once established, the spectacular show remains in varying forms, with changing tricks and elaborations. Its production is a matter largely, though not entirely, of technique; the effects that please one generation are not so attractive or wonderful for the next. Its spectacle is in terms of the developments and conventions of the period. Yet, if one takes a larger view, many of the ideas, themes, suggested movements, and scenic plans, of the Restoration "opera" might well be adapted for

modern stage presentation. The operas themselves have been revived
with some success with, on one occasion at least, even increased elaboration and attention to décor. Several plays from the Beaumont and
Fletcher group, such as *The Island Princess,* were converted into "opera"
by the addition of songs, requisite rewriting, and the splendour of
production which was an essential part of this theatrical genre. Finally,
one must stress again that such splendours, and even the machinery
of setting, were peculiar to these plays. From normal theatrical
practice, the spectacular show stood apart.

Towards the end of the period "blank-verse" tragedy is written
again, consciously taking the place of the rimed heroic plays which
attempted to regularise, to dignify English theatre, and to serve "neo-
classical" ideals. While in Lee and Otway something of Elizabethan
emotion and energy survives, the more typical tragedy of the coming
Augustan period may be studied in Congreve's *The Mourning Bride.*
Elegance of diction, the avoidance of the ill-bred, exaggerated, or
grotesque, the slow and stately movement and rhetorical beauty of the
so-called "classical" tragedies form yet another theatrical experience.
Nicholas Lee had himself earlier set the fashion for the "she tragedy"
with *The Rival Queens.* Indeed, it is difficult to separate the classical
tragedy from the beautiful and stately actresses, such as Mrs. Barry,
who spoke its lines to such effect. In these, rather than in the heroic
tragedies, English drama came nearest to the theatre of Corneille and
Racine. Critical writings of the time indicate the lines were spoken with
a recognised tune or cadence, a kind of melodious recitative, a conscious
stage convention and tune which, as Montague Summers once pointed
out, survived (and may still be heard almost as a natural redevelopment)
among the older English actresses down to the twenties of our own
century. Again, the aims and patterns of such dramatic pieces must be
fully accepted as a possible basis for theatrical presentation by the
producer before he undertakes to stage them.

THE PRODUCER'S APPROACH

Because the language, and the inserted stage directions, are much
closer to our own time, the producer may well tend to underestimate
the preliminary work which is needed before production of a Restoration comedy; contrariwise, he may avoid the presentation of a heroic
tragedy or a classical play, just because it seems so very different from
our style of theatre. A Restoration comedy of manners is just about
the final test of the producer's art. First, as we shall note, the actual
staging and running of the play, apparently so like our own, were in

reality based on entirely different assumptions, which are reflected in the play script. Secondly, while the actual unfolding of the plot, the course of dialogue, the characters concerned, seem fairly clear, we do not (we feel) need to consult lengthy volumes on the symbolism or metaphysical preoccupations of the period; but there still remain the less tangible but equally important assumptions and attitudes upon which the dramatic fabric is reared. Even in the matter of dress and fashions this is misunderstood. Too many productions (even professional) seem to assume that an appearance of exotic affectation is sufficient basis for the wit and action of the male characters. If a man dressed in the exaggerated style of the Restoration period today, he would undoubtedly seem dandified. But this, at the time, was accepted male attire. Make-up, jewellery, scent, were the perquisites of even the toughest. We have to secure the character variation, strength, weakness, honesty, and dishonesty, within the general appearance and manner accepted by all. And truly dandified or effeminate must be distinct from the rest. Each actor must be both "gentle"—polished, witty, elegant—and at the same time a credible "man". Unfortunately, today virility seems to be identified by many with rudeness, roughness, and uncouth dress. Yet the Restoration comedy has its tough characters, too; a thorough consideration of character and situation in the light of seventeenth-century ideals is needed. Lastly, we must note that during the so-called Restoration period a great change took place in male dress. The ribbons and excessive frippery of the early years gave way to the more tailored and elegant (many would think) fashions of the reigns of James, William and Mary, and Anne. Clearly actors need careful training in their movement with reference to costume, the bow, the curtsy, wearing of the wig, the use of accessories, typical stance and attitude, sitting and rising, and so on

Detailed and reasoned study of dialogue is important. Much drama now depends upon strife of characters through the spoken word, a contest of wit, the truly "dramatic" use of speech. Conflict and final resolution have never been, perhaps, so well presented in theatre as in the famous "proviso" scene between Mirabel and Millament, more exciting and strenuous than any physical battle and headlong action. At the beginning of the period, the self-revealing speeches of Sir Fopling Flutter are just as indicative of amusing event and dramatic struggle. Here is the essence of the comedy of manners—the strain and distortion introduced into society by the variant individual, who develops his own "manner" too far from the norm, and is held up to well-bred amusement. This apparently mild conflict is exciting. The sense of tension and opposition is communicated to us because their writer's own assumptions and views are obviously shared by others in the play. That is why correct speaking of the dialogue is vital. Again, no glib "patter" of speech in an "affected" voice will serve. Each thought, line, and inflexion, must be considered, the exact nuance decided, and then the rate of delivery speeded until it comes with apparent easy spontaneity and complete finality as the automatic response of the individual speaker. The pronunciation of the time must be used where possible, since the rhythm and point of a line depend upon it. This is an age of elegant diction, of sensitivity to the music of speech, vowel sounds especially, and to the balance and rhythm of statement—not less in prose than in the flowing beauties of the heroic couplet.

So far nothing has been said about plot. Naturally the producer will make a clear statement of the course of action. He will note the relationship of characters, the movement of events, minor crises, and the final climax. In the case of such a true comedy of manners as *The Way of the World* he may find some difficulty in sorting out the rather complex relationships to his own satisfaction. For while the Elizabethan dramatist is often typically concerned (whether in comedy or tragedy) with "theme", round which events and characters group and adjust through struggle, the Restoration dramatist is more concerned with relationship either in society (manners comedy) or in ideal action (heroic tragedy). How do characters relate to an accepted pattern of behaviour and thought? Further, what relationships are perceived by them in their thought and action—what "wit" is engendered? For "wit" involves the capacity to see relationship where none is obviously apparent. This is the grace of the cultured and civilised man—delightfully to express accepted truths, to illuminate and to perceive pattern and continuity within the fabric of the civilised community; to note, too, with incisive comment the aberrations from urbane (and urban) standards. It is thus within the situation that the delight of this comedy is discovered, rather than in the overall strife of the plot. Indeed, sometimes one feels that the play ends rather because it would be ill-bred to continue longer than because action has been now fully achieved, the climax reached and passed. After the curtain falls, the intrigues will recommence, entanglements and mischief develop anew. In someone else's play the dance will go joyfully on. It is this sense of continuity and permanence, of accepted standards and settled values, that makes comedy of manners possible. The producer must, therefore, not fall into the temptation of waiting for the amusing situation, the purple patch, such as Mrs. Pinchwife's letter-writing, or Valentine's "madness" in *Love for Love*. These plays afford such excerpts, often performed by students as test pieces; but too often full production seems to consist of such high moments linked by rather pedestrian passages which are less familiar to the producer and therefore less carefully worked. There must be an attempt to catch the real wit of each part of the play, and to secure, as far as possible, overall satisfaction and fulfilment in the comedy as a complete drama. Only then can the situations be really appreciated in their relevance to the whole character scheme and social pattern. And just because that social pattern is unfamiliar to us (and could be assumed by the Restoration audience and playwright) we must do our best to place the audience in position, as it were, to enjoy the play and to see its dramatic purpose. A brief programme note, a short description of each character (in the style of Victorian acting versions), may help, though anything lengthy defeats its purpose, suggesting the antiquary rather than the live performer.

All through this period and the succeeding century the producer must be familiar with the fashions and fads that excite satire and ridicule; we are nearing the great age of satire; and pointing of dialogue, whether or not the audience follows, is achieved only by knowing the writer's intent, and the relation of the speech to its speaker. The "provisos" of Mirabel and Millament are an encyclopaedic commentary on the tastes and manners of the period, and (further) a revelation of the essential good sense and healthiness of the two speakers; further still, a presentment of their own wit, wisdom, and zestful enjoyment of the social scene, their good-humoured mockery of its follies. Satiric intent is still more important in the "humours" plays of Shadwell, where the scope of characterisation is wider, even though the characters themselves are more "typed" than the elegant ladies and gentlemen of "manners" comedy. Finally, what is a manner, as distinct from the "humour" of satiric writing? It is defined in Wycherley's *Double Dealer* as "some distinguishing quality". It is the subtle variation —for better or worse—from the balanced and accepted courtly, fashionable, standards which adds vivacity and richness to the business of life, pleasure and individuality to the cultured in their daily (and nightly) business and diversion.

In the "heroic" plays, the producer has a fairly straightforward task, the actors a more difficult rôle. The theme is clear—the demands of honour, the duties of ideal love, the suffering to be borne, the emotions to be touched; all these are blended. There is little intricacy of movement. Where the stage is crowded, it is with the dignity of processions and courtly ritual. The producer contrives the picture and places his actors in suitable prominence and in pleasing attitude. He can ask them to accept the ideals and dilemmas of the characters. But once he has done that the actor has to learn to walk the stage and to speak the lines with clarity and beauty, without exaggeration, and at the same time with a sense of their subtly varying rhythms, always with the consciousness that this is far from naturalistic drama—significant attitude and rhetorical grace are essential. Once the actor over-emphasises and the note of falsity intrudes the whole fabric is shattered. How easy the style was to parody may be seen in satirical plays, such as Buckingham's *The Rehearsal*, which made fun of its solemnities and its obsession with "love" and "honour". Perhaps this is one dramatic form where the studied gesture of the old-fashioned "elocutionist" (and his sense of sound values and rhythms) is really useful. Long speeches must be studied in detail, and their real climaxes determined. An interminably monotonous vocal appeal, with a constant throb of emotion, would destroy the reasoned, patterned, movement of the rhetoric and its real dramatic pathos.

THE ORIGINAL STAGING

The Restoration theatre had its scenic effects. But in front of these, flanked on both sides by two large doors of entrance, was what we may term the "real" stage. The idea that the Restoration playhouse was overall a "picture-frame" stage is erroneous. It may be considered a logical development from the indoor Elizabethan theatre, with the curtained recess widened to allow of more complete setting, and containing the means of scene change. In this process the doors of entrance are pushed back to the side walls, and the stage follows them so that it now extends from side to side of the whole building, with extra doors of access from these sides. The balconies are still there above the doors of entrance as part of the acting area, and good use is made of them in such plays as Dryden's *Sir Martin Marrall*. Just as in the Elizabethan theatre, the entrance doorways and their associated areas can be the front entrances of a house, and the balconies part of the domestic architecture. The large forestage, now curved out into the audience (to compensate, one might think, for its closure to the side walls of the theatre) still gave the actor the chance to stand almost in the centre of the whole playhouse. Again, this real "stage" was imagined to be anywhere the actors chose: a house interior, a a street, a park. When necessary, furniture was carried on to it and set in sight of the audience. Most important of all (for the producer), nearly all entrances and exits were made on to the forestage by the proscenium doors. Only on very rare occasions (and then usually in later times) were entrances made into the scenery set back behind the proscenium arch. Actors could be "discovered" there, exactly as in Elizabethan practice such "discoveries" were made within the curtained recess. The scene was still only a useful adjunct of the "stage"; it was not yet (and would not be for a century or more) the main, or only, acting area. Actors came on front, by the "ceremonial" door, walked upstage into the "scene" (if this was in use—it might well not be), or walked down out of it and away through the door again. The importance of this to the producer as he studies the lines of the play is clear. Characters entering or leaving have a long and potentially elegant movement to make before reaching the actors who are within the scene. Remarks may be made by actors one to another as they leave the scene and make for the doorways; utterances made within the "set" as an actor is seen entering through a doorway—remarks which are audible to the theatre audience—will "by-pass" him completely. Even more theatrically significant (and still vital to the technique of the theatre in Sheridan's time) is the facility with which a character entering by the door can speak to the audience, involving them in the action, before he joins the party upstage within the proscenium. In this way the forestage could serve as a kind of no-man's-land shared (quite literally sometimes) by audience and actors; the so-called "aside" was simply a remark addressed to the audience as participants in the action. Note, also, that however bright the lights concentrated on the acting area, the audience also was clearly visible and sat in light. The intimacy was no less than in the daylit Elizabethan public theatre.

Two points emerge; the upstage entry of a character (necessitating the turning away from the audience of the group already there) is foreign to the technique of the Restoration playhouse; scripts, lines, patterns of action, are written for downstage entry; secondly, movements have to be considered as curves, distances, circlings, rather than as the naturalistic direct approach. Of such a play a professional producer said, "In the interests of costume and period I had to plan all movements of characters in terms of the greatest distance possible, with wide sweeping curves and indirect approaches." If he had considered also (he may have done) the conventions of the theatre itself, and the demands of the script, he would have been even more certain of the desirability of his planning.

Secondly, scene change did not interfere with continuity of running, any more than in the Elizabethan theatre. The emphasis and wit of the play depends upon immediately contrasting "scenes". Victorian revivals held up action, or even rewrote plays, so that elaborate settings of the box type could be provided. This is entirely foreign to the swift scene change, based on the later masks by Sir William D'Avenant, which was typical not merely of Restoration, but of British, theatre practice for the next one hundred and fifty years. Diagrams make this clearer than words. (See Figs. 28 and 30.) Flats, sliding in grooves, and similarly held above, could be pushed on from the sides, and if desired could meet in the middle of the stage to provide the backing, being then known as "shutters". Thus with sets of wings on each side of the stage stretching from the proscenium arch to the backing, the front wings on each set could be slid away by the "scene-shifters" revealing immediately a further pair of wings for the next scene. More important, as much or as little of the inner stage could be used as was desired. For scenes in an entry hall or the often mentioned vague "room in the house", where two or three actors met and talked briefly, only the forestage would be needed. The proscenium opening would be closed by two "shutters". Meanwhile, the next locality could be set in the "scenes". The "shutters" would be drawn off and the next acting area discovered. Alternatively, part only of the space behind the proscenium need be used. A further scene could be set behind. On some occasions scenes are set successively farther back, more and more of the inner stage being revealed as each scene "opens". Normally, however, the playwright would plan for a short forestage scene to give a chance for resetting behind. Only when there is a full (or nearly full) stage scene is furniture contemplated. This was, as in the Elizabethan theatre, merely functional, the chairs, the sofa, the table, needed for actions. There was little attempt to present an actual room with its accoutrements and elaborations. Restoration actors spend most of their time standing and moving. Even that bare fact might well be borne in mind by the set designer. Room, space for such movement, is essential. Another objective is speed, continuity, before a background in keeping with the flavour and atmosphere of Restoration playhouse, which was itself (in a very real sense) the "setting" for these plays.

A note may be added on lighting. Footlights were used, sometimes referred to more specifically as "the lamps". A large central candelabra and two smaller sprays of candles, one to either side, could light the main stage. Within the scenes lighting as yet was not so powerful. Wing lights, on large vertical battens, and some overhead illumination, were used. But by raising and lowering lights on pulleys, and by mounting the footlights on movable containers, similarly, the scene could be darkened or almost blacked out at will. "Sink lamps" is a common direction in prompt books. We must remember, however, that the audience still sat in light, and some scatter from this reached the forestage. Chandeliers were let down for "trimming" during the interval.

Finally, the curtain. This was ceremonially raised after the prologue to mark the start of the action. It was left up until the end. Not for nearly two hundred years was it to become the usual practice for the curtain to be raised and lowered to allow scene change during the action, although obviously irregular and special methods were used occasionally. For a hundred and fifty years the common terms, to be found in acting copies, were "the scene opens", "the scene closes", "the scene continues", which indicated shutters sliding apart, shutters sliding towards each other, shutters remaining in position—as they often did at the close of an act. The conclusion of a phase of action was simply the departure of actors from the stage.

APPROACH TO SET DESIGN

A simple solution is to reproduce the essential features of the Restoration theatre. Rostra are placed in front of the existing proscenium, and actors make their entry from the sides on to these. To secure their point of entry they may emerge from curtains at the side of the proscenium; or, even better, false proscenium doors can be contrived at the sides of the built-out rostra or forestage. This will depend on the amount of space available in the hall or theatre. Additional curtains may be draped as in the sketch (Fig. 29). Within the proscenium, wings or curtains are set in the convention of the Restoration period. The producer must, however, see that he can play scenes on the front stage only, with "tabs" in position, to give his stage assistants time to reset behind. Formal wings can be made as "bookflats" to stand as screens, although provision should be made to secure them by weights set on a projecting base extension. If decorated curtains are used, delightful possibilities of colour effect and design are at once possible. Any additional curtains used in front to screen in the doorways could repeat a dominant design. Again, over the proscenium arch some formal "neo-classical" device might be attached—the masks of comedy and tragedy, for example. In general, setting should strike a balance between decoration and an indication of locality. In the Restoration playhouse outside setting was presented by trees painted on flats, which had to be straight-edged to meet if necessary. Clearly, this is not naturalism. (Elaborate "operas" used other methods, as we have seen.) On the other hand, if the designer prefers to "cut out" the trees and place them formally as wings, he is still able to provide the general scene change, and open space for movement, that his play will require. There is no point in being antiquarian for the sake of antiquity. There is need, on the other hand, to provide conditions in which the play may be presented, the real play, not a rewriting to suit full picture-frame naturalism.

With a setting such as this, the producer will find (to his joy) that moves and grouping almost automatically adjust and create themselves, provided he is bold enough to use it in the convention of the period.

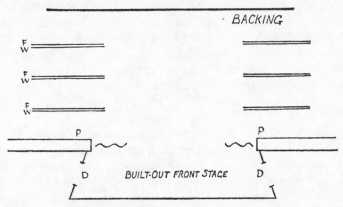

Fig. 31.—PLAN OF BASIC MODERN SETTING
P. Proscenium. W. Wing curtain or treewing for exteriors.
F. Formal wing flat.   D. Doors in booked flats.

Sometimes, critics glance deprecatingly at the seventeenth and eighteenth century habit of allowing actors to sort out their own moves and grouping, at their lack of real production discipline. The truth is, as bold working with this setting will show at once, that they were disciplined and grouped by the theatre condition and acting areas; the producer's main task will be to persuade his actors to trust themselves to the older convention, and all the difficulties which arise with the full picture-frame (the problems of asides, protracted entries and exits, separate groupings) will almost miraculously be avoided.

If, however, you have a large existing picture-frame stage, you may feel that it is better to set entirely within the area there available rather than to build out. The working plan may then be obtained by having a drape curtain four or five feet back from the footlights (if any), setting behind this, and entering from "proscenium doors" (or "tormentors") on to this "front stage" as in a music hall. Behind this drape all may be as outlined above. Again, you may wish to use all the stage most of the time and to be altogether more adventurous in setting, which is well, provided you observe the necessary requirements of the action and secure swift scene change. A formal setting, with possibilities of quick adaptation, has much to commend it. For

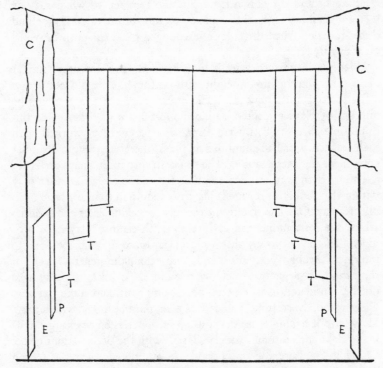

Fig. 32.—ELEVATION OF BASIC SETTING
T. Tree Wings.   P. Proscenium.
E. Entrances on to front stage.
C. Curtain draped down on to flats

example, three "neo-classical" archways may be placed upstage running across the acting area. Behind them a skycloth may be lit in various ways, or left dark. The arches may be filled with "walls", library shelves, fireplace and alcoves, according to locality, for interior scenes, and left as outdoor arches in a park or piazza for exterior scenes, with the skycloth lit behind. The "fillings" for the arches may be hinged ready and simply closed into position (scene shifters—garbed as servants in case glimpsed—moving first those at the sides). By setting the hinges back a little way it is possible to have two settings secured to each archway, one to each side. Curtains may be draped above to let down for a third possible setting. Further, the main upstage area may be raised to give further flexibility in movement. Furniture may be arranged by servants in audience view, although you can, of course, legitimately place your intervals where most convenient to allow resetting behind the drawn front curtain. Two sets of wings may be used for masking at the sides—plain curtains for interiors, and behind these, revealed when the curtains are looped back, cut-out tree wings permanently set.

Once you have such a set it may be used again for other similar plays. The Restoration and eighteenth-century theatre did not design a fresh setting for a new play. The quick change of programme, the number of plays presented within a short space of time, made this impossible. Sets of flats were kept, and playwrights worked with such stock material in mind. Their plays, therefore, required similar equipment in presentation. The modern producer may prefer to attempt a change of attitude and therefore of setting if another play within the period is presented, but basic requirements vary little from play to play. One has, in effect, to supply the acting areas and facilities which the Restoration and early eighteenth-century playhouse provided. That is not to say that a great deal more may not be done to interpret, through decoration and proportion, the general "feel" of the period, its elegance and neo-classical ideals, or that each play need not be considered in its especial needs, emphasis, and scene running. Clearly, too, the costume, colour, and plan, must be linked with setting. How far, for example, are the costumes to be stressed or exaggerated? If the elaborate costumes associated, say, with the presentations of the Comédie-Française for this period are attempted, then the setting will be correspondingly rich in the decoration of curtains, wings, furniture, and architecture. Again, these costumes must be linked with the producer's intention. How far is he planning to communicate through movement and gesture the essential elegance or affectation of the period? Or does he feel, that for his company and audience, he might do well to secure decorum and a less flamboyant approach, concentrating on verbal wit and the restrained good-breeding which may be equally effective? Figs. 31 and 32 show a possible "basic" setting. Instead of draping curtains down on to the proscenium doors you might attain a more solid and architectural effect by stretching canvas on wooden frames, painted to blend into the doors and placed above them.

Eighteenth Century, 1700-50: Formal Theatre

THIS is a neglected period, partly because its early years are included by many historians within the Restoration period; and partly because one's attention is attracted by the work of Goldsmith, and then Sheridan, immediately after the turn of the century. Yet there is much interesting dramatic material within the first fifty years—and the period has a style and interest of its own. The year 1700 saw the production of *The Way of the World*. Its reception, not very favourable, indicated the passing of the society who could accept the true comedy of manners and its moral assumptions and values. Collier's attack—*A Short View of the Immorality and Profaneness of the English Stage*—published a year or so earlier had voiced the objections of many, especially of the now wealthier middle-class, Whig supporters, who held places of prominence in the kingdom. The "genteel" was no longer the aping of French "manners" and courtliness, but rather the respectable, the desperate attempt of the social climbers to avoid anything "low". The vices, so easily accepted and elegantly indulged by the courtiers of Charles II, these new aspirants to upper-class status could not admit—they were too anxious to secure recognition as well-bred and correct in habits. They lacked confidence to sin openly; through the century the trend continues. Further, there was a general and genuine concern over disturbing and puzzling questions of life, and an attempt to secure genuine balance between passion and reason. Addison's good sense, Pope's superb exposition of "classical" ideals, self-control and avoidance of extremes, are powerful influences— subscribed to, at least outwardly.

> On life's vast ocean diversely we sail
> Reason the card, but passion is the gale. . . .

So said Pope. At the same time, middle-class anxiety over morality, its desperate desire for the respectable, created a new emotional situation—an almost neurotic sensitivity for right attitude and right feeling, which contrasted strangely with the amoral unconcern of the Restoration society in those very matters which the eighteenth century felt to be so important. So we find the desire for outward conformity united with increased moral awareness and feeling that people should concern themselves with individual and social welfare.

The increased moral awareness, the need for outward respectability and the wish to meet the demands of passion without disturbing society, to achieve some kind of acceptable solution which will send an audience home content, are most marked in comedy. Within this period fall the later plays of the so-called "Restoration" period—the works of Farquhar, and most of Vanbrugh's. While in the latter the classicism of well-balanced construction (he was an architect of plays as well as of Blenheim) is certainly evident, the moral codes of his characters and situations are largely those of the earlier gallants and their ladies. He solved the situation, however, by a characteristic sophistry; he had written with moral intent, to reveal vice, as it were, and his *Relapse*, or, *Virtue in Danger*, might find its place by a lady's prayer-book. The tendency to excuse "immorality" on the grounds of "moral instruction"—showing what should not be—is an unpleasant feature of eighteenth-century respectability. On the other hand, Farquhar moves quite definitely from the high life of London society to the country house and the bustle of rural townships in *The Recruiting Sergeant* and *The Beaux Stratagem*, after his earlier and coarser *The Constant Couple*. His plays are as charming as his own character. There is a foretaste of romanticism in the heroine who disguises herself as a man to achieve her love, and a serious reflection on the afflictions of the ill-matched wife in the fate of Mrs. Sullen. Had the climate of taste not changed earlier there would have been no need for Vanbrugh's later assumption of piety on the one side, and no essential problem for the unhappily married Mrs. Sullen of Farquhar on the other; marital infidelity could be more easily condoned earlier. But in *The Beaux Stratagem* there is a problem, an almost impassioned questioning which points us to the "feeling" of the later years of the eighteenth century, despite the contrived happy ending. Other dramatists solved new demands in other ways. Cibber, actor, manager, playwright and (not so efficiently) poet laureate, provided plays of theatrical appeal and excellent dramatic construction—his adaptation of Shakespeare's *Richard III* has been felt by some critics to be theatrically (even allowing for differing stage conventions) more striking than the original. His comedies *Love's Last Shift* (1696) and *The Careless Husband* (1706) bridge the transition period as public taste seems to be changed by

Collier's attack on the *Immorality and Profaneness of the English Stage* (1698). His plays are not "literary"—indeed, why should a play script be so?—but they are skilful and appealing. He can catch the character and affectations of the period; his later work probably also deserves revival. His is the "scripting" of the professional. In his *Apology*, he has left to us important information on acting conventions, styles, and staging of the period.

The tendency towards sentiment is shown in *The Funeral*, or, *Grief-a-la-Mode*, of Steele (1701), where he carefully depicts virtue and vice. His final comedy, *The Conscious Lovers*, serious in intent, though based on a Terentian model, again illustrates the entry of social problems into comedy. Primitive comedy had adjusted society through mockery and free expression, licence, and the inversion of established conventions. Now apparently it was to fulfil this traditional artistic function by thoughtful discussion on controversial themes. Yet another move is made away from the comedy of manners to treat middle class life and emotional attitudes; Lillo's *The London Merchant*, or *History of George Barnwell*, was produced in 1731. Its theme was a model for plays on "domestic" subjects, and Lillo's influence was felt in Germany; this examination of the feelings and sufferings of everyday humdrum life was another trend towards the sentiment and emotion of the early romantic period. The same moral intensity and carefully argued discussion is found in Addison's classical tragedy, *Cato*. This play is worth revival. The emotion of the Augustans is their impassioned appeal to reason, a passion which has itself to be satisfied in moderation. The struggle within the mind of *Cato*, expressed through long, yet beautifully constructed speeches, is highly dramatic, the drama of inner conflict. The play needs simple and dignified presentation, elegant speech, which on the one side avoids colloquial inconsequence, and on the other still possesses sincerity despite careful pattern and polish. The appeal to feeling continues in the work of Rowe, with his "she" tragedies. Phillips, in *The Distrest Mother*, blends emotion with classical dignity. His lines are in the "grand style"; again, feeling is expressed in reasoned argument.

The older style of comedy still found its exponents in Mrs. Centlivre and Fielding, yet often in the rather barren form of repeated situations and intrigues retained and used merely because they had entertained in the past and might entertain still. Once drama ceases to relate to life, fashion, foible and existing custom, it loses vitality. Precisely because of this, the actor must be imbued, imaginatively, with the spirit of the age to which his part refers and from which it emerges. The artificiality of many comedies is shown by the pious twist of their endings, where after more or less amoral adventures all is arranged according to the new social respectabilities, and a neat cliché ends the play, pointing out the solid rewards of virtue, however little suited to an evening's theatrical diversion.

So the epilogue to Conolly's *The Connoisseur* (1736) advises the author:

> I bad him, here and there, throw in a scene
> (But pray, says I—take care it's wrapt up clean)
> Of something—Psha——You all know what I mean.

There was, however, a new form developing which has not yet been fully exploited by the revivers of old plays—popular as this century has become nowadays. That was the ballad opera. A simple plot, a gay or satiric delineation of the more or less accepted life of the period, could be made attractive and exciting by the selection of popular song tunes to which fresh words were fitted. The "releasing" power of music which seems to strengthen every gesture and movement, and to sanction that theatrical enlargement of character and situation which most people find attractive (music removes the play from the conventions of naturalism), gave the new age its true and freer expression. For wit, the gaiety of music was substituted, and paradoxically in the situations and songs of *The Beggar's Opera* the "wit" (defined as the power to perceive relationships and significance in apparently unrelated affairs) came shining through. For most students of theatre, *The Beggar's Opera* and *Polly*, together with a few later "light" operas based on a similar plan of comedy script with interspersed songs, are the sum total. But scattered through old collections of plays are many more delightful "operas"; to the lyrics the producer may fit his own chosen popular tunes of the period. Entertaining in their way are Johnson's *The Village Opera*, Charles Coffey's *The Beggar's Wedding* and Fielding's *The Intriguing Chambermaid*.

Finally, new dramatic intent and thought found more savage expression in the burlesque (innocent enough in appearance) and the satiric political pieces of Henry Fielding. *The Tragedy of Tragedies* or *Tom Thumb* (1730) could be regarded merely as amusing fun, aimed at the highflown sentiments and wordy dignity of classical stage writing, but the Walpole administration were not pleased with such pieces as *Pasquin* (1736) and *The Historical Register for 1736* (produced in the following year). These dramatic satires, of the nature of "intimate revue" in West End theatres today, are hardly relevant for modern

production. They had two important results. One was a closer contro
on theatres other than the two patent houses—a monopoly not broken
for over a hundred years—and in addition a stricter stage censorship.
Fielding's own theatre was closed. Vested interest and political repres-
sion combined against him. On the other hand, the fun of the general
burlesque is still appreciated. Burlesque is an important form of
theatre—and in varying ways has survived to the present. Again,
hidden away in old play copies are many plays that could (perhaps with
judicious cutting) be revived today. The reversion of comedy to
Aristophanic directness and personal allusion was possible only for
a short time.

THE PRODUCER'S APPROACH

A pale reflection of Restoration style and grace will not do. As we
have seen, this period has its own ideals and positive motives in drama,
even though the later Restoration plays are included in its repertory.
Flamboyance and elegant mischief have yielded to precision and
polished decorum. Manners and modes are even more important, for
through studied correctness, the constant desire to be "genteel", there
can be perceived the spirit of revolt, of sentiment, and (though rarely)
of mockery. This last element is implicit rather than expressed. It is
sometimes sensed in the very moral ending, the formal bow to
accepted morality, and possibly influences much of a play. This spirit
is even more fragile and easily killed than that of the earlier Restoration
dramas. It is wistful, uncertain, and yet at times charming like the
behaviour of a shy and wayward child. Something can be learnt of
the styles of acting associated with the period, since Cibber has
recorded them. The producer has then some guide as to the original
presentation of any play by studying the cast list where this is available.
Some guide only, because we must not underestimate the versatility
of the actors of that time. Yet it was the custom for each established
actor to possess a certain number of parts, and for new plays to conform pretty much to a pattern in casting. The convention that a play
should involve a heroine, a second leading lady, and a more or less
comic elderly lady, is repeated again and again. Each actress had her
special set of parts, and might be expected to play one of these at a day's
notice. Production was simply a matter of muttering through the
play, leaving more emotional effects until performance. Acting was
still a matter of "walking the boards" to present one's interpretation
before friends in the "private house", not a deliberate and lengthy
preparation of an illusory world to which after careful planning

outsiders would be admitted, cut off from performers by a proscenium frame. Sense of social occasion marked the performance; some actors would greet friends they saw in the illuminated "house" before them. Yet there was a discipline, the discipline imposed by the stage and its accessories, the discipline of movement and attitude required by contemporary standards, a discipline imposed on each performer by each part he played.

What kind of acting was admired at the start of the period? Listen to Cibber. He is referring to Mrs. Mountfort.

"Melantha is as finish'd an impertinent as ever flutter'd in a drawing-room. . . . The first ridiculous airs that break from her are upon a gallant, never seen before, who delivers her a letter from her father, recommending him to her good graces as an honourable lover. Here now, one would think she might naturally show a little of the sex's decent reserve, tho' never so lightly cover'd! No, Sir; not a tittle of it; modesty is the virtue of a poor-soul'd country gentlewoman; she is too much a court lady, to be under so vulgar a confusion; she reads the letter, therefore, with a careless, dropping lip, and an erected brow, humming it hastily over, as if she were impatient to outgo her father's commands, by making a complete conquest of him at once; and that the letter might not embarrass her attack, crack! she crumbles it at once into her palm, and pours upon him her whole artillery of airs, eyes and motion; down goes her dainty diving body, to the ground, as if she were sinking under the conscious load of her own attractions; then launches into a flood of fine language and compliments, still playing her chest forward in fifty falls and risings, like a swan upon waving water; and, to complete her impatience, she is so rapidly fond of her own wit, that she will not give her lover leave to praise it. Silent assenting bows, and vain endeavours to speak, are all the share of the conversation he is admitted to, which at last he is relieved from by her engagement to half a score visits, which she *swims* from him to make, with a promise to return in a twinkling."

Of Mrs. Barry, famous in tragic roles, Cibber says that in such characters she had "a presence of elevated dignity, her mien and motion superb, and gracefully majestic; her voice full, clear, and strong, so that no violence of passion could be too much for her; and when distress or tenderness possessed her, she subsided into the most affecting melody and softness. In the art of exciting pity she had a power beyond all the actresses I have yet seen, or what your imagination can conceive . . . In scenes of anger, defiance, or resentment, while she was impetuous and terrible, she pour'd out the sentiment with an enchanting harmony." To exemplify further the taste of the new century we may quote his notes on the performance of Miss Santlow in *The Fair Quaker of Deal*: "The gentle softness of her voice, the compos'd innocence of her aspect, the modesty of her dress, the reserv'd decency of her gesture, and the simplicity of the sentiments that naturally fell from her, made her seem the amiable maid she represented."

The producer, then, has to examine each comedy for its particular reflection of the attitudes and conflicts of the period. The script must be taken at its face value, but also set against the background we have tried to sketch. Thus, Steele's characters in *The Conscious Lovers* may be accepted simply as the people of the period that they are. Their speech, their movements, their sentiments, are presented "in period"— which means that sentiments, however impossible to us, are said with belief. But, over and beyond this, Steele is trying to indicate, as a novelty, his own attitude to duelling and the correct behaviour of men to women. Again, while we accept these attitudes easily, the age did not. Here, therefore, there must be an emphasis on the struggle in the mind, the dramatic tensions; speeches which relate to these matters must be studied with care. The drama will then "communicate". Surprisingly, the audience will see the conflict in its period, just as they will accept its manners so unlike our own. The task for the producer lies in the words and opinions. Even where we cannot accept, the actors must "believe" and speak with sincerity. Where we accept easily, the actors may have to show reluctance and dramatically present a problem of the time. Just as in *Hamlet* the producer may have to explain to his cast the controversy concerning ghosts and purgatory which worried so many Jacobeans, so here he must put his cast "in the picture" about the assumptions and opinions of the age.

Strangely, perhaps, the classical tragedies, so scornfully dismissed by earlier critics of our own century, are much nearer to ourselves and to our own anxieties and life struggles. Again, plays where action is not so much *presented* as *suggested* through dialogue are with us again in the work of younger dramatists. Here the producer's task is to secure a delivery which reflects the inner conflicts of the mind. Each speech should be studied, and its sequence of thought considered and established. No matter how beautifully words are spoken, there will be no drama unless this careful orchestration (with operatic precision, maybe) of each speech is achieved. He must also establish within the overall pattern of his play the reality and relationships of the characters. The eighteenth century is the great age of character study—the "proper study of mankind is man", said Pope. Indeed, it was within the period under consideration that a start was made on detailed character interpretation of Shakespeare's plays, leading unfortunately to a distortion in their theatrical presentation. One has to realise that *Cato* produced enthusiastic and vociferous response from its audiences. True, it appeared to state the political crises of the age trenchantly. In fact both Whigs and Tories applauded; its problems and arguments, and the final tragedy, are still relevant and potentially exciting. The producer must give the play every chance—a dignified and simple setting, some assistance from lighting to enhance mood, beauty of group and gesture, and the conscious dignity of a high theme.

Ballad operas are, in a sense, outside our main theme. Yet they are often essentially straight plays, with songs added. Shakespeare's comedies also added song and dance; there is plenty of diverting situation and straightforward prose dialogue in the ballad operas, and light operas which followed. Gaiety, light-hearted amusement, and later a conscious unreality which reminds one of Dresden shepherds and shepherdesses, provide opportunities for colour, attractive costume and unpretentious but always bright setting.

More difficult to produce are the comedies of serious pathos (Mrs. Centlivre's *The Gamester*) or the domestic tragedies, such as Edward Moore's much later play of the same name. Here the sentiments are so exaggerated and the diction so stilted that one may despair of satisfactory revival on the modern stage. One can only warn against the temptation to "guy" and to play for laughs. After the first quarter of an hour the joke wears thin—and to the actors' surprise they find the audience either bored or (if they are acting well enough) seriously concerned and responding to the emotions of the play almost exactly as the dramatist had intended. Again, our mistake is to think that an alien form of theatre is something unsophisticated, childish, and merely laughable. When it is put into practice, this strange and apparently exaggerated dramatic sentimentality and mawkish emotion awakens from many a surprising response; they are genuinely moved. Yet it is doubtful whether afterwards they will view the experience as really worth while. What can be said is that an attempt to use these plays for purposes of burlesque will fail. A burlesque must be carefully written and cleverly contrived, and, moreover, requires highly competent actors, so serious and controlled that their efforts appear delightfully absurd. Once the actors share the joke, the burlesque ends. It is the audience's privilege to discover the absurdity—and to laugh at what they have, in their cleverness, discovered. Given actors who are willing to impersonate (but not to overact—the exaggeration is already secured in lines and situations) the larger than life figures of *Tom Thumb* and later burlesques, this can be a most entertaining form of theatre. Again, regretfully, one has to admit that unless the audience has (like the actors) been initiated into the background of eighteenth-century life much of the point in the lines will be lost; yet the mockery of certain recurrent stage exaggerations and mannerism will always be appreciated, as well as the general satire of pomposity and pretence.

THE ORIGINAL STAGING OF THE PLAYS

For straight plays general conventions remain as in the Restoration playhouse. "The scene opens", "the scene closes", and the "scene continues" monotonously as the century goes on. There were, however, developments. As might be expected, the area used for "setting" became gradually more important. The actor was being forced back from his "stage" and into the picture-frame—but only slowly and under protest. Even then the reasons were partly economic. Cibber becomes eloquent and indignant on the matter. "By the original form the usual station of the actors, in almost every scene, was advanc'd at least ten foot nearer to the audience, than they now can be; because not only from the stage being shorten'd in front, but likewise from the additional interposition of those stage-boxes, the actors (in respect to the spectators that fill them) are kept so much more backward from the main audience than they used to be. But when the actors were in possession of that forwarder space to advance upon, the voice was then more in the centre of the house. . . . Nor was the minutest motion of a feature (properly changing with the passion or humour it suited) ever lost—and how valuable an advantage the facility of hearing distinctly is to every well acted scene, every common spectator is a judge. A voice scarce raised above the tone of a whisper, either in tenderness, resignation, innocent distress or jealousy suppress'd, often have as much concern with the heart as the most clamorous passions." All this has been lost. For what? For ten pounds more in a full house, answers Cibber bitterly. This change may be dated roughly to the start of the eighteenth century. A closer study of the full passage in Cibber's *Apology* will reveal some puzzling features in his account; but for the practical purposes with which we are now concerned the general result is clear enough. The actor from Elizabethan times had been able to stand almost in the middle of his playhouse, when he so desired. The slight quirk of an eyebrow, the drop of a lip, the whisper, the sigh, the slight expiration of breath—all these things had been obvious to his audience and a means of communication. On the other hand, in tragedy he had been able to walk the boards with dignity and grandeur, dominating the hearers with nodding plumes and measured utterance. The idea that this early theatre was a place of exaggerated and noisy rant is surely wrong. In comedy the acting stylised normal manners and good breeding. In tragedy, it was solemn, sonorous, and weighty

Fig. 33.—DEVICES IN FORMAL THEATRE

—but Garrick's new and lively manner was not so much a protest against exaggeration or falsity as an attempt to secure a more natural-istic and sympathetic treatment of human emotion in serious plays. It was part, if you like, of the trend to portray the sentiments and anguish of an ordinary man placed in circumstances which the audience (being ordinary mortals) could presumably share. The hieratic and ritual gestures and studied movement of the older tragedians were to be avoided.

Yet, in all these matters the change was gradual and slow. Popular engravings show the tragedian a hundred years later still dressed in his nodding plumes, still posed on the forestage in front of the proscenium, still making his entry through the formal proscenium doors. The existing order was perpetuated by the building throughout the country of many small playhouses, all basically on the plan of the larger (but not very large) theatres in Drury Lane and Covent Garden. The intimacy and charm of these little theatres, used on "circuits" by companies settled at larger centres, such as York, can be discovered even today in such remaining buildings as the Georgian Theatre at Richmond. Indeed, there were more theatres (relative to population) in the later eighteenth century than there are in England today. For a hundred years the conventions of performance were retained; the actors knew the traditional moves and business which had to be fitted to the stage plan and the limited acting area available. As with the Restoration playhouse, the scripts more or less produced themselves, so far as moves and grouping went.

During the period a new form of spectacular entertainment is found—the pantomime. Starting as a kind of offshoot from the *commedia*—retaining the characters which most appealed to the English—Harlequin, the athletic and resourceful, in particular—and showing action in mime (whence its name) it then sought novelty by adding dialogue. Because variety was needed, Harlequin was (in true *commedia* tradition) involved in various places with various adventures. He visited the South Seas, he explored China, as well as living a gay life in various parts of Britain. Because this was a "show" and not a legitimate play, spectacle and machinery, as in the opera, were expected and were used freely. Soon the "introduction" setting out the story which was a basis for the adventures of Harlequin became an important part of the whole production; then came the actual "pantomime", the harlequinade. These could be linked by a "transformation" scene, on which great care was expended; this was the miracle which "transformed" an ordinary world into the world of Harlequin, Columbine, and the clown. Some of these early scripts might be revived, much as Victorian pantomimes have been re-staged with success. They would, however, be essentially "period pieces", very different from the period play which has lasting relevance to human affairs. In any case, they depended largely for effect on athletic prowess and the carefully organised dives, leaps, and tricks, of Harlequin, a matter for the professional acrobat rather than the actor *per se*. These "pantomimes" are important in the development of the more exact pictorial scenery, which, encouraged by Garrick, was later to change the balance and style of British theatrical presentation, with effects that were felt fully in Victorian theatre.

THE APPROACH TO SET DESIGN

Clearly there must be room for movement, grouping, and the dances so often suggested. The same general requirements are demanded by both straight plays and by comic operas and burlesques, for primarily the early eighteenth-century stage is a bare and partly open setting, with ample space for actors. They, as in the Elizabethan theatre, dress the stage themselves. Such scenery as there is furnishes decoration (from the modern viewpoint) rather than provides precise locality; it is the symbolism of the formal wing, the looped curtain, with the simple architectural features of proscenium door and balcony above.

Fig. 34.—PATTERNS IN FORMAL THEATRE

This, too, suits the statuesque and formal groupings of classical tragedy. Perhaps there is no period when such use may be made of formal devices, emblems, columns, and arches—for these were painted in this "Augustan" age upon wings, and formed part of the theatre decoration, not imitating three-dimensional reality, but simply as an expression of the neo-classical taste of the time. A glance at contemporary illustrations of theatres will show this almost intangible and pervasive "feeling", more easily recognised than described in factual terms.

The designer has for many plays quite consciously to "set" the action of plays with this sense of period attitude. Formal doors or arches for entrances from the side front (as previously suggested) but having something more of functional dignity, lacking softer touches of decoration, or erected in chosen positions within the set, are obvious devices. Their importance will serve to adorn an otherwise comparatively bare stage, which must be left free for movement. The stage may (further) be built out in front of the proscenium, and a formal pattern be placed above the arch. Backcloth and wings, stylised (or modified pictorial) in intent, may clearly be used, and afford a

Fig. 35.—FORMAL THEATRE
After the frontispiece in Tonson's edition of *Twelfth Night*

wide variety of possibilities. Scene change on this basis is quite easy. Wings and backing are arranged simply in the desired order and drawn off as required.

Further suggestions follow from the consideration of the plays to be staged. For such a classical tragedy as *Cato* light pillars on weighted bases can be arranged, and rearranged behind a traverse while the forestage is in use. Again, part of the stage may be raised, with the formal approach stairways which are so useful for rhetorical speeches, variety of attitude and pointed climax, and easier and more attractive grouping. Outdoor scenes in such an opera as Bickerstaff's *The Maid in the Mill* may imitate the original setting of the play with simple "tree" wings and landscape backing. There is no need, of course, to retain the straight edge of the eighteenth-century "shutter", but the general effect should not be over-decorated or challenge detailed representation. "Trees" should be simple—and repetitive. Otherwise, the light drama of the original will be overweighted by lush setting. Street scenes, again, while not representing classical buildings (unless appropriate to a wealthy locality) may have the same formality and repeated pattern, for the terrace house is popular, and the town street has the same balance and precision. Again, the naturalistic and photographic set must be avoided; it just doesn't help these plays. Leave as much space as possible for walking, talking, and dance. The actors in early eighteenth-century plays are on their feet most of the time. Domestic interiors are best indicated by formal wall backing and wings. The need for quick change is still paramount. An interesting study is the examination of various settings for *The Beggar's Opera*; those of Nigel Playfair's production at the Hammersmith Lyric are an education for set designers. In general, scene change can be based upon use of the front curtain, if there is a stage in front of this, with or without the aid of a traverse on the main stage itself. In some plays a charming effect may be obtained by use of simple cut-out pieces, card supported on a framework of laths; these are carried on stage and supported (like portraits) by struts behind and anchored by stage weights. With the further use of a sky cyclorama and formal curtain wings you have a quickly changed and extremely flexible set. Fig. 35 shows some aspects of the "formal" theatre. It is taken from the frontispiece to Tonson's *Twelfth Night* (1714). We notice the costumes, the decoration, and the use of the proscenium door as an entrance to Malvolio's prison. Figs. 33 and 34 illustrate designs and ornaments from play books at the end of the period, especially from a 1754 edition of *The Old Batchelor*, printed for S. and R. Tonson and S. Draper.

The Later Eighteenth Century

THIS is the period of Sheridan, Goldsmith, George Colman, and Hannah Cowley, a writer whose work was once famous. Classical tragedy continues, though it is really outmoded and ready to yield to "romantic" plays of high adventure and deep emotion. The sentimental comedy (satirised by Goldsmith and Sheridan) gradually leads to plays of serious thought, with sympathy for classes and people up to now mocked or despised, as in Cumberland's *The Jew*, though the original style is continued in Holcroft's *The Road to Ruin*. Domestic tragedy blends with this serious treatment of social evil in such a play as Moore's *The Gamester* at the beginning of the period. Social awareness, sentimentality, moral purpose, sincere or assumed because fashionable, give the period, whether positively in support, or negatively in satiric opposition, its particular character. To this general "feeling" for others must be added the "feeling" for other localities, ages, and societies, which develops into exploratory romanticism. And all this is linked with corresponding changes and developments in theatrical presentation, growing technical ability to portray the wonders and (often) supernatural events which such "romanticism" demanded.

Events in the period show in themselves how completely the old patterns and ways had been destroyed by the new emotional attitude to life. The French Revolution had its effect in our own country. Germanic opposition to French classical ideals in the mid-eighteenth century had been inspired by a new discovery of Shakespeare, with his all-embracing vision of human life and action; this wider view encouraged attempts to treat of the total experience of mankind, the development of "sturm und drang" writing, with outlaws and titanic heroes obviously in revolt against the well proportioned classical edifice of society. More important, lesser writers copied the current enthusiasm for the wild and remote; their work was translated into English —and Kotzbue's "melodramas" (the term is used loosely) were popular on the London stage, so that to raise money by a popular success Sheridan himself adapted *Pizarro*—one of the most lucrative of his ventures—for his own theatre.

Our own rediscovery of Shakespeare had begun in the 1730's when the "romantic comedies" (previously regarded as "non-acting" plays) were revived. Garrick's productions and the "Stratford" festival which he sponsored in 1769 witnessed to a growing enthusiasm which bordered on idolatry. The eighteenth century, however, approached Shakespeare with their own prejudices in mind. Garrick prided himself on removing the "rubbish" of "comic" scenes from *Hamlet* and *Macbeth*, showing that he really missed the dramatic issues which Shakespeare presented. The "character" approach encouraged by the critics ("the proper study of mankind is man") led many productions even down to our own time, into by-paths and perplexities. (Only recently have we begun to free ourselves from the eighteenth century partial appreciation of Shakespeare, in which he becomes a character analyst.) This rediscovery was in the 1780's and 1790's linked with a greater respect for the past, a love of the medieval and "Gothic", which would soon create a demand for correct costuming and historical setting. Until this time, the costume of the day had been generally worn, save for some distinctive characters and occasional symbolic dress. Further, the new "romantic" adoration led away from classical tragedy to imitations of Elizabethan writing, not always completely worthless.

Pantomime became even more popular, and here, too, Garrick's influence was important. His own productions developed more elaborate setting and pictorial effect, which again reacted upon, and with, new romantic naturalism as contrasted with eighteenth-century formality and style. Yet, above all, the period is most famous for the great achievements of the "classical" Georgian playhouse—Sheridan's *School for Scandal* or *The Rivals*, Mrs. Cowley's *The Belle's Stratagem*, for over a hundred years a stock acting test for the comedienne, or Goldsmith's *She Stoops to Conquer*, regarded by Horace Walpole as unutterably vulgar. It was in such reaction against the new and (possibly) false tastes and enthusiasms that the theatre found most vital expression. These plays, using only the conventional staging and elegance of accepted social behaviour (or consciously vulgar contrast to this), held the stage with resounding success, perhaps because they reflected opposition to movements which men could not stop. Because they show the comic treatment of certain recurrent human emotional trends, there is also universality—at least in Sheridan's plays—which makes them truly great theatre. Against all the weepings and anguishes, the exaggerated heroics of anti-social heroes, and the rising spectres of Gothic romance (both in story and theatre), these comedies present their gay mockery of a society in transition, poised between over-emphatic authority and reason on the one side and on the other sentiment, feeling, the lending library, and the mutterings of scandal which attend high moral protestations. At the same time, Goldsmith dares to run counter to public taste and the exaggerated gentility of aspirants to upper class status; when early in the period he brought bailiffs on to the stage in *The Good Natur'd Man* (its central figure a representative of the foolishly sentimental heroes of the *comédie larmoyante*) he was forced to see his play presented for some time without this vulgarly funny scene which reduced the hero to common clay. *She Stoops to Conquer* also angered the over-refined; the idea of a young "lady" pretending to be a barmaid was too horrible. You will note also Goldsmith's subtle satire of the genteel and the sentimental in the inn scene, where even the low life characters protest their culture—the genteel thing is the genteel thing, and the bear dances only to the most refined tunes. Sheridan, a far greater dramatist, works with elegant precision to give in *The School for Scandal* not only the essential life of a changing society viewed almost in its entirety, but also a genuine comedy of manners based on London upper-class social conventions before this society was fragmented by the strains and stresses of the eighties and nineties; he did more—he caught some eternal human situations and attitudes, which will last so long as there are men and women, communities, and codes of behaviour.

THE ORIGINAL METHODS OF PRESENTATION

The producer's approach to plays of this period must be with full understanding of the conventions and developments upon which they were based. At first the conventions shaped the play; later, new methods of elaboration, scenic device, and artistic ideals, were largely the *material* of the play. Here is the climax of one theatrical style, and the start of another. In Sheridan's work the instinctive stagecraft "built into the script" makes the great drama; the script cannot be thought of apart from its theatre, the fully developed playhouse of apron, proscenium doors, and rear stage, side wings, and shutters. On the other hand, again, the new "pictorial" plays, the pantomimes, and the lighting devices of De Loutherbourg, mirror the material and actions of a new theatre, its style, its dramatic emphasis. Before, then, we can discuss the producer's approach to the script we must study methods of presentation.

A script such as Burgoyne's *The Maid of the Oaks*, "a new dramatic entertainment, as it is performed at the Theatre Royal, in Drury

Lane" (1774) will serve to illustrate the gradual invasion of the normal conventions by pictorial effects. *The Maid of the Oaks* is a musical play; typically, it could be played straight—the omission of the songs would not wholly impair its story and effect. Like so many of the ballad and light operas of the eighteenth century it is essentially a dramatic piece with inserted songs and dances. The preface claims that the piece owed much to the encouragement and approval of Mr. Garrick; but the inspiration was originally the "Fête Champêtre, given by a noble Lord last summer. . . . Accordingly, permission having been obtained to employ the music and to copy some of the decorations, a plan was projected for adapting them to the Stage". The author acknowledges further how much he owes to "the Actor, the Musician, and the Painter."

The normal method of flats and shutters, part stage and whole stage, is adopted for much of the play. The first scene is simply "part of an ornamented farm"—a term which in itself is indicative of "taste". The talkers who start the story are cleared from the stage, and then we "draw" on to the second scene where we have "an outside Building, workmen of all sorts passing to-and-fro", with an architect who opens his remarks "as speaking to persons at work behind the Side-scenes". Act II is labelled "Scene the Oaks", with Maria "sitting under a great Tree". This is clearly a full stage scene, since no change takes place through the Act, which finishes with a grand dance of shepherds and shepherdesses. Act III starts with a front stage sequence (Scene, the Garden Gate); when the stage has been cleared by the usual "exeunt", we find our next set is "A Flower Garden", which takes up the major portion of the Act. Act IV opens with a brief scene, presumably front stage, for the next scene is "Arcades of Flowers", with a procession, which does not occupy all the stage, for "After the Song, the Scene opens, and discovers the GARDENS illuminated" and actors already "on" go upstage to join those discovered by the "opening". A note tells us "The Painting of this Scene is taken from a Portico, in the Gardens of Lord Stanley, as illuminated at his entertainment last Summer". Act V shows us "The Saloon". This is explained as a "representation of the temporary saloon, as designed by Mr. Adam, and erected at Lord Stanly's [*sic*]." Now comes the interesting direction "The Character of FOLLY enters from the Top of the Stage to lively Symphony". After which all the company retire to the wings on each side, and the curtains of the "saloon" are drawn up "to discover the company at supper". A Druid enters; after singing he waves his wand and "The Scene breaks away, and discovers the PALACE OF

CELESTIAL LOVE" which remains until the play ends with a grand dance.

Here we have, first, the simple and traditional arrangement of front stage and doors, painted wings and shutters behind. "The scene opens", the scene "breaks away"—i.e. existing flats are drawn off to reveal the fresh setting, while short scenes are played on the apron with entrances and exits formally through proscenium doors. But alongside this, notice the emphasis on painted scenery; at the same time, it *is* "painted" (it is not three-dimensional) and the view of the building and garden is specifically noted as such. Extra emphasis on the setting within the proscenium arch suggests the wings as means of entry—though this final stop is not taken. People simply retire to the wings, people talk to others "at work behind the side scenes". On the other hand, a definite instruction tells Folly to enter right upstage, which is in effect a wing entry by the top shutters. Finally, we note the erection of an elaborate piece of "furniture"—the saloon in the garden, with its surrounding curtains. This was a suitable elaboration, since the original "saloon" was only a temporary frame building, and the dramatist's intent was to transfer this to the stage. Again there is no "three-dimensional" attempt at presenting a permanent building; this, when needed, is painted on the back shutters.

General trends are, however, clear. The front stage is losing its importance—the emphasis is on pictorialism—the representation in detail of the pageantry of the outside world. We quote again the author's words: "They who suppose an English audience, because used to plain entertainment, are incapable of relishing the most refined are greatly mistaken. . . . The middle class and bulk of the assembly, like that of the kingdom at large, will ever be on the side of nature, truth, and sense. Let the piece be founded upon those principles and applause will follow every circumstance of elegance and decoration that can accompany them."

So the show of effect and spectacle blended with normal stage practice. The pantomimes of the Christmas season were recognised as distinct and legitimately elaborate, appealing through song, dance, décor. Garrick was again here an influence in the increasing importance of scenery. He employed De Loutherbourg as his designer, and sent him, for example, to Derbyshire to study settings for the pantomime *Harlequin in the Peak*. The peculiarly exaggerated and emotional interpretation of "mountain" scenery, romantic in its appeal, became the stock English style for plays requiring a setting of woodlands, ravines, and chasms, and many plays did require that, since romantic

"subjects" were outlawry and brigandage. In addition, De Loutherbourg was an artist in lighting. His colour effects, shadows, simulated
storms, and gauzes, were so popular that he was able to open a show
based on these illusions alone. The concentration of interest on the
area within the proscenium arch could not fail to lessen the importance
of the apron and the formal convention of stage doors. The pretence
of reality within the scene clashed with the front stage, related so
intimately with audience and contradicting the carefully simulated
other world within the arch. Further, we have the start of building
another stage floor. Gradually, though slowly, raking pieces are set
on the stage floor within the scene, so that actors may walk up the
heights and move behind rocks and walls. The three-dimensional set
is with us. Yet—and this must be stressed—for another fifty years the
main emphasis will be on flat painting, and not on sets actually built.
Wings and backing, cleverly executed to suggest perspective and
solidity, will still be general practice. Only slowly will the usage of
built-up levels be established. "Straight" plays will continue the
convention of quick moving, stylised, wings and shutters well into
the nineteenth century. In the smaller theatres of the provinces this
normal practice will survive longer. The last half of the eighteenth
century was a great age of theatre building. Despite the prohibition of
theatres, other than the patent houses, in London, there were probably
many more theatres in proportion to the population than at the
present time. Each little country town had its playhouse, used maybe
only at certain seasons of the year—but still there. These, built to
function according to the established practice of the "Georgian"
playhouse were naturally a conservative influence, though inevitably
in the early nineteenth century the fashion for "spectacular" shows
spread, and what effects could be introduced were utilised.

Let us look finally at the early "melodrama"—melodrama in spirit,
if not in fact. Here are the settings required in *Pizarro*, Sheridan's
adaptation from Kotzbue. The settings are (clearly) painted, and the
haste of production (and even uncertainty as to some scenes in the
play) precluded anything beyond the use of quickly contrived flats
and backings. The presentation involved: Act I, scene i, Pizarro's Tent
with a view of the Spanish position on the coast of Peru. Act II,
scene i, A sheltered Room, with view of the garden of the Royal
Palace; Scene ii, The Temple of the Sun—A solemn march; Scene iii,
Peruvian landscape. (This very brief scene is probably front stage to
allow the setting of the next—though this also is noted as a "view");
Scene iv, A Mountainous View near the City. Act III, scene i, A

Wild Retreat—the secret refuge amidst the rocks; Scene ii, Same as
Act II, scene i; Scene iii, Pizarro's Tent, distant view of the city.
(Perhaps the same wings as Act I, scene i, with different painted view
as backing shutters): Act IV, scene i, A Dungeon. (References to
"cavern" and "recess" suggest that this was front stage and part of the
rear area—but not all. Characters retire to this area when others enter,
presumably by the normal doors, suitable for dungeon doors because

Fig. 36.—A GEORGIAN PLAYHOUSE
From a contemporary print

of their massive nature.) Act IV, scene ii, Pizarro's tent (As before but
with the entrance curtains closed. The view is therefore not seen.
Pizarro is discovered on a couch, the shutters backing the previous
scene having been drawn off.) Act V, scene i, The Entrance of a thick
Forest—a storm. (Here are the chances for lighting effects; but note
again the use of only part of the possible area—"The entrance of a thick
forest"—so that it can be painted across shutters a little way within the
proscenium arch. This is necessary to place the possibly one solid
and three-dimensional setting needed, which follows.) Scene ii, The
Outpost of the Spanish Camp—the background wild and rocky—a

M

trunk of a tree thrown over a ravine, over a torrent. (It is necessary for Rollo to cross the tree bridge later and to throw it down into the stream. This is the one "big" effect in setting, and is intended as a climax much as the "saloon" noted in *The Maid of the Oaks*. Clever scene painting is needed to blend the raking pieces with the "wild and rocky background". At the end of the scene all "exeunt"). The remaining scenes are very brief and follow quickly by use of sliding shutters. Scene iii is the Peruvian outpost—Rollo dies, although he has saved Cora's child. Again it is necessary (still as in Elizabethan times) to carry his body from the stage. Scene iv is the "Exterior of The Temple of Rocks". In a brief scene Pizarro is slain. Again, "exeunt". "A solemn march". And so to the final spectacle, scene v—Interior of the Temple of the Sun. There is a procession with the body of Rollo—and the sole dialogue of the scene is

> Let tears of gratitude and woe
> For the brave Rollo ever flow.

The need for quick and instantaneous scene change during the final act is obvious. This is in the style of melodrama—to progress at ever-increasing pace, move to its most elaborate use of "practicable" setting, and then to end with a flurry of action, few words, but a great many stage directions to guide the often involved fighting and final spectacle. One gets the impression that the dramatist and actors have wearied themselves in emotional entanglements and have no breath to say more. They leave the climax of the drama to setting, lighting, frenzied event, and go from the stage just as quickly as they moved on to it— to seek refreshment and grateful relief. The staging of *Pizarro* has been quoted in detail since it links its period to Victorian practice, and serves as the basis for the description of later theatre technique.

There was another change which affected greatly both plays and actors; that was the rebuilding, with greatly increased size, of both Drury Lane and Covent Garden. In a sense again, cause and effect were confused. Demand for more elaborate presentation put up costs; managers needed larger audiences, or at least the possibility of accommodating them; theatres were built with larger stages—which required spectacle to fill them; the intimate eighteenth-century playhouse disappeared. But when theatres are so large, actors are heard only with some difficulty. Cibber's ideal of the audible whisper, the breathed aside, has passed for ever; and, more, even gestures are seen only with some concentration of attention, for the actors are dwarfed by setting and the distance. Acting has to be enlarged, meaning telegraphed by attitude and formidable arm movements (no longer Cibber's minute motion of feature) to the distant parts of the house. The actor is lost in the pictorial whole—and the process of dependence on elaborate presentation is accelerated by a natural impetus, like a snowball gathering pace, weight, and momentum, as it rolls downhill.

THE PRODUCER'S APPROACH

The most famous plays of the period were, of course, produced in the smaller playhouses; their general nature and "quality" remain unaffected by these later developments. Examine *The School for Scandal*, and in imagination re-create its performance in the theatre of its own time. Luckily, some illustrations of setting still remain, notably of the "screen scene". How would a manager present this play? And what impact would the outward technique of scene change and physical arrangement of entrances have upon the audience? Act I, scene i, is Lady Sneerwell's dressing-room. Two chairs and two tables are needed, and the actors are "discovered". So the scene is set some way behind the proscenium arch. Scene ii is an often repeated direction "Sir Peter's House"—and like some other scenes so designated is a comparatively brief exchange between two speakers. At the end of the Act, there is of course no curtain. The "scene continues" for the next Act when (for scene i) Sir Peter and Lady Teazle enter through the proscenium doors. For the next scene we draw off again for a room at Lady Sneerwell's. Some early nineteenth-century acting versions suggest this is the same as Act I, scene i. Others indicate that a greater depth of a stage is used. However, the next scene closes the shutters again for Sir Peter Teazle's house—to end the act. Act III, scene i, "continues" (in the original version). In the early nineteenth century, it was apparently set back—so that it secured the alternation of "front stage" and "inner stage" which was so loved by some producers, for the next scene has again to be front stage, the conventional "hall" using the main proscenium doors of entrance, this time in Charles Surface's house. This front stage scene of arrival is needed so that we can set behind the proscenium arch "a handsome Chamber", where Charles and his friends are roistering. We notice throughout the particular use of the proscenium doors. Trip shows the visitors in by one door, and the company are shown out by the other—"the dice", says Charles "are in the next room". The act ends, as Sir Oliver, walking down to the proscenium door, tells the audience, "I'll never forgive him— never, never." Act IV opens on the "picture room" for the famous auction of ancestors. Here our manager would have to secure two shutters on which portraits were painted; the point is covered in the dialogue where Charles asserts that the pictures "are all stiff and awkward as the originals, and like nothing in human nature besides". We should probably set in the "second" grooves. Scene ii is a short front interlude, to allow us to arrange the full stage "library scene", which will be required for various main actions and which has to accommodate most of the cast at the end. Here we have a contemporary picture to help us, which shows the painted wings and library backing, not forgetting the window alluded to in the dialogue, and the use of a proscenium door as a hiding place. The furniture is simply that needed functionally, chairs and screen. Apart from the brief use of a front

Fig. 37.—SCHOOL FOR SCANDAL
Screen scene in performance

stage scene, indicating the visitors who invade Sir Peter's house following the scandal concerning Lady Teazle, the library is used for the remainder of the play. Note again the reference to proscenium doors in the front stage scene, "No, but she has left the door of that room open, you perceive."

As the producer examines this possible reconstruction of the action on stage, he will become aware of many points significant in presentation. The entry by the door often introduces a move upstage "into the picture" where the others are gathered. As a character enters he stands for a moment poised between audience and the stage group, and he can speak to the audience almost unheard by the others on stage. So Sir Peter bows formally as he enters, and tells the audience

"Mercy on me, here is the whole set". Again, the long entries accord deliciously with the dialogue (naturally enough since the latter has been planned for such entries). So Mrs. Candour sweeps on, talking as she comes, after her hurried curtsy, "Oh, my dear Lady Sneerwell, how do you do? Mr. Surface, your most obedient? Is there any news abroad? No, nothing good I suppose. . . ." So, too, the entry of Crab-tree, as he enters, bows, speaks, proceeds further towards the group, bows, and speaks again. Even more beautifully arranged are the "talking" exits. Sir Benjamin and Crabtree can only work their suggested exit, following the stage directions, if they use space which corresponds with the comparatively lengthy (and audience facing) withdrawal possible in Sheridan's theatre.

SIR BENJAMIN: And I'm very sorry also to hear some bad stories against him.
                     (*Going*)
CRABTREE: Oh, he has done many mean things, that's certain.
SIR BENJAMIN: But, however, as he's your brother——
                     (*Going*)
CRABTREE: We'll tell you all another opportunity.
                     (*Exuent*)

Of course, some way round can be found, even in a box setting with an upstage exit, but the producer should at least consider the action involved in the play itself, Sheridan's play in Sheridan's theatre, before too hastily blaming the dramatist (as some have done) for poor stage-craft. Having noted the close relationship between actors and audience when needed, the graceful movements which can accompany the dialogue, and the elegant clothes of the actors, the producer may consider Sheridan's phrasing and words further. Here is stage dialogue at its best and most polished. It is not artificial, because the normal thought and speech patterns of the age were very much thus. Even a superficial acquaintance with the reported conversation and everyday writing of the literate classes of this period will reveal the same easy grace and balanced pattern of statement. What Sheridan did was to use this existing speech dramatically, not distorting but adapting natural and accepted expression perfectly to situation and character. There is magnificent pleasure in speaking the lines, and no sense of artificiality. They accord exactly with the stage reality of situation. Consider even such a simple opening as "When an old bachelor marries a young wife what is he to expect? 'Tis now six months since Lady Teazle made me the happiest of men—and I have been the most miserable dog ever since". To analyse in detail would be pedantic. What Sheridan did so instinctively and well must be left—but note, as Sir Peter speaks the lines, the accord of phrase with phrase, point with point. As for the opening scene of Act II, nothing finer has been constructed for any English comedy. The producer may note a possible danger—that while enjoying the easy flow of words sweet on the tongue, the actor or actress may fail to give the pointing, the gradual build-up of retort and counter-retort, climax and anticlimax, which is the joy of the scene. It is in dramatic construction that Sheridan excels—all the more since the play is a *mélange* of two themes which he had partially worked. Granted, the age helped the man; the instinctive sense of words and epigram were there to be used, and elegance and style were thus possible without the least artificiality. There could be a comedy of manners; manners were there.

Note also the quick and startling effect of scene changes secured by the presentation. This rivals the changing views made possible by the cinema camera. The almost instantaneous switch from the quarrel scene between Sir Peter and Lady Teazle to the crowded room full of gossips is equalled only by the dramatic effect of Sir Peter's exit to be reconciled with his lady, with his final rejection of all "sentiment" and the immediate appearance, back at Joseph's, of the two thwarted "lovers", Lady Sneerwell and Joseph, with the speech of frustration, "Oh I was a fool, an idiot, to league with such a blunderer", and Joseph's indignant, "Surely, Lady Sneerwell, I am the greatest sufferer. . . ." This swiftness and pointing must be retained if the real play is to be presented. The same requirement is met in most plays of this period—not forgetting *The Rivals, She Stoops to Conquer*, and *The Belle's Stratagem*. Yet how often are we forced to wait for scene change, until the whole issue and contrast of the struggle before us has been lost?

Finally, the producer will not forget how much the ceremonial bow, curtsy, and correct use of costume—which should inform the action and use of hand and arm, not hinder them—are part of the entire play. In just the same way the existing stage conventions and possible acting areas, the agreed methods of entry and exit, control and shape the play itself. Sheridan has the quick wit and the instinctive sensitivity to use of setting, which seem to stem from the ready apprehension of the Anglo-Irish, their appreciation of any suitable vantage point for action and speech. It is this acceptance and creative use of stage discipline which unify his play and its double plot. How powerful this discipline was may be realised when one remembers that there was rarely any actual direction of eighteenth-century productions. The actors knew their parts. Their moves were governed

Fig. 38.—IMPRESSIONS OF EIGHTEENTH-CENTURY STAGE COSTUMES
AND ATTITUDES

by the physical conditions of the acting area, the few pieces of necessary furniture within the arch, and the normal rules of deportment and behaviour. True, at times a Garrick would insist on a united and reasoned approach. Any new play might have special consideration. But basically they could ignore such "production". If you would test this, mark out the eighteenth-century stage on your floor space, set as suggested above, and give the actors their scripts. Let them move according to the conventions—and you will find that the time and effort needed in the naturalistic setting are neither necessary nor (perhaps) desirable; your attempts to create a picture, to work entries and exits are here forgotten; the script and the stage manage by themselves. You will probably not choose in performance to emulate eighteenth-century conditions, but at least (once again) you will have gone some way to experiencing the actual play, and can plan your own production accordingly.

In imagination we have witnessed something of the eighteenth-century presentation. What was the theme of all the action we saw? Garrick's prologue tells us in brief: "Cut Scandal's head off, still the tongue is wagging".

The Town and Country Magazine, the moral (or mock moral) attitudes, the man of "sentiment", all are included in the treatment of gossip-mongering based on pretended concern for right attitudes and feelings.

APPROACH TO SETTING

As noted, it is important to secure continuity and speed of action. There must be ample room for grouping, movement, and for effective entrance and exit. Some pictorial background is suggested even in "legitimate" plays, beyond the customary wings and shutters. The complete formality associated with the first part of the century has passed. Even in the comedies of manners (such as *The Rivals*) which attack sentimentality (see the second prologue) there is a suggestion of romantic love and fancy. The set designer has therefore more scope. He will hardly go as far as the Bancrofts did in naturalistic detail when, in their production of *The School for Scandal*, they aimed at reproducing the lavish interior scenes of the eighteenth century, and were then necessarily forced to rewrite the play. It is almost impossible even with all the stage machinery and staff imaginable to secure the quick changes needed if you persist in setting heavy scenery and massive furniture. At the same time he has scope for imagination and more extensive scenic effect.

Two doors of entry, whether placed in front of the proscenium by a built-out forestage, or situated within the proscenium, up or down stage, may be found a good functional starting point, since most plays plan script round these. The doors can be decorated or adapted during presentation; curtains may be used instead, draped or allowed to hang, and are easily involved in the more exotic scenes in such a play as *Pizarro* where they become part of a tent or hangings in a palace. To secure the contrasting localities desirable (in place of the forestage and inner stage), a rostrum or platform within the proscenium will differentiate groups and allow definite and dramatic movement on to and from the stage. As we come nearer to the end of the period, plays suggest further use of lighting; the caves, recesses, and gloomy woods, of the "melodrama" will be presented more vividly by careful light and shadow than by over-elaborate setting. Such practicable additions to the basic stage setting may be contrived by small lath frames covered with cloth which can be folded for easy storage. Hardboard cut out, braced and weighted, may indicate the necessary irregularity of rock or earthy bank.

For front stage scenes a curtain or dropcloth may be placed a yard or so within the proscenium. A formal street design, perspective or otherwise, will be sufficient—this is an age of transition, which the scripts reflect; the mixture of formalism with pictorial precision corresponds with the mixed intent and content of the plays themselves. From the street in Bath (of *The Rivals*) we move finally to the parkland outside with the distant view of the city. If considered more challenging or affording more variety in grouping and movement this curtain could be angled across the stage, involving, however, setting mainly from one side while the curtain is in place for front action. The advantage of the curtain parallel with the stage front is the easy re-arrangement of all furniture behind while the front stage scene is in progress. Entrance can now be made straight from the wings without necessarily invalidating the conventions of the script. While I would always design with front stage doors and "front" entries, these plays offer the possibility of designing for work entirely within the proscenium arch. Earlier eighteenth-century plays may be set thus, but much is lost unless part of the space immediately behind the arch is then treated as a forestage with formal entrances. Now, in later plays of this period, there is an integration of fore and main stage, and direction of attention to unified visual effect. Yet there is still the need, as stated above, to give the actors enough room to move and to group. Hence the desirability of varying levels, whether imagined as slopes on a hillside in outdoor scenes, or varying floor levels in a reception-room.

Clearly, in setting these plays the painter comes into his own—and the use of light, shade, and perspective, the suggestion of solidity, the consideration of overall colour effect in conjunction with costuming, give him ample opportunity and challenge. Fig. 38 illustrates some eighteenth-century costumes and attitudes, based on contemporary theatrical prints.

Romantic Theatre 1800-50

IMPORTANT technical advances in this period changed the whole emphasis of theatrical work. First, the continued policy of building large theatres demanded further scenic development. Acoustics were not satisfactory, and some concession had to be made to audibility. Still, scenic elaboration went on. In the mid-nineteenth century a new method of "setting" was developed—"set pieces" and furnishing could be lowered from above. Ingenious machinery had long been used; flats had been changed by winches controlling wires attached, and so on. Basically, however, as the low roofs of Georgian playhouses evidence, change had been horizontal removal from stage to wings, or vertical from below *via* traps upwards. Now came a new technique— a whole setting could be held in position above and lowered on to stage with approximate accuracy. Also during the twenties and thirties, built-up, three-dimensional, "set scenes" become more usual. In the opening decade Capon's sets for Kemble at Covent Garden, while historically "accurate", were still painted wings and backing in principle. This is the great age of the scene painter. Again, for the first time, with the new emphasis on visual effect, completely accurate historical costumes and accessories are demanded. J. R. Planché's designs for the costumes of *King John* in 1824 are famous. He had still to meet opposition from traditionalists, but he won, and his method of presentation was elaborated further and further with long scholarly programme notes and painstaking research in the mid-century productions. The play itself was (it seemed) almost forgotten in the desire for complete and instructive historical realism in the stage picture. Moreover, there was an attempt to force imaginative plays into the same exact historical and precise naturalism, inventing a fictitious reality (to be paradoxical) from which the exact stage effect might be justified. Thus, Charles Kean's presentation of *The Winter's Tale*, which is set "accurately" back in a Syracuse supposed to mirror ancient Athens, and a "Bithynia", since the Shakespearian "Bohemia" will not possibly fit what I have termed above the "fictitious reality". Costume and all properties had to be minutely in accord. So, Bohemia changed to

Bithynia, the vegetation of this place had to be from sketches taken by George Scharf, Esq., F.S.A., "on the spot".

Even more striking in its effect was the introduction of gas lighting (September, 1817, for the stage at Drury Lane), which completed the process of concentrating attention on the stage picture, and, at the same time, broke the eighteenth-century "entre-nous-ship" (as Charles

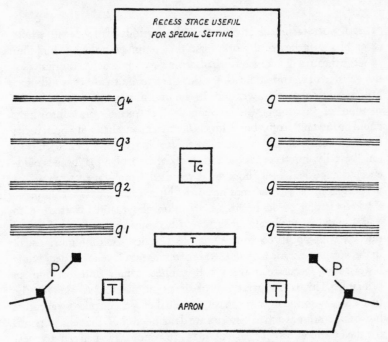

Fig. 39.—PLAN TO SHOW POSSIBLE ARRANGEMENT OF LATE EIGHTEENTH OR EARLY NINETEENTH CENTURY STAGE AREA.
G. Grooves for wings and shutters.
T. Traps (Tc—cauldron trap as for *Macbeth*)
P. Proscenium door

Lamb phrased it) between audience and actors. At first gas was used only for the auditorium; but even here its effect was great. It was now possible to darken the auditorium during performance. In their own world of blackness the audience looked away into the "other world"— a world of light, colour, and costume beyond the barrier of footlights (still, by the way, on an extensive forestage).

This is an age, in serious drama, of expensive and elaborate revival rather than a time of original composition. Many plays we do recall from this period are actually imitations of earlier drama, now studied afresh with the enthusiasm of the Romantic revival and the approval of such critics as Lamb, plays of which Shelley's *Cenci* with its Websterian and Shakespearian echoes may serve as a favourable example, rather than the professional stage productions of Sheridan Knowles. On the other hand, Byron, an underestimated dramatist, did some original and vivid work, produced later (in the case of *Sardanapalus*) with most impressive sets—in a wave of enthusiasm for Assyrian antiquities. The admiration of earlier writers (and their freer emotional expression) is paralleled by love of historical accuracy and the fascination of past scenes; so that themes and sets can accord.. On the other hand, Byron's more original poetic drama *Manfred*, which foreshadows the rebirth of original (not pseudo-Elizabethan) poetic drama in the 1930's remains almost unknown as a stage piece.

The developing barrier between audience and actors led not only to the pictorial detail and technical skill of outdoor scenes (attempting to ape precisely the external world) but also to an equal care with interior setting. This took longer. Flats and shutters were less inadequate to present a simple indoor scene. Under Madame Vestris, however, at the Olympic (1831) attempts were made to attract the public by a detailed and refined attention to the interior setting. Later under her management with Charles Mathews at Covent Garden, such plays as Boucicault's *London Assurance* are clearly to be considered as naturalistic—using a "box setting", and basing on the convention (not yet clearly enunciated) of the fourth wall. The audience "look in" on the lives of others; the old demand that the audience, as it were, play the action through with the people on stage, using imagination and constructive participation (i.e. accepting doors as various entrances in various houses and quick changes of locality without demur), has largely been abandoned. Instead, the audience are required to accept the stage picture and events as "reality". Every effort is made to suggest that the scene is as in "real" life. Ultimately, of course the attempt must fail without *some* audience co-operation. But the emphasis is on separation, with, across the footlights, fuller and fuller presentation of the outward appearances and behaviour of actual life. A new style of acting develops as a result. A famous early play (still revived) of this kind is Lord Lytton's *Money*. Characters are observed and presented from the contemporary world, with little exaggeration. Yet this is not realism; it is the outward that is stressed. Many plays produced are merely efficient readjustments of stock stage characters, a hopelessly (if charmingly) theatrical world, later to be described by Jerome K. Jerome in *Stageland*. On the other hand, there is much material that could be revived, provided the producer accepts the plays for what they are—*commedia* stock characters in early nineteenth-century dress and setting. Many of the farces produced as after-pieces are hilarious in the style of the early films, depending greatly on the improvised business of some popular comedian. They can be found in early acting editions—and several are listed below. Some complete comedies and dramas, such as Morton's *Speed the Plough*, are equally amusing, and have sufficient character reality to entertain.

Yet if serious comedy indoors was verging towards restraint, while farce clowned over the stage rejoicing in new trick settings, plays with emotional subjects and outside location became pictorially more intricate, and necessarily more exaggerated in gesture and action. Large theatres, elaborate scenery, and high passion, demanded such a style from the actors. This kind of play, the "melodrama", is for many producers the most familiar product of the period. And, again, other circumstances contributed to its development. Only two theatres legally could function without let or hindrance in the capital. These were Drury Lane (which possessed the Killigrew patent) and Covent Garden (owning the D'Avenant grant). Other theatres could operate only at certain times and in a limited way. One method of evading the prohibition on presenting stage plays was to convert the performance into a musical piece. In the eighteenth century a concert of music would be given. During the "interval", as an extra, a play might be presented. This, however, and other pretences, were abandoned as the law gradually dealt with the attempted evasions. There remained the conversion of a whole presentation into a musical piece, or "burletta". The law pursued its tortuous course. How many songs should be introduced to qualify a piece as musical? How much incidental music should accompany actions? How much recitative? And so on. Whatever the exact conclusions, "melodrama" (literally—adopting a French term—a play with music) was also established as a particular form of drama. Obviously, the employment of music removed the style from "naturalism", and since the appeal was to be popular, scenic effect was usual; the "pirate" theatres had to pack in large audiences with spectacular and vivid dramatic pieces. Music has a releasing and heightening emotional effect. All worked together to produce the kind of effect that we call "melodramatic". We have never abandoned the essential elements in this form of drama. Straight plays in acting versions of Victorian times have often, during an exciting passage, the direction "melodrame until curtain"—indicating *pizzicato* violins and suitable musical effects to build up the tension. Film and television employ the background "melodrame" incessantly. In addition, the legitimate theatre has learnt something of the value of suitable incidental and atmospheric music, while in training actors improvisation to music is used extensively. The producer's approach to melodrama must be very careful—it is a complex form, and by no means to be dismissed as trivial or merely ludicrous.

There is abundant material from this period—not, perhaps of the highest dramatic quality, but lively, varied, and theatrically efficient. George Colman's (the younger's) comedies—including the famous *John Bull*—are typical of many other comic dramas which could be revived successfully. The characterisation is not deep or subtle; we are somewhere between the types of *commedia* and realistic "roundness" of character—a kind of workaday domesticated *commedia* which is not without theatrical point and vitality. The versatility of these working dramatists or perhaps "men of theatre"—for their experience was wide and related closely to the bread and butter imperatives of the trade—is impressive. Colman wrote other dramas which may serve as typical examples of the period—a long and elaborate historical drama, *The Battle of Hexham*; a melodramatic tragedy, *The Iron Chest*; a romantic drama, *The Mountaineers*; a musical farce, *The Wags of Windsor*; and an indefinite number of short one-act farces. Such styles of drama may be paralleled again and again in the general theatrical activity of the period. The new emphasis on spectacle is reflected very clearly in the writing of Fitzbell, for example, with spectacular plays, nautical dramas, as well as lavishly mounted melodramas, with thirteen or fourteen settings. These are romantic dramas set in remote places, historical dramas relying on wonder and rather overwrought emotional appeal, and such histrionic use of the supernatural or the tortured mind as Irving found in *The Bells*. At the same time, poets and the more scholarly writers attempt to revive the Elizabethan verse drama and themes, with varying success. Where, as Shelley, they had the sensitivity, they lacked the theatrical knowledge; where they had theatrical knowledge, they copied too slavishly. Yet the scornful rejection of the work of such a writer as Sheridan Knowles is not really justified. Turgid and false though his blank verse dramas may seem, in presentation good qualities emerge. Perhaps if more producers risk an actual performance we shall discover, as so often, that one or two at least of his tragedies, carefully directed, merit revival. They are not so far removed from some of the theatrical styles and themes which have succeeded on the London stage in the last twenty years or so. And our taste for verse drama—often of a most involved and derivatory kind—seems to have been reawakened; through music and incantation of the voice, event and emotion emerge in reality.

Which brings us to the most striking feature of this period. Music is everywhere. Music in melodrama, music in song and dance, music in all kinds of dramatic developments of almost unparalleled ingenuity. Many of the dramatists—Fitzball, for example—wrote also opera librettos. No rigid barrier divides the straight play from the opera. Songs are introduced into melodramas and musical accompaniment to action is accepted as normal even in otherwise "straight" plays. This had been necessary to escape the effects of the laws forbidding performance of legitimate drama elsewhere than the patent houses. So melodrama—music drama—was first a necessity and then shaped by the emotional power of the music into a spectacular and exciting form. Indeed, if one can rid one's mind of prejudice, one suddenly has a vision of a theatre as rich and varied in its approach as the traditional Eastern, with all the devices of dance, clowning, mime, music, irrational and fantastic costume, crowd effects, elaborated skilfully because of the new technical resources of the period. Pantomime continues, with surviving harlequinade and increasing pictorial effect; burlesque acquires fresh importance. Technically, as we have seen, burlesque is the presentation of a serious theme, play, or story, in a spirit of satire, derision, parody, and general good humour. The last quality is important in the early Victorian theatre. A stage success would almost immediately be put on in a "cod" version; and usually the general characteristics of the leading players in the serious play would be guyed and the events exaggerated until the whole situation and theme became ludicrous. If the Victorians had pomposity and falsity at times, they balanced these self-important attitudes with healthy derision and good-humoured satire, possibly quite unequalled in our day. (Modern impersonators show us a little of this art; the distinction between good humoured—and often extremely perceptive—criticism, and cruelty, is obvious.) But the burlesque became, not merely a broad term for a particular dramatic approach, but a technical and clearly defined form of theatre. It now involved singing, dancing and show; naturally the dancing and show encouraged the use of many "supers", especially dancing girls. In this form it might be said to dominate the popular musical stage until the coming of "musical comedy", another example of general approach evolving into specialism. In America the burlesque show survived, but more and more as a "girls' and glamour" presentation, until it faded, or merged with strip shows in clubs, in the 1940's. In the nineteenth century, however, it was a popular, witty, and versatile, entertainment. The burletta, though technically and legally defined with precision, in practice overlapped (once monopoly ceased) and came to mean much the same. Planché's *Olympic Revels*, and his *Paphian Bower*, or, *Venus and Adonis* (with a cast of seven men, twenty women, and an indefinite number of supers) represent the use of classical legend, while such a piece as Byron's *La, Somnambula!* or, *The Supper, the Sleeper, and the Merry Swiss Boy*, indicates the "codding" of contemporary taste. Perhaps equally important and popular was the extravaganza. A basic fairy-story was developed with song, dance, spectacle; it shared Christmas popularity with the pantomime—from which we should find it hard sometimes to distinguish the form. Planché's work is again outstanding. Much of our traditional fairy-lore and pantomime material was staged (and established as part of popular "culture" by him) in such extravaganzas as *Beauty and the Beast* and *The Sleeping Beauty in the Wood*. The curious *mélange* which was acceptable is illustrated in such an "extravaganza" as *The New Planet*, or *Harlequin Out of Place*. In short, anything was material for the extravaganza; nothing too far-fetched, as its titles would indicate. Yet from these fantasy plays emerged real beauty. The apparent abandonment of all canons of realism produced a vital theatrical style which drew upon the very foundations and archetypes of human dramatic activity. Further, as recent London revivals have shown, there is (by any standards) real artistry and poetry in the work of Planché. Some of his stories are original in concept, and possess, despite the puns and apparent nonsense, a genuine poetic quality, fairy-tale beauty, and delicacy of invention. Horror and joy, monster and fairy, are blended; even the prying psychologist, who contrives (by some mental dichotomy of his own) to denigrate fairy-stories on the one side as unhealthy and to justify horror comics on the other as furnishing an outlet for children's urges, will hardly be able honestly to fault this Victorian work. A glance at the play list will show the scope and variety of material. It becomes richer and more varied as the century proceeds—but evolves into newer and more adult forms through the opera bouffé (again Planché helps the process) into comic opera, and thus to the work of Gilbert and Sullivan.

The abundance of short farces from the period may be understood when we remember that the "bill" was often threefold—a short one-act play, a main item (tragedy, comedy, or longer musical play), and finally a farce to send the audience away in a cheerful mood. Many farces from the period are well worth consideration. Unfortunately we seem to demand such an impeccable standard from the play script of

N

earlier periods. Examine the words of a modern farce or broadcast script and they are—in themselves—devoid of humour, flat, meaningless, heavy. Yet we judge farces from earlier periods on just such a casual reading. They are not meant to read well, but to act well. As the words given to the Clown and Wagner in *Dr. Faustus* appear dull and trite, until brought into being with action and comic imagination, so with these farces. If you doubt this, try reviving one or two of these farces with the approach and awareness of comic possibilities that you would bring to a modern farce. Clearly, we are under one disadvantage. We do not know the actors for whom the farces were designed; the characteristic gesture and by-play taken for granted by the writer is lost. But the same difficulty exists with every revival; and study of the theatre and conventions of the period are just as helpful and just as necessary for the production of the farce as for the presentation of *The School for Scandal*. You must, of course, have actors who can attempt farce with some hope of success. Lack of such is perhaps the real difficulty, not the poverty of the script, which is a basis for comic invention and timing.

Finally, look at some of the charming little musical pieces, or "vaudevilles", such as Planché's *Loan of a Lover*, in which Vestris played the lead. The dialogue is superior to that in most modern musical plays, there is a real plot, amusing characterisation (within the limits of such a slight dramatic form), and you can set the songs as you wish, to accord with your own interpretation of the script.

APPROACH TO PRODUCTION

Much of what has already been said relates to the producer's task. Let us summarise:

Farce: The producer must examine the text very carefully, reconstructing for himself a satisfying pattern of action and movement. He should consider in detail the stage position of actors at particular moments to emphasise comic point, fear, despair, exultation, triumph. This may sound obvious, but it is the successful pointing of situations which take control of the helpless human, reduced almost to an automaton, which makes the successful farce. If, of course, with all his care the producer still cannot see a really "audience-proof" series of absurdities, catastrophes, and surprises, or (as in the farces associated with the comedian Robson) the unending angularity of character which persistently impedes the efforts of others—if no such plan or pattern can be achieved, clearly the play is useless to him. What *he* cannot

see, his actors will not; or, more awkwardly, one or two will see
opportunities for by-play and personal clowning, will dominate the
rest and destroy the situation. Farce demands technique; it is a difficult
form of theatre for the less skilful actor. An absolutely firm production
plan is needed.

Comedy: In this period type character is still predominant. But
the types can be filled out with a kindly humanity. The producer must
now begin his task of suggesting "character building". Lines here and
there in the text will suggest possibilities. At the same time, he must
keep in check any effort by an actor to regard his part as a serious
psychological study and to distort the play and the performances of
others to his own taste. Character must be kept in accordance with the
events of the whole play. Within these limits interesting individual
work is possible. Again, the comedies of the period are light and do
not pretend to penetrate far below the obvious, but they do portray
very clearly (consider Mrs. Grundy) certain trends, tendencies, patterns, in human behaviour, and from these emerge amusing characters
(who are not unreal). Don't let the pace get too slow; don't over-
emphasise or suggest subtleties. Allow clear presentation of well-
marked peculiarities to speak for itself. Outward human behaviour
has tended (during the last forty years or so) to conform (in accepted
respectable circles) to a more uniform pattern. Yet those who live in
the country, or recall Edwardian days, can point to many people who
had even more marked eccentricities than, and whose hearts were
just as golden as, the apparently unreal creatures of Morton and the
younger Colman. These register on stage because (deep down) we
recognise them as portraying certain genuine human attitudes, and
we welcome the refreshing clarity and directness of their behaviour.
But don't over-emphasise—play "straight". Words and situations
will do the rest. Where events or phrases seem too exaggerated—or
have changed their meaning for a modern audience—cut or paraphrase
carefully. A measure of rearrangement is normal practice when such
plays are revived professionally, and from Shakespeare's day onwards
such readjustments (not radical but to secure audience understanding
and interest) have been accepted. The aim always is to allow the real
play to make its full impact.

Tragedy: Play straight, don't guy, cut where Victorian verbiage is
too overpowering or tedious for a modern audience. Character motive
is needed to bring life and reality to words. Some actors may welcome
the chance to experience the larger passions and agonies of the Victorian
tragedy, but insincerity will wreck the effort. It was well said that if

you are sincere—if you "believe" in the character—the most exaggerated speech and situation will become real and convincing. If you do not "accept" your unbelief will be at once apparent, and in trying to "cover", you will inevitably overact. In verse tragedy, consider the whole technique of verse-speaking. It may not be Shakespeare's work, but it must receive the same consideration as his poetry.

Melodrama: Again, approach sincerely and act as convincingly as you well can. If your version is going to "burlesque", a "serious" approach is all the more important. Once the actors start to laugh at themselves the audience loses interest. It is the high seriousness, slightly overdrawn, that will secure hilarity. On the other hand, it may be true that, like the scoffer in Goldsmith, those who come to laugh remain, if not to pray, at least in an enjoyably chastened mood. This is true of the actors themselves. Drama is more powerful than the merely rational. Looking at the script, one is inclined to smile, but once start acting and emotions and situations grip, and one begins to fill out the barren words with life. So be prepared for a flexible approach to the script; attitude may change as you go on. As to burlesque, it is a fine art. I have seen many attempted burlesques of melodrama, yet never one that was really successful, pointed, and amusing. Too many are merely silly, feeble, and in the end fatuous.

Musical Plays: Here the producer must be ready to study the whole involved business of moving and grouping large crowds, working with an expert on dance routines, and co-operating carefully with set designer and costume maker. But he must not allow his own concept of the play to be overruled. There must be space for movement, quick scene change, and a colour scheme overall which reflects the general fairy quality, fantasy, unworldliness, which he regards as typical of his play. Musical accompaniment is essential—not recorded music—and ample rehearsal with the musicians, whether piano and violin only, or full orchestra, is necessary. Amateur work suffers inevitably from the difficulty of getting everyone together at the same time; the elaborate play is sometimes best not attempted.

ORIGINAL METHOD OF PRESENTATION

We have plenty of evidence, in the stage settings supplied for toy theatres—"Penny Plain, Twopence Coloured"—of general décor and styles of presentation used in the more melodramatic plays, the tragedies, and the musical or dance plays. Very lovely some of these were in colour and general effect. They are, for the toy theatre, contrived mainly on the system of wings and backing, although some envisage doors in flats, and interesting moves towards full three-dimensional settings, wings being angled back to form a "solid" house. Even after "solid" sets are introduced, a study of acting editions shows the con-

Fig. 40.—EARLY NINETEENTH CENTURY THEATRE
Based on an illustration in Pierce Egan's *Life of an Actor*

tinued use of grooves in conjunction with the constructed settings well into the second half century.

The original settings and style can clearly best be appreciated by securing a model theatre of the Regency period, with its still existing curved apron stage, and building up the actual material supplied, say, for such a ballet drama as *The Silver King*. We shall note the use now of "ground rows", overhead masking, each set of wings having its corresponding ground and sky piece. We find that the setting can be changed quite easily, even though the staging is so much more carefully contrived—the basis is still simple, the elaboration being in the painting and the colour effects. It is a fairy world, an unreal but strangely attractive creation, that the theatre presented in such pieces.

Further, it is possible to secure thus the evidence for the original staging of the more famous melodramas, such as *The Demon Barber*, and to use these for a modern revival. We cannot overlook the pride taken in transformations and trick effects. Stage machinery was almost (like the Grand Turk in puppetry) an art form in its own right. Two influences were important. First the pantomime, with its frankly spectacular aims—especially the grand transformation. Lighting, gauzes, traps, revolves, all were thoroughly exploited. The other influence was the continuing romantic drama—which explored not only time, space, and character eccentricity, but also (as enthusiastically as a Gothic novel) the supernatural. Ghost appearances were necessary, and the aim was to make these as "natural" as possible. If ghosts existed, then this was how they would behave; the audience *must* be convinced. So came the famous Corsican trap. By this a ghost would rise from the floor, glide across, and gradually sink—all without any visible means of support, or any apparent cleavage in the solidity of the boards. The illusion was complete. Of such effects the Victorians were justly proud. On the other hand, development of box setting leads on to our own picture-frame stages. The aim here was gentility and respectability, in contrast with tatty wings, torn hangings, tables rough and old, and chairs that might be functional, but had no fitting reference to the place or rank of the users. This, again, was as revolutionary as were the real carpets in place of baize, covering the stage floor. Efforts were made with ornaments and accessories, mirrors, and hangings to suggest the refined interior of the day.

The Miller and His Men, by I. Pocock, first produced in 1813, is typical in both "setting" development and dramatic content. Robert Louis Stevenson was familiar with the version published for the toy theatre by G. Skelt (and still obtainable); I have referred to this "juvenile drama" (sub-titled the *Bohemian Baditti* and "written expressly for, and adapted only to, Skelt's characters and scenes") but the rather differing emphasis of timing and presentation in the toy theatre renders its evidence a little dubious, however informative the actual "scenery" and "dresses" are. Music directions, etc., are omitted and characters changed. For the reconstruction of action and setting methods, the edition in Lee's *British Drama* will be used. The varied and elaborate demands of the various scenes comprise in themselves a whole theatrical history, a collection of various conventions and methods to be used during the nineteenth century and the present day in some types of presentation. Further, they indicate the demands made by nineteenth-century scripts, and the tasks facing producer and designer today.

> "Act I, scene 1. The Banks of a River. On the right, in the distance, a rocky eminence, on which is a windmill at work—a cottage in front. Sunset."

Later in the scene Kelmar enters the cottage. We find that the river is navigated by "practicable" boats. Further, the Miller appears "in perspective coming from the crag in the rock". There is also a tree behind which robbers retire.

Here, then, we have wings and backing; the cottage may be painted on a flat with a door; the windmill has sails that turn—a common stage device even in the eighteenth century—and towards the back a raked piece is built up from stage level. The cottage is placed front right (according to Skelt's plan) and masks out the continuing "river" —so that boats may appear from the wings here, or vanish behind the cottage "structure". Tree wings are added, including a decayed tree on the left by "1st entrance". Grindoff the miller seeks the hand of Claudine, in love with the penniless Lothair. Two robbers have been sent to kidnap her. They pursue her to the cottage, and see Lothair inside. There follows:

> GOLOTZ: Lothair! 'twas he, then, that marred our purpose; he shall smart for't.
> RIBER: Back! back! he comes. On his return he dies; he cannot pass us both.
> *Music.*—They retire behind a tree—A boat passes in the distance, from the mouth of the cavern in the rock beneath the mill, and then draws up to the bank. Enter GRINDOFF the miller, in the boat, who jumps ashore.

He and Lothair meet, and the robbers' plan is thwarted. Only the great depth of stage at Covent Garden would, surely, enable the effect of distance to be convincingly sustained. The use of music at every exciting turn in the action is essential in the melodrama, Victorian or modern, romantic theatre or television screen. The unlucky pair emerge from behind the tree:

> RIBER: Curse on this chance! we have lost him!
> GOLOTZ: But a time may come.
> RIBER: A time shall come, and shortly, too.

Such "exit lines" were just as necessary on the vast stage expanse of nineteenth-century theatre as they were with the proscenium doors of the smaller eighteenth-century playhouses.

We move to Scene 2. "The Forest—distant thunder—stage dark." This short scene concerns only the returning ruler, Count Friberg, and the lamentations of his comic servant, especially as "the storm increases". All that is needed is a forest "cloth" dropped not too far back within the proscenium, to allow the setting of the next main scene, "A Room in the Cottage", which, after his exit from the preceding scene (marshalled by his servant, "This way, sir—this way"), the Count inevitably reaches, to find Grindoff with Claudine and Kelmar her father. The Count suspects Grindoff; he and his servant have just escaped from robbery; they plan to leave, but the storm has swept away the "ferry barge". The scene ends with a "sestette" led by the gentle Claudine, "Stay, prithee, stay—the night is dark" and the final stage directions "CLAUDINE tenderly detains the COUNT—KELMAR detains KARL, and scene closes".

Again we switch to a "front stage scene". "The Depth of the Forest —Stage dark." Lothair has disguised himself to penetrate the robbers' hideout. He has tracked Riber and Golotz, as he carefully explains, "as the moon's light burst from the stormy clouds".

> *Music.*—Enter RIBER, GOLOTZ follows—they look round cautiously, then advance to a particular rock, which is nearly concealed by underwood and roots of trees. (Lothair challenges them, persuades them of his loyalty to the cause.) *Music.*—GOLOTZ leads LOTHAIR to the rock, pushes the brushwood aside, and all exeunt, followed by RIBER, watching that they are not observed.

The technique of exit will again be noted. (From such beginnings stem a whole series of training exercises in the textbooks of picture-frame presentation in the twentieth century.) Since we next "discover" one of the most elaborate scenes in the play, and since the preceding scene is brief, it seems reasonable again to suppose that the forepart only of the darkened acting area was needed. The simple "built up" brushwood piece by a tree wing would, with a "cut out" rock, be quickly set and sufficient in realism. Through the yielding "bristles" of brushwood the three could exit to the wings. The abandonment of entry by proscenium doors for such spectacular pieces is clear, although they were retained and could be brought into use if desired. So to:

Scene V—A Cavern
BANDITTI discovered variously employed, chiefly sitting conversing around tables, on which are flasks of wine, etc.—steps rudely cut in the rock

in the background, leading to an elevated recess, on which is inscribed "POWDER MAGAZINE"—Other steps lead to an opening in the cave—a grated door.

Here, then, is a "raked" and "built-up" setting. Probably this was simplified in later presentations at less ample theatres. Skelt, for example, shows merely a ladder in place of the "steps cut in the rock". The banditti sing an opening chorus, during which, in best musical comedy style, they "all rise and come forward" for the second half of their song. To them enters the gangster's mistress, Ravina, and is told that a new lady is to come to the cave. To more music, the trap in the floor is thrown up and Riber, Golotz, and the new comrade, Lothair, appear. Almost immediately the leader arrives, and "descends the opening" (i.e. comes down from the entrance to the cavern shown at the back) and (not to our great surprise) is seen to be the wealthy miller, Grindoff. The murder of Friberg, whose return to his domains threatens the end of Grindoff's career of violence and robbery, is planned. The act ends as the robbers drink to "the miller and his men", and Grindoff dresses again as the miller. They go out by the rock door, singing a closing chorus.

Act II takes us again to Kelmar's cottage. The interval has given time for resetting. Scene ii takes us to the "front" forest scene, again brief. Scene iii repeats the full cavern set, where Lothair is on guard. "Could I but reach the magazine," he reflects.

Music.—LOTHAIR retires cautiously—he places his foot over the body of a ROBBER who is seen asleep on the steps leading to the magazine—by accident he touches the carbine which slips down—the ROBBER being disturbed alters his position, while LOTHAIR stands over him, and again reposes— LOTHAIR advances up the steps—as he arrives at the magazine, WOLF's signal, the bugle, is heard from above—the ROBBERS instantly start up, and LOTHAIR, at the same moment, springs from the steps, and, seizing his carbine, stands in his previous attitude.

Such action, free from the intrusion of dialogue, links the melodrama almost symbolically with earlier dramatic forms and origins. Later, Lothair secures the help of the jealous Ravina, now that Claudine has been brought to the cavern; even more typically, come the directions:

Music.—LOTHAIR points to the magazine—shows the train to RAVINA, and explains his intention—then gives a phosphorus bottle, which he shows the purpose of—she comprehends him—CLAUDINE's action, astonishment, and terror—LOTHAIR opens the trap up the stage,

Scene iv is at first glance a little more involved than the usual alternating scene—"The Cottage of RIBER—The sign of the Flask at the door". Study of the action and stage directions, however, shows that only the flat exterior of the cottage is needed, with a window from which Wolf (the miller) looks out. So we reach the climax of all the effects and spectacular action and the end of the play. Scene v shows "A near view of the Mill, standing on an elevated projection—From the Foreground a narrow Bridge passes to the rocky promontory across the ravine."

Bustle, struggle, hand-to-hand combat, build up to the pyrotechnic horrors of the end, devoid, of course, of dialogue:

> LOTHAIR instantly sets fire to the fuse, the flash of which is seen to run down the side of the rock into the gully under the bridge, from which RAVINA has ascended, and the explosion immediately takes place—KELMAR, rushing forward, takes CLAUDINE in his arms.

The "explosion" is the destruction of the mill, "crowded with banditti". Here, the collapsible canvas frame, with suitable wire-drawn fragmentation will obviously be needed—and use of lighting, and/or flash powder.

Yet with all the setting complications, the speed of running was obviously carefully preserved. The story—like the staging—constantly anticipates (or repeats) certain recurrent trends in this kind of dramatic presentation, even in character. Ravina, the dishonoured girl with a heart of gold, who plots against her seducer, and then at the last moment cannot execute her revenge—she loves him yet—will be found in many later plays. So, too, will the Jekyll and Hyde character of Grindoff–Wolf, who seems (as Stevenson himself indicated) to have haunted this great novelist's mind throughout his life, and still appears, under various names, on screen and television. Despite the critics who look with some scorn on such dramas, such characters perhaps symbolise and present archetypal human experiences. Are they real in some sense, beyond easy naturalism, modern representatives of the old morality tradition away in some eternal country of the mind the never-never (or always present) land of Bohemia?

For the development of the "set piece", "set scene", and our own term "setting", consult Richard Southern's *Changeable Scenery*, page 249ff.

Fig. 41 is based on an illustration in Dibden's edition of Sheridan's *The Critic* (Chiswick Press, 1814). It shows the blending of eighteenth and nineteenth-century styles—the proscenium door, the raised curtain, the painted "scenes". We note that the text is "correctly given, from the latest representations, by Thomas Dibden . . . prompter of the

Theatre Royal, Drury Lane", and that "the supposed extracts from newspapers, names of, and compliments to, particular performers, with other temporary or local passages occurring in this excellent afterpiece have been always varied to suit the times and purposes of current representation".

The frontispiece shows the developing pictorial stage. It is taken from an illustration to *The Infant Phenomenon* by H. Horncastle (adapted from *Nicholas Nickleby*) (Strand Theatre, 1832). Note the

Fig. 41.—THE CRITIC IN PERFORMANCE, EARLY NINETEENTH CENTURY

romantic "drop" scene and the built-up "flowery bank" or set piece on which Crummles has placed a foot.

Fig. 40. Early Nineteenth-century Theatre. Based on an illustration in Pierce Egan's *Life of an Actor*. Proscenium door, side wings, and painted back scene in grooves 2, are clearly shown.

Fig. 42. This sketch from Dolby's *British Theatre*, Volume 2, shows a reference plan for curtain fall. Note the front curtain, the drop, and the persisting proscenium doors. The attitudes of the figures are interesting. Here is the new pattern of dramatic construction—the working for the effective "act" or "final" tableau curtain.

APPROACH TO SET DESIGN

The play text must now be considered carefully so as to envisage necessary movement and action. Before this period the stage floor had largely determined the form of the text and the movements therein suggested. Now with increased technical possibilities and the use of doors within the set each dramatist could be, to some extent, a law unto himself; and the set has to be based on his individual script. Thus in Morton's famous *Speed the Plough*, Act I, scene i, asks for "In the Foreground a Farm House.—A view of a Castle at a Distance— FARMER ASHFIELD, Discovered with his Jug and Pipe". Act II, scene iv, demands "An extensive view of a cultivated country—a ploughed field in the centre, in which are seen six different ploughs and horses—at one side a handsome tent—a number of country people assembled". Act IV, scene iii, is "A gloomy Gallery in the Castle—in the centre a strongly barred Door—The Gallery hung with Portraits". Act V, scene iii, is "The Garden of the Castle". The castle is now on fire and we read. "The effects of the fire shown on the foliage and scenery". Yet to meet these demands, the play could probably be staged in the eighteenth-century convention if necessary. The emphasis is almost entirely on scene painting "in the flat". The modern designer will, however, accept the *intention* of the nineteenth-century theatre—to give adequate pictorial background and setting—and will be able to carry out this desire more effectively. The important consideration is that we are no longer bound to relate the script to a conventional stage; we are free to implement the dramatist's intention as we feel best. Incidentally, of course, once we abandon the Georgian playhouse, we also lack its guidance as to moves intended; it may be well sometimes to comfort ourselves by the realisation that many managers would still stage by earlier conventions, and these must have been in the actors' minds, even when they strove for full pictorial effect and grouping.

In melodramas much will be lost unless we give some equivalent for Victorian detail, colour, and desire for verisimilitude which might make most grotesque events credible. Half the horror of later melodrama is that it occurs in the streets and tenements that we can see around us. There is, too, the need to evoke the period in which the events take place. Trick "machinery" and lighting must be carefully contrived. If these are too difficult, the script must be so adapted as to make the omission seem unimportant. To attempt the scene change or effect crudely is to wreck the dramatic style. Lastly, all setting must be planned with costume and movements, including the gestures to be held dramatically, by the actors. The model theatre setting will assist you in every way. Don't exaggerate in design—the actual straight naturalistic décor of the period (with slightly emphasised lines and colours) is grotesque enough.

The basis of setting for musical plays and extravaganzas may well

R.   RC.   C.   LC.   L.

Fig. 42.—FORMAL DIAGRAM USED IN DOLBY'S *BRITISH THEATRE*
Indicating stage positions with characters in typical positions

be wings and backcloth; but these can be very carefully designed and painted in relation to costumes and movements. The advantage of such a setting is the ample space it leaves for grouping and entries. Lighting, however, and gauzes may well supplement the total effect. Costumes may be simple; total colour is important rather than detail; lightness and freedom of movement are essential, with the possibility of quick change. Sometimes in fantasies a basic costume of leotard and tights may be worn throughout, and trimmings, garlands, head-dresses, or robe, worn over these. Note especially (a point often forgotten) the use that may be made of half-masks, which are quickly slipped on and obviate elaborate change of make-up. Approach the whole script imaginatively—stress the positive, the things which can be achieved and which will appeal; omit the less promising material. This is not a crime in so mixed and composite a form as the burlesque or extravaganza, so long as you compensate for omissions by re-adjustment and keep the same overall emphasis.

Naturalism and Picture-frame, 1850-1900

CAREFUL revivals, and expensive productions of new costume plays, continue. Time, however, softens the academic enthusiasms of Charles Kean into the beautiful Shakespearian productions of Irving. The melodrama comes to terms with the demand of naturalism towards the end of the period, so that at Drury Lane with Augustus Harris as manager, the appearance of contemporary life is united with ingenious pictorial effect and high adventure. In the popular suburban theatres again melodrama has a more up-to-date appeal—the life of the wicked city, the fate of helpless maidens, and the career of the crook, are set against the Victorian background. A version of *East Lynne* was first performed in Whitechapel (1864); Merritt's detection thriller *The Golden Plough* at The Surrey in 1877. The Adelphi Theatre was especially associated with melodrama of the newer style. After the end of the period, the film began to use this kind of dramatic material, and in the end produced it rather better, with the complete illusion of naturalistic detail, and less exhausting presentation, whatever the initial effort and expense.

The most important original plays of the period are probably those associated with this move towards naturalism in style, theme, and presentation. It is almost impossible to dissociate in discussion content from setting, character, and costume. Tom Robertson, an actor who felt the need for greater accuracy and care in stage setting, was fortunate enough to be called to work with Marie Wilton, soon after she took over the little "Dust Hole" theatre off the Tottenham Court Road, now the New Scala. She determined to make her "house" respectable, attractive in Victorian eyes, and fashionable. With redecoration of the auditorium went tasteful setting, the depiction of the fashionable interior, when possible, and unexaggerated behaviour of ordinary life. Robertson's first play for the Bancrofts (for Marie soon married her leading man, Squire Bancroft) was appropriately termed *Society*. It deliberately attempted to present life in the contemporary setting, and incidentally to satirise certain literary "sets" and figures. The scenes vary (just as in melodrama) from exteriors (but only the mild atmosphere of a London square) to various interiors, including the scene at the "Owls' Roost", a haunt of identifiable writers and journalists. Mrs. Bancroft and her helpers were frightened that this scene would prove dangerous; luckily, the fun and point of the characterisation were appreciated; the time was ready for relevance to actual life. The extent to which Robertson and the Bancrofts did deal with topical crises is hard to realise. Looking back, we may see the sentiment as exaggerated, the fears and enthusiasms as unreal. Yet the central problem in *Caste*, despite the occasional apparent falsity and the contrived happy ending, is a real issue; the character studies are not only appealing and theatrically moving but also rooted in reality. This is shown when the play is acted. More than one company has attempted *Caste* as a period exercise, prepared to "guy" and have (to their amazement) been forced by experience and the audience's reaction to play completely straight. The critics of the time were not all in favour of this new style of play—"cup and saucer" comedy, as they called it, from the close attention to naturalistic detail, washing-up, and other "chaws" of everyday existence. Further, the actors moved and grouped as in real life; they were hardly" audible" in speech, grumbled one critic. Study of original stage directions shows that they sometimes stood and spoke back to audience. Most important was the method of production; the author and Squire Bancroft worked together to direct an organised team, aiming at overall effect and as complete an illusion as possible. Again, they did not build the play necessarily round a star, differing here from Irving's methods at the Lyceum. Both Mr. and Mrs. Bancroft took whatever parts suited; needless to say they saw that as often as not suitable parts were there; but they did not lead; they concentrated on character work. The company became a training ground for young actors in the new style. Admired by Continental visitors it was styled the English "comédie française"; the hope was that it might become a permanent institution. It did not; but Bancroft was one of those who worked for the establishment of an Academy of Dramatic art. What the Bancrofts did achieve was the naturalistic school of presentation and new ideals and techniques of acting associated with this. When they moved to the Haymarket, rebuilt for their use and reopened in 1880, the ultimate was achieved in the pictorial approach to presentation—a picture-frame was set round the proscenium. Bancroft was at great pains to point out that he was the first to construct a stage thus. In every way, the detail of setting, the completely satisfying moving picture of actors within the scene, must be contrived and executed. Many entries in their autobiographical memoirs record their triumphs in this way, and the letters from more than satisfied admirers of outward appearances and replicas of things as they are.

Robertson's other plays, such as *M.P.*, *Ours*, *Play*, deserve examination. Strangely, as it seemed to Mrs. Bancroft, the most fanciful and "stagey", an adaptation from the German entitled *School*—a simple and unlikely Cinderella theme—was the best loved and most successful, perhaps because it was fantasy in modern dress—and a girls' school is not an unattractive setting. Besides which, in the character of Naomi Tighe, Robertson, like Shakespeare, introduced a very real and lively person against a romantic and unlikely background, thus suggesting by implication the possibility of fairy-tale events for the "real" people in the audience; fantasy and "naturalism" were reconciled. Recent revivals have not lacked success—although the effort to make *School* into a full musical play missed the whole point of its charm.

From Robertson onwards one notes the increasing skill of dramatists in blending contemporary life with satisfying dramatic pattern of their plays. The period achieved a compromise between (*a*) the observation of outward modes of behaviour, credible characters, ideas in the air at the time, and (*b*) the need to present an entertaining and artistically balanced sequence of action. The skilful naturalistic technique of the Bancrofts in acting joined with an equally skilful technique in patterning events, and over all was the illusion of normal appearance and everyday possibility. Problems (not too deep) are solved to the satisfaction of the audience. Yet one must not underestimate the vitality and relevance of these plays. Time has dulled the immediacy of their challenge; manners which then seemed natural seem exaggerated now. Yet in the end one is conscious that it was in convincing appearance, technical proficiency, restraint and polish of performance, that these plays made their contribution to the style and content of English theatre and actor-training. From France our dramatists brought the model of the "well-made" play; sometimes in A. W. Pinero and H. A. Jones contrivance seems to subdue life; yet obviously a play SHOULD be "well-made", whatever its theme. The only reservation is that the pattern may be too neat, the trick too obvious; yet in performance dialogue and character in their plays carry (through easy fluency and confidence) conviction and acceptance. Among the lesser plays of the period are some, listed below, well worth revival; sometimes

o

the passage of time has brought added reality to their subjects; sometimes they are frankly now "period" plays (as Boucicault's *London Assurance*), but valid and sincere within that convention.

It must be noted that not all producers of the time followed the scenic elaboration and/or naturalism which seemed dominant. Phelps at Sadler's Wells presented Shakespeare, Elizabethan, and other standard plays, with simple imaginative staging, using selective effects and sensitive décor, which elicited high praise from such critics as Morley, who deplored the over-elaborate setting which stifled the real play. Irving, for example, had to cut very large and sometimes dramatically important passages from his Shakespearian presentations in order to make time for scenic effects. Thus the work of Craig (himself at one time a member of Irving's company) and of Poel did not emerge from a vacuum; the tradition of imaginative and stylised décor was not entirely lost.

FURTHER MATERIAL

From this period come a great number of amusing farces—Pinero's *The Magistrate*, *The Schoolmistress*, not the least. Again, they appeal because they deal with real people, who become involved in impossible situations presented with the illusion of reality. Disbelief is suspended; naturalism triumphs over the wildest adventures. Moreover, the people are largely (we admit) ourselves, our own prejudice, affectations and stupidity. The panoply of pride, costume, and furniture, with which the characters are surrounded in this farce make the essential human frailty all the more significant and comic. Man—even Victorian man—puts on a brave show—but . . . !

Society, during the long reign, became stabilised after Chartism and the uncertainties of the first half of the century; thus a comedy of manners again becomes possible for a short while. The ruling class, as the Empire expanded, became the aristocracy of a great cosmopolitan capital. True, the nature of the "aristocracy" is a little dubious—but such circumstances only give Wilde more material, point, and epigrammatic opportunity. *The Importance of Being Earnest* is a true comedy of manners.

Material available includes most of those dramatic forms discussed for the early part of the century. The pantomime becomes, indeed even more spectacular and elaborate especially at Drury Lane under Augustus Harris, but tends towards its modern construction, the use of variety acts linked rather loosely by the fragments of the original story. There is little motive for reviving the post-1880 pantomimes;

one can construct one's own show on this formula. (Indeed, Messrs. French have issued some excellent basic pantomimes for use if you wish to do this.) The burlesque still offers interesting possibilities—to be used selectively. Probably the best hunting ground is among the writers of comedy and farce. Sidney Grundy (with suitably small cast lists), Alfred Sutro, Palgrave Simpson, John Madison Morton, R. C. Carton, all have plays worth examination. Pinero, Robertson, and Gilbert, are still very much on our "acting list". It is interesting to note how "modern" many of these plays are, once an obvious variation in common phrase and expression is accepted and in some way "cushioned" in production. Yet for most people the period is associated only with the later melodrama which, mixed with Victorian moral purpose, has become only a subject for mockery, difficult even to burlesque; the joke is obvious, and its repetition wearing. Humorous criticism of Victorian attitudes, and their cult of respectability, is better achieved by their own writer—Pinero and Gilbert. Seeing their plays we find that we (and possibly human beings at most times) are guilty of similar pretence, stupidity and weakness.

PRODUCER'S APPROACH

The use of complete box settings discouraged change of scene within the Act. Each act thus tended to become a complete unit in itself progressing steadily towards the "curtain". This developed a new technique in play-construction, for which the producer must make due allowance. So marked was this rhythm of action that at the end of each act in Victorian times a curtain was often taken with the actors in position for a "tableau". The curtain would close again, and then a second "tableau" would be presented with varying positions. Hence the term "tabs" for this curtain. How different this was from the practice of seventy years earlier (with its laconic comment at the conclusion of the act "scene continues") is obvious. What is not so obvious is the change in play form and dramatic intent involved. The producer's task is more clearly defined technically; he has to work within the three or four act convention and pattern, but within each act there is definite movement and rhythm, point and emphasis to be marked, which emerges in a halting place, the temporary destination of "tableau".

Because we are now so near our own day, much of the producer's work is essentially that at which he is prepared to labour in any presentation, and the problems of understanding older plays in terms of theatre are not so acute. Yet just because of this apparent outward similarity, the difficulties of accurate interpretation for the modern

audience are sometimes even more intricate. A period play can be staged
as such; what of these later Victorian dramas? Are we to stress that
they are period plays? Or are we to accommodate them to modern
taste, to avoid the obvious jar when words and situations may evoke
the wrong response? We may illustrate from plays even nearer our own
time. In a play dating from a few years ago the heroine is made to say
that a statement is a "corking whopper". The remark evoked from
students, who were examining the play, the expected derision. The
rest of the dialogue was easily acceptable as speech of our day; there
was no point in treating the play as anything else but contemporary.
So the offending phrase was cut. Had the characterisation and situations
of the play been typical, say, of the twenties, then the whole presentation
could have been in period—indeed, such treatment was mooted. But
the plot was essentially a recurrent problem and the people such as
one meets today in general social position and attitudes. In a very
much more striking way, the producer of the later Victorian play
must decide whether this is to be in period—or whether, even if events
are regarded as happening in Victorian times, dialogue is to be treated as
if by a modern writing of that period. Will the dialogue and attitudes
presented ring true if played exactly as written? If they provoke
laughter and upset the balance of presentation, so that what you
intended as serious becomes farcical, then period must be stressed, not
only in costume and setting, but also in mannerism and behaviour.
"This", you indicate, "is how those people behaved and thought
at that time. Their phrases, their inhibitions, their manners and
hypocrisies, may seem ludicrous—but we are accepting all these things.
Humanity will shine through." (It may be that the early plays of Shaw
can be treated only as period comedies nowadays. Time has destroyed
the originality of the characters; there is now general acceptance of
ways and views which gave piquancy to his original dialogue.) You
carefully prepare the audience for attitudes and expressions which
seem to them prudish or naïve by emphasising that you are reviving
a period comedy or "drama", just as certainly as if you were presenting
The School for Scandal. On the other hand, the work of Robertson often
needs no such emphasis. Even in the fanciful *School* much of the
dialogue is absolutely acceptable and "pointed" to modern ears.
(Examine the exchanges on the subject of military service between
Naomi and Jack Poyntz.) Thus, while the behaviour, the costume,
the movements, are all in period, there is no need to "cushion" the
audience by suggesting (through attention to details slightly over-
elaborated) that this is a different social scene from our own and that

they must be prepared to accept statements and phrases that seem insincere and over-dramatic. Revivals of Robertson's plays, initiated with some hesitancy, are found (surprisingly to some) to carry the audience so completely that they can be played perfectly straight; there is no need to underplay situation and dialogue on the one side, or to emphasise the difference in conventional behaviour on the other. The plays of Pinero and Wilde, naturally, rely on their relevance to the period which is best presented without exaggeration, but with sufficient emphasis; and, of course, the dialogue itself demands and communicates a sense of period and character. The better the dramatist, the less difficulty there is, for the great dramatist has that inner sense of fitness which avoids insincerity and contemporary falsities, or else deliberately exploits and shares them with the audience. What must be constantly studied is relationship to setting. The producer and the cast who can satisfactorily (without overplaying but securing complete fullness of effect) stage *The Importance of Being Earnest* have probably achieved one of the most difficult and technically demanding tasks in theatre. A final word—often the apparent Victorian exaggeration is not in the script as a whole, but in the character who speaks the lines, placed there deliberately by the dramatist, who would share our sense of falsity in the views expressed. The long quotations by the March-ioness from Froissart in *Caste* were surely intended by Robertson to show an essentially untenable position. Yet, again, is this attitude not still with us? Time and again, when we tend to deride Victorian sentiments we find them, on reflection, surviving.

Henley and Stevenson wrote in 1885 the play *Beau Austin*, set in Regency times at Tunbridge Wells. Despite the literary nature of the dialogue there is much dramatic opportunity and value in the play. When the play was recently revived the audience was slightly sur-prised by the frank statement in the prologue (originally delivered by Beerbohm Tree when the play was first produced at the Haymarket in 1890) that "the great duel of Sex"—"that ancient strife"—was the "very central fact of life". Although the happy ending may seem contrived, the problem of the betrayed heroine, and the amorality of the elegant Beau (who nevertheless has his own very exacting code of behaviour) in his sexual relationships are presented with honesty and without any prejudice—indeed, if there is any warping of artistic integrity, it is in the Beau's favour. There is so much "realism" (es-pecially in the fascination of the older man for the girl) that the play is potentially good theatre—apart from charm of dialogue and attrac-tiveness of costume and décor associated with its period. Unfortunately, the heroine has lines which may seem to a modern audience melo-dramatic and exaggerated, understandably, since Henley and Stevenson, newcomers to theatre, imitated what they thought to be good stage effect. (Stevenson was educated in the drama of "Skeltdom".) The producer had two possible lines of action. Either the "melodrama" could be exaggerated and the weeping heroine secure only mock sympathy from the audience, or the over-emphatic and "insincere" lines would be cut. Since the revival was based on faith in the essential virtues of the play, the real dramatic value of situation and character (despite the inexperience of the writers), the second course was, rightly or wrongly, taken. No violence was done to the play—the heroine's situation and predicament were presented just as strongly as in the original, but shorn of the "literary" oratory that the writers had added to her part. On the other hand, the speeches of the Beau himself needed no change or cutting at all; they were completely acceptable, as were the utterances of the other characters. This is a special case, but it illustrates, I think, the restraint which can make plays acceptable to the modern audience. It is a matter of communication. Where today a comparatively brief speech will convey quickly all that is needed (more would be wasted and over-emphasis disastrous) the Victorian audience liked to luxuriate in the situation. *Judicious cutting rescues the play.* Further, by this cutting, the Regency period was established more fully. Stevenson and his collaborator had other-wise caught the flavour of the earlier times as well as any dramatist. Costume, setting, and words blended pleasantly.

Finally, in all plays of the later Victorian period, the producer should enlist the use of music. It can suggest or exaggerate period and event, it can modulate and mediate dramatic crisis. Further, the use of melo-drame—accompanying the start or ending of a scene with appropriate music, which fades out or plays softly in to close the scene—is just as effective as in the modern screen play. I am not suggesting that more than a few bars should actually accompany dialogue—unless for a full melodrama—but simply that the pleasant leading in of the audience, or leading out from an emotional scene, which music achieves, creates atmosphere, and puts the hearers in a receptive mood. At the same time, music may be used satirically and even brutally, as Gilbert and Sullivan showed when it served their purpose.

Essentially, then, the producer must decide on his own attitude to the play. Granted that he feels it worthy of revival, what will be the best line of approach so that the audience can share its dramatic qualities? What points in the script will need stressing or readjustment to mediate the essential drama to his audience? The suggestions given above may furnish him with a starting point, at least, for his planning. Every play is, of course, a separate problem, not merely in itself and its theatrical relevance, but in its potential cast, presentation, and audience.

The producer might ask himself questions about any play, Victorian or modern, in some such order as the following. Drama is action, doing, events. First, then, what action takes place? This is fundamental; yet many producers begin elsewhere in their consideration of a play. Secure quite firmly and coherently the course of action, shown or implicit; never mind as yet about motives and character. What happens? Next, what is the theme of the play? We have discussed this earlier. If you have difficulty in separating actions from themes, think of a proverb. Then consider some of the plays which might illustrate the chosen proverb; invent a few more relevant sequences of action for yourself. The theme is similar. It furnishes a thread, running through actions; it is a centre, round which action builds; it is a dominant aspect of human experience, which the actions mirror; it is an archetype, on which the actions build. Because a work of art is living it will at different times and for different people present events, seemingly, in varying patterns and with varying relevance to human life. But, for his own day and for his task, the producer must decide what this central core in the play is. He sees then how action and event group around this theme. His next task is to examine carefully the whole play—not merely the script; what were the realities of its presentation? What was, indeed, the real play in its theatre? At this point, he reconsiders carefully his earlier decisions regarding theme and events. Usually he finds that his earlier thoughts are reinforced; but he may decide to pattern action rather differently around the theme, to change emphasis, to reject some ingenious theory, when he discovers that this does not accord with the play as originally presented, and was, therefore, presumably not in the dramatist's mind, either. Now, and not before, he considers carefully the characters involved in the action. What kind of people were responsible for such actions? What motivated them? The study and building of character becomes a main task in naturalistic and realistic nineteenth-century drama, whatever its place before. It must still be fitted into the whole theatrical pattern; any theory of character which contradicts the action established is false. You will have to write a new play. (Which has been done!) The producer must now work on each character's relation to the whole of the existing play. From available actors he casts the play, remembering that character can be interpreted only in terms of the individual actor's physical, mental, living experience, and abilities. Each actor has his own work now—he studies his part, building his character in accordance with the overall needs outlined by the producer. Some adjustment and development inevitably and rightly take place, as rehearsals proceed, from the relationship of character with character, and the modification of emphasis made necessary by the individual actor's powers and particular personal qualities. Through all the producer patiently co-ordinates and creates the organic play, within the setting he has planned with the designer, helping the actors to achieve the necessary actions. Movement, the apparatus of presentation, scene change, and the correct flow of the play, are included in

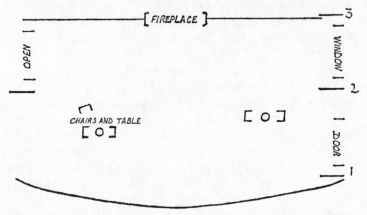

Fig. 43.—SETTING FOR ACT I OF *DAVID GARRICK*
(T. W. ROBERTSON, 1864)
Based on a diagram in acting version 1889

his task. The basic pattern of events, its inception, development, movement to climax, is to be realised and emphasised in the completed art-form, the living theatrical presentation which has life itself as its material and ultimate discipline.

Some such consideration of his task may enable the producer and designer to organise, and then to begin, the real work. There are books enough for them to consult, with varying views of the theatrical experience, from Stanislavski to Brecht, from Craig to Whistler.

ORIGINAL PRESENTATION

During the period the box set became a normal setting for naturalistic comedy. Fig. 43, taken from the Sampson, Low, and Marston edition of Tom Robertson's plays shows the final stage of change from grooves and wings to box setting; though the term "grooves" was used still as a technical term of useful reference for stage planning. Here we have a transitional setting. Note the remnant of curved apron. Instructions read "Interior, on three grooves". The set (1864) is partly enclosed. Fig. 44 shows a fuller box setting for a later play by Robertson, *M.P.* (1870). Fig. 45 illustrates romantic setting in a naturalistic play. This is the "castle scene" from Robertson's *Birth* (1870). His instructions are typical and sum up the whole matter. "No moon to the cloth. The moonlight to be on the grass. The ivy is to be real ivy, and the grass to be grass matting—not painted."

At the same time, external settings were often required even in

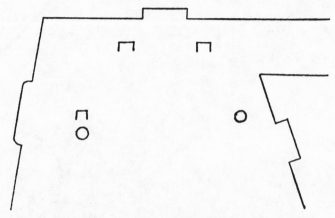

Fig. 44.—SETTING FOR ACT IV OF *M.P.* BY T. W. ROBERTSON
Based on a diagram in acting version 1889

comedies. Rising costs had not yet curbed the tendency to use three or more sets for a straight play. Indeed, when one considers the flexible and easy movement of an eighteenth-century play, it is matter for wonder that actors and dramatists accustomed themselves so soon to the fewer settings possible when each scene was elaborately and massively presented. Gradually the clogging effect of naturalistic scenery slowed scene change to a minimum, but "a single play a single set" did not become the desirable rule until well into the twentieth century. For external settings wings and backing were often used. Of course, for spectacular plays involving large crowds traditional staging, with added machinery and lighting effects (electricity became available for stage illumination in the 1880's, although not welcomed by some who thought gas lighting more mellow, more atmospheric, and wonder provoking), was still followed. These methods are retained today, and can be studied in, for example, "off West End" pantomimes. The Victorian wing flat with inserted door is often used; the ways in which wings and backing can be modified in setting, the use of ramps, drop scenes, and gauzes, may be studied conveniently from a seat in the second or third row of the circle, preferably well to the

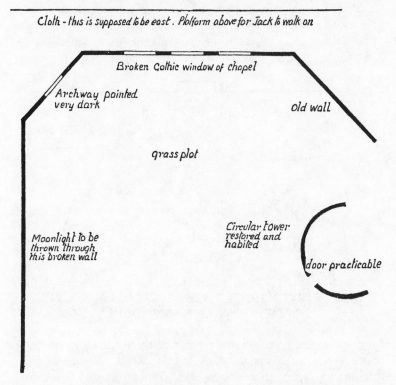

Fig. 45.—A ROMANTIC SETTING IN A NATURALISTIC PLAY
The Castle scene in *Birth* by T. W. Robertson, 1870

side of the theatre, which normally gives a view into the wings, and at the same time enables one to see floor-cuts, traps, and the general juxtaposition of set pieces. West End shows are usually too carefully disguised and finished to give real opportunity for studying methods of setting and scene change. The importance for the producer is that he can (by seeing such presentations) envisage the staging of his own play, and can deal with the questions of his set designer, or suggest ways round difficulties, so as to secure the space and ease of movement which his actors need. Less experienced designers often wish to clutter the stage—disastrous to the "many set" melodrama or musical play.

APPROACH TO SET DESIGN

Basically, there is in this period little to be added to information given in normal textbooks on set design. The danger of confusing naturalistic methods of setting with the needs of the spectacular or melodramatic musical play has been suggested. At the same time, it is essential that exact and careful naturalistic setting should be used where it is demanded, as in Pinero, Robertson, Simpson, and Sutro. It constitutes an integral part of the action and its requirements. "Cup-and-saucer comedy" requires cups and saucers and all that goes with them. The difficulty today is to secure adequate setting and flexible scene change. Materials are expensive. The settings for a play must be conceived as a whole. In other words, the various apparatus needed must be listed, and then patterned so that one set may fit within, or be rapidly moved from, another. Further, where possible parts of a setting should be left in position for the next scene if such a compromise is possible without spoiling effect. The plans shown in Figs. 46, 47 and 48 for *School* give some tentative suggestions for sufficiently accurate presentation without too much difficulty or expense. Woodland, garden, and schoolroom, are needed. Tree wings (W) and backing (B) secured the first. A "red brick" wall (S.P.) was pushed on in two halves from each side of the stage, and secured by weighted braces. An arched gate was built into one half. Similar flats (screwed to a wider plank base) were the back wall of the schoolroom. Self-standing booked flats (F) made the side walls. Benches and blackboard were also set. Flats were stacked ready along walls in the wings.

Significant details, the overmantel, the antimacassar, achieve the period impression that holds the audience and helps the actor. This, however, must not strive too far towards stylising; a sense of over-crowding and functionless ornament are in themselves part of the necessary Victorian "style". In the better plays of the period, with that poetic quality of imagination that inspires great drama, the designer has ample chance of helping, provided again the emphasis does not go too far towards distortion. Period and manner in settings for Oscar Wilde's plays have engaged some of our greatest stage workers; and, again, the heightened apprehension and comic implications of farce may well be expressed in plans for *The Magistrate* or *The Schoolmistress*. For the theatre of today, general principles of design are described and exemplified by many writers and authorities. Only, listening to their theories, aims, and techniques, one has to strive to remember, ever and again, that the play is the important thing; the setting is there to present the whole play, the true play, and nothing but the play.

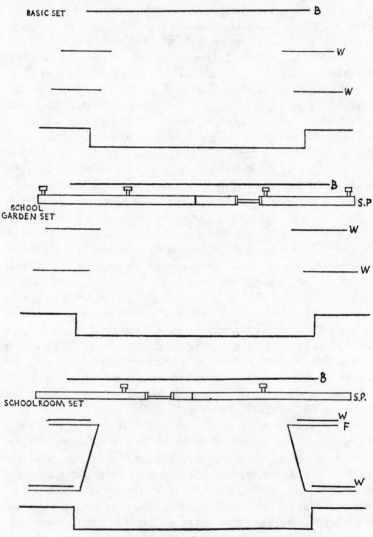

Figs. *46, 47, 48.*—TOM ROBERTSON'S *SCHOOL*
Three settings for the revival of Victorian Plays

Appendices

Appendices

LIST OF PLAYS

THE list is selective. Notes are added where specially relevant. Accessibility in library or publication has influenced inclusion. Even so, many of the plays noted (especially nineteenth-century publications by Lacy and French) are out of print, but may often be consulted, for example, in the British Drama League Library; further, a search of second-hand booksellers' shelves often yields bound volumes of these older scripts.

Students who wish to explore further material must refer to the fuller lists, often with valuable annotation, given in the various volumes of Allardyce Nicoll's *History of British Drama*.

If a writer's work does not fall clearly within a particular period, it is listed in that which seems most appropriate to his approach and style.

ABBREVIATIONS

BDLC   British Drama League Library Catalogue. *The Player's Library.*
       (British Drama League and Faber and Faber)
BD   1, 2, etc. *British Drama* (Jones)
BP   1, 2, etc. *Bell's Plays.*
BP   1, 2, 3, etc. *British Plays.* Ed. M. Moses (Little, Brown, Boston)
CED   *Chief Elizabethan Dramatists.* Ed. W. Neilson (Harrap)
CMP   *Chester Miracle Plays* (S.P.C.K.)
CPSD   *Chief Pre-Shakespearian Dramas.* Ed. J. Q. Adams (Harrap)
EABSP   *English Association Book of Short Plays.*
EED   *Earlier English Drama.* Ed. F. J. Tickner (Nelson)
EM   *English Masques.* Ed. H. A. Evans (Blackie)
EMP   *English Miracle Plays.* Ed. A. Pollard (O.U.P.)
EOI   *Everyman and Other Interludes.* Ed. E. Rhys (Dent)
ET   *English Theatre* (Lowndes)
LS   1, 2, 3, etc. *London Stage* (Sherwood)
OTEL   *Oxford Treasury of English Literature.*
PBS   *Plays before Shakespeare.* Ed. E. Smith (Dent)
POTR   *Plays of the Restoration.* Ed. D. Macmillan and H. Jones (Allen and
       Unwin)
RBD   *Readings from British Drama.* A. Nicoll (Harrap)

RBD *Representative British Dramas.* Ed. M. Moses (Little, Brown, Boston)
RC *Restoration Comedies.* Ed. M. Summers (Cape)
REC *Representative English Comedies.* Ed. C. M. Gayley (Macmillan)
RMTP *Representative Medieval and Tudor Plays.* Ed. R. Loomis and H. Wells. (Sheed and Ward, N.Y.)
SPSD *Specimens of Pre-Shakespearian Drama.* Ed. J. M. Manly (Ginn)
TEF *Ten English Farces.* Ed. L. Hughes and A. Scouten (Univ. of Texas Press)
TEP *Typical Elizabethan Plays.* Ed. Schelling (Harrap)

Burl.	burlesque, burletta.
Com.	comedy, comic.
Dom.	domestic.
Dr.	drama, drame, dramatic.
Ext.	extravaganza.
F.	farce.
Fant.	fantasy.
Hist.	history play, historical.
Melo.	melodrama.
Mus.	musical.
Op.	opera.
Panto.	pantomime.
Rom.	romance, romantic.
Trag.	tragedy, tragic.
Tragi-com.	tragi-comedy.
V.	verse.

m = men; w = women; sprs = supers;
ch = children; g = girls; b = boys

RITUAL AND FOLK-DRAMA

The following will be found in CPSD:
Tropes and Liturgical Plays:
 The Quem Quaeritis Trope
 The Easter Sepulchre
 Sepulchrum: The Visit of the Marys
 Sepulchrum: The Visit of the Marys: The Race of Peter and John
 The Appearance to Mary Magdalene
 The Wayfarers
 The Shepherds
 The Magi

Herod
The Prophets
Conversion of the Blessed Apostle Paul
Ludus Super Iconia Sancti Nicolai
Tres Clerici
Adeodatus

Introducing vernacular:
  The Sepulchre, The Wayfarers, The Shepherds (Fragmentary)

Plays not in cycle:
  The Conversion of St. Paul
  Mary Magdalene
  The Play of the Sacrament

Folk Plays:
  Robin Hood and the Sheriff of Nottingham
  Robin Hood and the Friar
  Sword Play
  St. George Play (Oxfordshire)
  St. George Play (Leicestershire)

Separate plays:
  King George and the Turkish Knight (Sussex) (St. Dominic's Press, Ditchley)
  The Mummers' Play (Three Arts Magazine, Jan., 1923)
  The Peace Egg, or *St. George*. Yorkshire Folk Play (Edward and Bryning, Rochdale)
  St. George and the Dragon, or *The Peace Egg*. (Derbyshire Folk-Lore Society)
  For other versions see BDLC

  For reference:
Chambers, E. K., *The Medieval Stage*. (Clarendon Press) 2 vols.
Chambers, E. K., *The English Folk Play*. (O.U.P.)
Tiddy, R., *The Mummers' Play*. (O.U.P.)
Young, Karl, *The Drama of the Medieval Church*. (O.U.P.)

MEDIEVAL RELIGIOUS PLAYS

Abraham and Isaac (Brome Play). 5m EMP and CPSD
Abraham, Melchisedec, and Isaac (Chester Play). EOI
Childhood of Man. Adapted I. and O. Bolton King. CMP
Creation and Fall of Lucifer (York). 5m EMP
Creation (with the Fall of Man) Coventry) 2m 2w sprs EED
Creation of Eve (Norwich). 6m 3w choir CPSD, SPSD
Crucifixion (Cornish). 6m 1w EOI
Doomesday. 8m sprs. EED

P

Harrowing of Hell (Chester). 15m sprs EED, CPSD
Harrowing of Hell (Wakefield). 10m 1w EOI
Jacob (Wakefield). 2m 2w SPSD
Judgement Day (York), 12m CPSD
Judgement Day (Hegge MS.). 6m sprs RMTP
Killing of Abel. 4m sprs CPSD
King, I. and O. Bolton (edrs.)
    The Chester Miracle Plays: Done into modern English and arranged for
      acting. (S.P.C.K.)
The Play of the Maid Mary (Coventry) Ed. by E. Martin Browne. 14m 12w
    5g sprs (Allan)
Mary Magdalene. 33m 2w CPSD
The Play of Mary the Mother (Coventry). Ed. E. Martin Browne. 14m 9w sprs
    (Allan)
Miracle of St. Nicholas and the Virgin. 5m 3w
Miracle of St. Nicholas and the Schoolboys. 2m 1w 3b RMTP
The Pageant of the Nativity (Chester). 19m 6w 4b EMP
Noah (Wakefield). 5m 4w CPSD, SPSD, EED
Noah and Lamech. 9m 4w SPSD
Noah's Flood (Chester), 5m 4 or 6w CPSD, EMP and various school editions
Pageant of the Shearman and Taylors (Coventry Nativity Play). 15m 4w ch sprs
    CPSD, EED, etc.
      (Many adaptations for school use)
The Passion (Chester). EMP
The Passion and Resurrection. EED
Passion Play (Hegge MS.). 35m 5w RMTP
Pharoah (Wakefield). 6m sprs CPSD
The Prophets (Coventry). 17m RMTP
The Prophets (Chester). 16m CPSD
Raising of Lazarus (Wakefield). 5m 2w EED
Raising of Lazarus (Hegge MS.). 6m 2w RMTP
Salutation and Conception (Hegge MS.). 4m 1w 6m or w EMP SPSD
Play of the Shepherds (Chester). 6m 1w EED
Second Shepherds Play (Towneley, Wakefield). 5m 2w CPSD, SPSD, EOI, etc.
Mak and the Shepherds (A new acting version). 4m 1w (New Theatre Play
    Service)
York Nativity Play. Arr. E. Martin Browne. 12m 5w sprs (Allan)
Slaughter of the Innocents (Chester). 5m 2w ch sprs EED
Trial of Christ (Coventry). 13/14 m 2w sprs EED
    For reference:
Cawley, A. C., *The Wakefield Pageants.* (Manchester Univ. Press)
Chambers, E. K., *The Medieval Stage.* (Clarendon Press) 2 vols.
Brooke, I., *English Costume of the Early Middle Ages.* (Black)
Craig, H., *English Religious Drama.* (O.U.P.)
Purvis, J. S., *The York Cycle of Mystery Plays.* (S.P.C.K.)

Wickham, Glynne, *Early English Stages, 1300–1660*, Vol. I. 1300–1576 (Routledge and Kegan Paul)

Young, Karl, *The Drama of the Medieval Church.* (O.U.P.)

MORALITY PLAYS AND SOCIO-RELIGIOUS DRAMA

Bale, John, *God's Promises.* 8m EOI

    Kynge Johan. 19m SPSD

Castle of Perseverance. See R. Southern: *Medieval Theatre in the Round* (Faber)

Everyman 16m or w EOI

        (For other editions see BDLC)

Everyman, The Interlude of Youth, The World and the Child (Ed. Hampden) (Nelson)

Hycke-Scorner. 6m or w SPSD

Interlude of Youth, 6m or w (Cowans and Gray)

Lindsay, Sir David. *The Satire of the Three Estates.* Two parts arr. Kemp. 23m 9w sprs (New Alliance and Scots Review)

    Acting version, The Drama Library (Heinemann)

Mankind, 7m or w SPSD

Rastell, J., *The Four Elements.* 4m or w EMP

Redford, J., *Wit and Science.* 2m 2w 16m or w SPSD, CPSD

Skelton, J., *Magnyficence.* 5m or w EMP

    Morality of Wisdom. 5m 6w sprs EED

    World and the Child. 5m 9ch SPSD

For reference:

Brooke, I., *English Costume in the Later Middle Ages.* (Black)

Houston, M., *Medieval Costume in England and France.* (Black)

Farnham, W., *The Medieval Heritage of Elizabethan Tragedy.* (O.U.P.)

For modern religious plays, see:

A Catalogue of Selected Plays: The Religious Drama Society (in association with S.P.C.K.)

LIGHTER ENTERTAINMENT: THE INTERLUDE

Heywood, John, *The Pardoner and the Frere.* 4m EMP, etc.

    A Play of Wytte and Wyttles. 3m (See *John Heywood*, by R. de la Bere)

    The Play Called the Foure PP. 4m CPSD, SPSD

    A Merry Play between Johan, Johan, the Husband, Tyb his wife, and Syr Johan the Priest. 2m 1w EEDS

Ingelond, Thomas. *The Disobedient Child.* 7m 2w PBS

Interludium de clerico et puella (incomplete). RBD

The Nice Wanton. 4m 3w 3m or w SPSD

Thersytes. 3m 1w 1ch EMP

Tom Tiler and His Wife. "Mock moral" farce in verse. 4m 3w 2m or w (EEDS. Two Tudor *"Shrew"* plays)

For reference:

De la Bere, R., *John Heywood, Entertainer* (Allen and Unwin)

Baskerville, C. R., *The Elizabethan Jig and Related Song Drama.* (C.U.P.)

RENAISSANCE DRAMA

Boas, F. S. (Ed.) *Five Pre-Shakespearian Comedies.* (O.U.P.), esp.
    Fulgens and Lucrece. (Medwall, H.)
    Ralph Roister-Doister. (Udall, N.)
    Gammer Gurton's Needle. (Stevenson, W.)
    Supposes. (Gascoingn, G., from Ariosto)
Cunliffe, John W. *Early English Classical Tragedies.* (O.U.P.), esp.
    Gorboduc. (Sackville and Norton)
    Jocasta. (Gascoingn and Kinwelmersh)
    Gismond of Salerne. (Various hands)
    Misfortunes of Arthur. (Hughes)
Preston, *The Life of Cambises, King of Persia.* 12m 5w 13m or w (Planned for 8 to play) CPSD SPSD
Udall, N., *Ralph Roister Doister.* Com. 9m 4w (Malone Society, etc.)

For reference:

Boas, F. S., *University Drama in the Tudor Age* (O.U.P.)

Kermodle, G., *From Art to Theatre: Form and Convention in the Renaissance.* (University of Chicago Press)

Mackenzie, A. M., *Playgoer's Handbook to the English Renaissance Drama.* (Cape)

Reed, A. W., *Early Tudor Drama.* (Methuen)

(The above books are wider in scope than the specific material of the chapter—but the conventions of the "learned" theatre also involve many later plays and practices. Other plays might be added to the above list from Mie Elizabethan period as suitable for treatment as "Renaissance" drama of the pseudo-classical type.)

EARLY ELIZABETHAN DRAMA

Anon., *Edward II.* Chronicle. 40m 3w sprs (Dent)

Anon., *The Merry Devil of Edmonton.* 19m 3w sprs (Dent)

Anon., *Mucedorus,* "a most pleasant comedie". 11m 4w SA

Anon., *Fair Em, the Miller's Daughter of Manchester.* Com. 12m 4w sprs (Malone Society)

Chettle, Henry, *The Tragedy of Hoffman*. 13m 2w sprs (Malone Society)

Edwards, R., *The Excellent Comedie of Two the Moste Faithfullest Friends, Damon and Pithias*. 12m CPSD

Greene, R., *Plays* (Fisher Unwin), inc.

    Alphonsus, King of Arragon. Com. 19m 13w sprs

    A Looking Glass for London and England. Morality (with T. Lodge) 24m 4w sprs

    Orlando Furioso. Rom. com. 19m 2w sprs

    Friar Bacon and Friar Bungay. Com. 24m 4w sprs

    George-a-Greene, the Pinder of Wakefield. 20m 4w sprs

Kyd, T., *The Spanish Tragedy*. Trag. 39m 5w sprs

Lodge, T. (See Greene, R.)

Lyly, J., *Alexander and Campaspe.* Com. 20m 3w sprs CPSD, etc.

    Endimion, the Man in the Moon. Com. 13m 8w sprs CED, etc.

    Midas. Com. 11m 1w sprs (Adapted E. Smith, *Plays from Literature*, Senior Book, Dent)

    Mother Bombi. Com. 9m 4w (Malone Society)

Marlow, C.,*Works and Life.* (Gen. ed. R. H. Case) Methuen. Many separate editions. Besides *Dr. Faustus*, consider for production *Tamburlaine, Edward II, The Jew of Malta*, and also two plays in which Marlowe's share is uncertain—*The Tragedy of Dido* and *The Massacre at Paris*

Peele, G., *The Arraignment of Paris.* Com. Masque. 17m 15w sprs

    Edward I. Hist. 30m 9w sprs OTEL Dent

    The Love of King David and Fair Bethsabe. Biblical drama. 23m 4w sprs SPAS

    Old Wives' Tale. Folk-lore fantasy, 13m 3w 3m or w (Sidgwick and Jackson)

Porter, H., *The Two Angry Women of Abington.* 11m 3w REC

(Several of the above might be included under Renaissance drama, morality, or religious plays.)

For reference:

Chambers, E. K., *The Elizabethan Stage.* (Oxford, Clarendon Press) 4 vols.

Joseph, B. L., *Elizabethan Acting*

Brooke, I., *English Costume in the Age of Elizabeth.* (Black)

Baker, H., *Induction to Tragedy.* Louisiana State University

Cunliffe, J. *The Influence of Seneca in Elizabethan Tragedy.* (Macmillan)

THE HALL THEATRE—DÉCOR AND DANCE

Browne, W., *The Inner Temple Masque.* 3m 2w sprs EABSP

Campion, T., *Lords Masque.* 9m 5w sprs EM

Daniell, S., *The Vision of the Twelve Goddesses.* 2m 18w sprs EM

D'Avenant, W., *Salmacida Spolia.* 12m 13w sprs EM

Day, J., *The Parliament of Bees.* 35 characters, sprs (See *Nero and other plays*)

Gentlemen of Grays Inn. *The Masque of Flowers.* Masque for a Court Wedding, 1614. 4m 1w sprs EM

Jonson, B., *The Fortunate Isles.* 7m choir sprs EM

    The Golden Age Restored. 6m 3w sprs EM

    Lovers Made Men. 4m 3w choir sprs EM

    Hue and Cry after Cupid. 3m 5w sprs TEP

    Masque at Lord Haddington's Marriage. 3m 5w sprs EM

    The Masque of Augers with several anti-masques. 5m 3w sprs EM

    The Masque of Christmas. (Feasey: *On the Playbill in Old London*)

    The Masque of Queens. 1m 25w EM

    Neptune's Triumph for the Return of Albion. 8m 1w EM

    News from the New World Discovered in the Moon. 5m sprs EM

    Oberon, The Fairy Prince. 11m 2w sprs EM

    Pan's Anniversary, or *The Shepherd's Holiday.* 2m 3w sprs EM

Milton, J., *Comus* (as staged in nineteenth century) 7m 6w BD2. BP. (Adapted Lucy Chester) 6m 3w sprs (Allen and Unwin) (other editions easily available)

Peele, G., *Arraignment of Paris.* 17m 15w sprs (Dent)

Shirley, James, *The Triumph of Peace.* 11m 9w sprs (Fisher Unwin)

For reference:

Nicoll, A., *Stuart Masques and the Renaissance Stage.* (Harrap)

Simpson, P., and Bell, C. F., *Designs by Inigo Jones for Masques and Plays at Court.* (Walpole and Malone Societies)

Sullivan, M., *Court Masques of James I: Their Influence on Shakespeare and the Public Theatre.* (Pitman)

Welsford, Enid, *The Court Masques.* (C.U.P.)

WILLIAM SHAKESPEARE

Consider presenting the less popular plays. Consult, also, scholarly editions that give you a fresh and more accurate view of the plays, e.g.

    The Player's Shakespeare, with prefaces by Harley Granville Barker. (Benn)

    The Swan Shakespeare (notes on production by C. B. Purdom) (Dent)

    The Works of Shakespeare (The New Shakespeare) Ed. J. Dover Wilson (C.U.P.)

So-called "acting editions" are often int resting as showing the interpretation, staging, and sometimes misunderstanding of Shakespeare at various periods. Eighteenth-century versions have a flavour of their own. Thus you may study *As You Like It* as it is acted at DL and CG in 1777 (Warman), "as performed at the Theatre Royal" (1842) (Lacy), and "under the management of Mr. Hare and Mr. Kendall" (1885) (J. Miles). More instructively, one can consult Facsimile reprints from the First Folio (Faber and Faber) or from the Quartos (Sidgwick and Jackson).

There are many editions of extracts, shorter acting versions, and adaptations. Several are listed in BDLC.

Examine also *The Shakespeare Apocrypha* (O.U.P.) ed. C. F. Tucker Brooke. The first two listed contain almost certainly some work by Shakespeare, and the fir.t named (revived professionally in 1955 by Brian Way's company in London) is important for its information on early Tudor acting companies and their material:

> *Sir Thomas More*
> *The Two Noble Kinsmen*
> *Arden of Feversham*
> *Mucedorus*
> *Sir John Oldcastle*
> *Thomas Lord Cromwell*
> *The London Prodigal*
> *A Yorkshire Tragedy*
> *The Puritan,* or *The Widow of Watling Street*
> *Locrine*

For reference:

Adams, J. C., *The Globe Playhouse*. (O.U.P.)

Agate, J., *Brief Chronicles: A survey of the Plays of Shakespeare and the Elizabethans in actual performance*. (Cape)

Baldwin, T. W., *The Organization and Personnel of the Shakespearian Company*. (O.U.P.)

Barker, H. G., *Prefaces to Shakespeare*. 5 vols. (Sidgwick and Jackson)

Bethell, S., *Shakespeare and the Popular Dramatic Tradition*. (Staple Press)

Campbell, Lily, *Shakespeare's Histories: Mirrors of Elizabethan Policies*. (C.U.P.)

Campbell, O. J., *Shakespeare's Satire*. (O.U.P.)

Clemen, W., *The Development of Shakespeare's Imagery*. (Methuen)

Davies, W. R., *Shakespeare's Boy Actors*. (Dent)

Farjeon, H., *The Shakespearian Scene*. Dramatic Criticism

Flatter, R., *Shakespeare's Producing Hand*. (Heinemann)

Greg, W. W., *The Editorial Problem in Shakespeare: A Survey of the Foundations of the Text*. (O.U.P.)

Hodges, G. W., *The Globe Restored: A study of the Elizabethan Theatre*. (Benn)

Hotson, L., *Shakespeare's Wooden O* (Hart Davis) (Fascinating and erudite—but conclusions dubious)

Kelly, F., *Shakespearian Costume for Stage and Screen*. (Black)

Knight, G. W., *The Wheel of Fire*. Essays in the Interpretation of Shakespeare's sombre tragedies. (Methuen)

Knights, L. C., *How Many Children Had Lady Macbeth?* (Heffer, Cambridge) (One of the first books to challenge the "traditional" approach to production and character emphasis.)

Nagler, A. M., *Shakespeare's Stage*. (O.U.P.) (The most recent—1960—work.
  Deals with both indoor and outdoor presentation.)
Palmer, J., *The Comic Characters of Shakespeare*. (Macmillan)
Speaight, R., *William Poel: The Elizabethan Revival*. (Heinemann)
Sprague, A. C., *Shakespeare and the Actors*. (O.U.P.)
  Shakespeare's Players and Performers. (Black)
Sisson, C., *New Readings in Shakespeare* (2 volumes). (C.U.P.)
Spurgeon, Caroline, *Shakespeare's Imagery*. (C.U.P.)
Watkins, R., *On Producing Shakespeare*. (Joseph) (Relates the work, practically,
  to the original conditions and conventions.)
Shakespeare Survey (Annually). Ed. A. Nicoll. (No. 12, 1959)
Companion to Shakespeare Studies. (C.U.P.)

LATER ELIZABETHAN (JACOBEAN AND CAROLINE) DRAMA

Beaumont and Fletcher, *Best Plays*. 2 vols. (Fisher Unwin), esp.
  The Maid's Tragedy
  Philaster
  The Wild Goose Chase
  The Knight of the Burning Pestle
  A King and No King
  The Spanish Curate
  The Faithful Shepherdess
  Merchant of Bruges or *Beggar's Bush*. (ad. Kinnaird) LS4
Brome, R., *The Antipodes*. Com. 8m 3w sprs REC
Chapman, George, *Works*. (Chatto and Windus), inc.
  All Fools. Com. 1m 3w
  Gentleman Usher. Com. 12m 4w sprs
  Monsieur D'Olive. Com. 7m 14w 2b
  Bussy D'Ambois. Trag. 14m 7w sprs
  The Revenge of Bussy D'Ambois. Trag. 16m 4w sprs
  May Day. Com. 16m 3w
  Revenge for Honour. Trag. 10m 5w sprs
  Eastward Hoe (with Jonson and Marston). Com. 17m 6w sprs
  The Ball (with Shirley). 11m 6w sprs
Cowley, A., *Essays, Plays, and Sundry Verses*. (C.U.P.), inc.
  The Guardian. Com. 6m 4w sprs
  (Later version—*The Cutter of Coleman Street*)
Day, John, *Humour Out of Breath*. Com. 12m 3w sprs
  (See *Nero and other plays*).
Dekker, Thomas, *Best Plays*. (Fisher Unwin), esp.
  The Shoemakers' Holiday
  Old Fortunatus
  The Witch of Edmonton

Field, N., *Amends for Ladies*. Com. 19m 5w
    A Woman is a Weathercock. Com. 12m 5w
Fletcher, J., *The Chances*. Com. 15m 5w TEP (Garrick's version in Bell's Plays)
    Rule a Wife and Have a Wife. Com. REC III, TEP
    The Faithful Shepherdess. Pastoral. 7m 3w sprs (Williams)
Ford, J., *Best Plays*. (Fisher Unwin), esp.
    The Lover's Melancholy
    The Broken Heart
    'Tis Pity She's a Whore
    Love's Sacrifice
Heywood, T., *Best Plays*. (Fisher Unwin), esp.
    A Woman Killed with Kindness. Trag. 17m 3w sprs
    The Fair Maid of the West. Rom. com. 21m 2w sprs
    The Wise Woman of Hogsdon. Com. 14m 7w, also
    If you know not me, you know nobody. Chron. 2 parts. (Malone Society)
Jonson, B., *Complete Plays*. (Dent)
    Works (Ed. Herford and Simpson)
      Consider some of the lesser known plays:
    Cynthia's Revels. Fant.
    Sejanus, His Fall. Trag.
    Catiline, His Conspiracy. Trag.
    Bartholomew Fair. Com.
    The Devil is an Ass. Com.
    The Magnetic Lady. Com.
    Volpone, Epicoene, The Alchemist, are known to everyone
Marston, J., *Plays* (3 vols.) (Oliver and Boyd), esp.
    Antonio's Revenge. Trag. 10m 2w sprs
    The Malcontent (with Webster). Tragi-com. 11m 5w (Also Dent)
    Sophonisba. Trag. 13m 5w
    The Dutch Courtezan. Com. 11m 5w
    What You Will. Com. 20m 6w
Massinger, P., *Best Plays* (2 vols.). (Fisher Unwin), esp.
    The Duke of Milan. Tragi-com. 20m 5w sprs
    A New Way to Pay Old Debts. Com. 12m 5w sprs
    The Maid of Honour. Tragi-com. 19m 3w sprs
    The City Madam. Com. 18m 6w sprs
    The Roman Actor. Trag. 15m 5w sprs
    The Fatal Dowry. Trag. 20m 3w sprs
    The Guardian. Com. 13m 4w sprs
    The Virgin Martyr. Trag. 18m 4w
Middleton, T., *Best Plays*. (Fisher Unwin), inc.
    A Trick to Catch the Old One. Com. 18m 5w sprs
    The Changeling (with Rowley). Trag. 11m 3w (CED also)
    The Spanish Gipsy (with Rowley). Rom. com. 12m 6w sprs
    A Fair Quarrel (with Rowley). Com. 11m 7w sprs

The Roaring Girl (with Dekker). Com. 24m 5w
The Witch. Tragi-com. 16m 8w sprs
A Chaste Maid in Cheapside. Com. 15m 10w sprs
The Mayor of Queenborough. Trag. 20m 2w sprs
Rowley, W., *All's Lost by Lust*. Trag. 12m 4w sprs (Heath)
    A New Wonder, a Woman Never Vext. Com. RBD
    (See also Middleton, Massinger, Webster)
Shirley, James, *Best Plays*. (Fisher Unwin), inc.
    The Witty Fair One. Com. 13m 4w sprs
    The Traitor. Trag. 11m 3w 5m or w sprs
    Hyde Park. Com. 9m 3w sprs
    The Lady of Pleasure. Com. 10m 6w sprs
    The Cardinal. Trag. 12m 4w sprs
    The Sisters. Com. 14m 3w sprs (Wells, Gardner, Darton)
Shirley, James (ad. by Garrick)
    The Gamesters. Com. 13m 2w (John Bell)
Tourneur, Cyril, *The Atheist's Tragedy*. 10m 4w sprs
    The Revenger's Tragedy. 11m 3w sprs
    (Both in *Best Plays of Webster and Tourneur*) (Fisher Unwin)
Webster, J., *Complete Works*. Ed. F. L. Lucas. 4 vols. (Chatto and Windus), esp.
    The White Devil. Trag. 20m 5w sprs
    The Duchess of Malfi. Trag. 14m 3w 3ch sprs
    The Devil's Law Case. Tragi-com. 11m 4w sprs
    A Cure for a Cuckold (with Rowley and Heywood). Com. 18m 6w
    Appius and Virginia. Trag. 15m 4w sprs
    Anything for a Quiet Life (with Middleton). Com. 16m 4w 2ch
    The Fair Maid of the Inn (with Massinger, Fletcher, Rowley and others).
    Tragi-com. 21m 5w sprs

For reference:
Bentley, G. C., *The Jacobean and Caroline Stage*. Dramatic companies and players. (O.U.P. 2 vols.)
Bradbrook, M., *Themes and Conventions of Elizabethan Tragedy*. (C.U.P.)
    Elizabethan Stage Conditions. (O.U.P.)
Ellis-Fermor, U. M., *The Jacobean Stage*. (Methuen)
Greg, W., *Dramatic Documents from the Elizabethan Playhouse*. (O.U.P. 2 vols.)
    A Bibliography of the English Printed Drama to the Restoration. 4 vols. (O.U.P. for the Bibliographical Society.) [A monumental and scholarly work included for reference (if obtainable) because it gives some idea of the scope and magnitude of the necessary research on theatre and allied problems.]
Hosking, C. L., *The Life and Times of Edward Alleyn*. (Cape)
Hotson, Leslie, *The Commonwealth and Restoration Stage*. (O.U.P.)
Isaacs, J., *Production and Stage Management at the Blackfriars Theatre*. (Shakespeare Association)

Leach, C., *John Ford and the Drama of His Time.* (Chatto and Windus)
    John Webster. (Hogarth Press)
Reynolds, G. F., *The Staging of Elizabethan Plays at the Red Bull Theatre
1605-25.* (O.U.P.)

RESTORATION DRAMA

Behn, Aphra, *Works.* Ed. Montague Summers (Heinemann) (4 vols. of plays)
(Her work includes comedy, tragedy, and farce—amoral often, but lively
nearly always.)
    Consider esp.
    Sir Patient Fancy. Com. 14m 8w 1g sprs
    The Town Fop. Com. 11m 3w sprs

Congreve, William, *Plays.* (Benn)
    Comedies. (O.U.P.)
    Works. (Peter Davies), inc.
    The Old Bachelor
    The Double Dealer
    Love for Love
    The Way of the World, and the "classical" tragedy:
    The Mourning Bride, 8m 4w sprs

Crowne, J., *Sir Courtly Nice*, or *It Cannot Be.* Com. 9m 4w sprs RC
D'Avenant, Sir William, *Love and Honour.* Heroic drama. 12m 4w sprs
    The Seige of Rhodes. Heroic drama. 9m 2w sprs (Heath)
Dryden, J., *The Dramatic Works.* Ed. Summers (Nonesuch), esp, the comedies:
    The Wild Gallant
    Sir Martin Mar-all
    An Evening's Love
    Marriage à La Mode
    The Mistaken Husband
    The Spanish Fryar

    The heroic tragedies:
    The Indian Queen (with Sir Robert Howard)
    The Indian Emperor
    The Conquest of Granada
    Aurengzebe

    The blank verse tragedy:
    All for Love, or *The World Well Lost*

    The adaptations of Shakespeare:
    The Tempest, or *The Enchanted Island*
    Troilus and Cressida
    and the very interesting "opera":
    The State of Innocence and the Fall of Man

(This looks forward to the modern verse drama of inner predicament and struggle in a metaphysical context.)

and the dramatic opera:

> King Arthur, or The British Worthy

Etherege, Sir G., The Man of Mode, or Sir Fopling Flutter. Com. 13m 9w sprs POTR

> She Wou'd if she Cou'd. BP1

Farquhar, George, Best Plays. (Fisher Unwin)

> The Constant Couple. Com. 8m 4w sprs
>
> The Twin Rivals. Com. 10m 4w sprs
>
> The Recruiting Officer. Com. 12m 4w sprs
>
> The Beaux Stratagem. Com. 11m 5w sprs
>
> The Inconstant. Com. 5m 3w sprs LS1 BD1
>
> Sir Harry Wildair. Com. 10m 3w sprs BP 32

Howard, Sir R., The Committee, or The Faithful Irishman. Com. 17m 4w sprs (J. Bell)

Killigrew, Thomas, The Parson's Wedding. Com. 14m 7w sprs RC

Lee, N., Alexander the Great. Trag. 11m 4w sprs LS1 BD2

> Lucius Junius Brutus. Trag. 13m 3w sprs (Bell's Plays, 33)
>
> The Rival Queens. Trag. 12m 4w sprs (John Bell)

Milton, John, Samson Agonistes. V. trag. Classical in form.

> (Almost any edition of the collected poems)

Otway, T., Best Plays. (Fisher Unwin), inc.

> Don Carlos. Trag. 6m 4w
>
> The Orphan. Trag. 8m 3w sprs
>
> The Soldier's Fortune. Com. 9m 3w sprs
>
> Venice Preserved. Trag. 17m 6w sprs

Ravenscroft, E., The Anatomist. F. 6m 4w TEF

> The London Cuckolds. Com. 8m 6w sprs RC

Sedley, Sir Charles, The Poetical and Dramatic Works. (Constable), inc.

> The Mullberry Garden. Com. 11m 5w sprs
>
> Bellamira, or The Mistress. Com. 8m 5w sprs

Shadwell, Thomas, Complete Works. Ed. Montague Summers. 5 vols. (Fortune Press)

Besides "humours" comedies, there are interesting adaptations from Molière, and some "operatic" versions of Shakespeare.

> The Sullen Lovers, or The Impertinents. Com. 12m 5w sprs
>
> The Humorists. Com. 7m 6w sprs
>
> The Miser. Com. 17m 6w sprs
>
> Epsom Wells. Com. 12m 7w sprs
>
> The Tempest, or The Enchanted Island. 11m 3w 1m or w sprs
>
> The Virtuoso. Com. 9m 7w sprs
>
> The Squire of Alsatia. Com. 15m 8w
>
> Bury Fair. Com. 11m 9w sprs
>
> The Scourers. Com. 10m 8w sprs

The Volunteers, or *The Stock-jobbers*. Com. 11m 7w sprs

Southerne, T., *The Fatal Marriage*, or *The Innocent Adultery*. Trag. 11m 2w sprs BD1 LS2

   Oronooko. Trag. 9m 4w sprs (J. Bell)

Tate, Nahum, *A Duke and No Duke*. F. 7m 3w sprs TEF

(He also wrote, among many dramatic works, the "happy ending" version of *King Lear* which held the stage during the eighteenth century.)

Vanbrugh, Sir John, *Plays*. (Fisher Unwin)

   The Relapse, or *Virtue in Danger*. Com. 13m 4w sprs

   The Provok'd Wife. Com. 7m 4w

   The Confederacy. Com. 6m 6w

   The False Friend. Com. 6m 3w (Tonson and Watts)

   The Mistakes. Com. (from Molière) 8m 4w (Tonson and Watts)

   The Provok'd Husband, or *A Journey to London* (with Colley Cibber). Com. 6m 7w (T. Lowndes)

Villiers, George, Duke of Buckingham, *The Rehearsal*. Com. and burl. 23m 7w sprs (Shakespeare Head Press, etc.)

(An amusing satire on theatrical themes and styles—the first of many such topical comments.)

Wycherley, W. *Plays*. (Fisher Unwin)

   Love in a Wood, or *St. James's Park*. Com. 7m 9w

   The Gentleman Dancing Master. Com. 7m 6w sprs

   The Country Wife. Com. 8m 7w sprs

   The Plain Dealer. Com. 7m 5w sprs

For reference:

Brooke, I., *English Costume of the Seventeenth Century*. (Black)

Deane, C., *Dramatic Theory and the Rhymed Heroic Play*. (O.U.P.)

Dent, E., *The Foundations of English Opera*. (C.U.P.)

Kritch, J. W., *Comedy and Conscience after the Restoration*. (O.U.P.)

Spenser, Hazelton, *Shakespeare Improved*. (Restoration versions of his plays) (O.U.P.)

Summers, Montague, *The Playhouse of Pepys*. (Kegan Paul)

   The Restoration Theatre. (Kegan Paul)

FORMAL THEATRE—EARLY EIGHTEENTH CENTURY

Addison, Joseph, *Cato*. Trag. 6m 2w sprs (Bell)

Baker, T., *Tunbridge Walks*. 5m 5w sprs ET7

Carey, H., *Chrononhotonthologos*. Burl. v. trag. 11m 5w sprs (Lacy)

   The Dragon of Wantley. Burl. opera. 4m 1w sprs (Dicks)

Centlivre, Susannah, *The Gamester*. Com. 11m 6w ET3

   The Busie Body. Com. 6m 4w ET

   A Bold Stroke for a Wife. Com. 8m 4w ET

   The Wonder, a Woman Keeps a Secret. Com. 7m 4w sprs ET7

Cibber, Colley, *The Careless Husband*. Com. 3m 4w sprs BP1, ET3
  The Double Gallant, or *The Sick Lady's Cure*. Com. 10m 6w (John Bell)
  The Lady's Last Stake, or *The Wife's Resentment*. Com. 4m 5w (BP 25)
  Love Makes a Man, or *The Fop's Progress*. Com. 14m 5w sprs (Bell's
    Plays, 4)
  (One of the most persistently popular plays of this century.)
  Love's Last Shift, or *The Fool in Fashion*. Com. 8m 6w sprs
    (In *Plays of the Restoration*, Macmillan and Jones)
  The Refusal, or *The Ladies Philosophy*. Com. 5m 4w sprs (Bell's Plays, 18)
  She Wou'd and she Wou'd not. Com. 6m 4w sprs (Bell's Plays, 18)
Dodsley, R., *Cleone*. Trag. 6m 2w 1ch sprs BP11
  King and the Miller of Mansfield. Dr. 3m 3w sprs LS4
Doggett, T., *Hob*, or *The Country Wake*. F. TEF
Fielding, H., *The Intriguing Chambermaid*. F. 12m 3w BD2
  The Mock Doctor. Com. 10m 5w sprs (Nelson)
  Tragedy of Tragedies, or *The Life and Death of Tom Thumb the Great*.
    Burl. v. trag, 10m 5w (O.U.P.)
  Pasquin. Satiric drama.
Gay, John, *Acis and Galatea*. Opera libretto. 4m 3w sprs (Johnson)
  The Beggar's Opera. Ballad opera. 14m 12w (French, O.U.P., etc.)
  Polly. Ballad opera. 10m 6w sprs (Gowans and Gray). A version by Clifford
    Bax (Chapman and Hall)
Glover, R., *Boadicea*. Trag. 5m 2w sprs (Bell's Plays, 9)
Hill, Aaron, *Alzira*. Trag. 4m 3w sprs (Bell)
  Merope. Trag. 5m 2w sprs (J. Bell)
  Zara. Trag. 6m 2w BD2 LS4
Hoadley, Benjamin, *The Suspicious Husband*. Com. 13m 7w (J. Bell)
Johnson, Samuel, *Irene*. Trag. (v). 9m 2w sprs (Bell's Plays, 30, etc.)
Lillo, George, *The London Merchant*. Trag. 7m 3w sprs (Heath)
  Fatal Curiosity. Trag. 4m 3w sprs
  When Crummles Played. (*The London Merchant* arr. by Nigel Playfair, 1927)
    (Chapman and Hall)
Mallet, David, *Eurydice*. Trag. 6m 2w sprs BP27
Moore, Edward, *The Foundling*. Com. 6m 2w sprs (John Bell)
  The Gamester. Trag. 7m 3w (Longmans, Hurst)
Phillips, Ambrose, *The Distrest Mother* (fr. Racine). Trag. 4m 4w sprs (J. Bell)
Rowe, Nicholas, (Writer of so-called "She" tragedies)
  Dramatic Works. (W. Feales)
  The Royal Convert. V. trag. 5m 2w sprs
  Jane Shore. V. trag. 6m 2w
  Lady Jane Grey. V. trag. 8m 2w sprs
  The Fair Penitent. V. trag. 5m 3w sprs
  Tamerlane. V. trag. 11m 2w sprs BD2
  The Biter. Com. 9m 5w sprs
    (also some published by Heath).

Shadwell, C., *The Fair Quaker of Deal.* Com. 6m 8w sprs ET3
Steele, R., *Complete Plays.* (Fisher Unwin)
    The Funeral. Com. 10m 7w sprs
    The Lying Lovers. Com. 8m 4w sprs
    The Tender Husband. Com. 6m 5w
    The Conscious Lovers. Com. 8m 5w
Thomson, James, *Sophonisba.* Trag.
    Agamemnon. Trag.
    Tancred and Sigismunda. Trag. 4m 2w sprs BD1 LS4
    Coriolanus. Trag.
Whitehead, W., *Creusa, Queen of Carthage.* V. trag. 4m 3w sprs BP34
    The Roman Father. V. trag. 5m 2w sprs BP17, LS3
    The School for Lovers. Com. 5m 3w (J. Bell)
Young, Edward, *The Brothers.* V. trag. 8m 2w BP34
    Busiris, King of Egypt. V. trag. 8m 2w BP31
    Revenge. V. trag. 5m 2w LS1, BD1
See also: Restoration period play list.

For reference:
Bateson, F., *English Comic Drama,* 1700–80
Berbaum, E., *The Drama of Sensibility.* (O.U.P.)
Cibber, Colley, *An Apology.* Everyman's Library, Dent
Laver, J., and Brooke, I., *English Costume of the Eighteenth Century.* (Black)
Pearce, C., *Polly Peachum.* (Stanley Paul)
    (Much interesting and relevant information about early and mid-eighteenth century theatre and presentation.)
Schultz, W. E., *Gay's Beggar's Opera: Its Content, History and Influence.* (O.U.P.)
Nicoll, A., *A History of English Drama, Vol.* 2 (C.U.P.).

LATER EIGHTEENTH CENTURY. 1750–1800

Bickerstaff, Isaac, *Lionel and Clarissa.* Com. opera. 6m 4w (Secker)
    Love in a Village. Com. opera. 8m 6w (Secker)
    The Maid of the Mill. Com. opera. 7m 5w (Longmans)
    Thomas and Sally. Miniature opera. 2m 2w chor. LS4
    (Also in Herbert and Playfair: *Riverside Nights*)
Brooke, Mrs. Frances, *Rosina.* Com. opera. 7m 3w sprs BD1
Bourgoyne, J., *The Heiress.* Com. 8m 6w sprs LS3
Cherry, A., *The Soldier's Daughter.* Com. 13m 6w (G. H. Davidson)
Cobb, James, *The Doctor and the Apothecary.* Com. 7m 3w BD1
    The First Blow. F. 9m 3w LS3
    Paul and Virginia. Musical entertainment. 6m 3w LS4
Colman, George (the elder), *The Deuce is in Him.* (ad. W. Graham Robertson)
    F. 4m 3w (Nelson)
    The English Merchant. Com. 7m 4w sprs

The Jealous Wife. Com. 12m 5w (O.U.P.)

Polly Honeycombe. Com. 3m 3w LS2

The Clandestine Marriage. (With D. Garrick) Com. 10m 6w (French)

Cowley, Hannah, The Belle's Stratagem. Com. 9m 5w (Cumberland)

Cumberland, R., The Brothers. Com. 10m 6w sprs (Longmans, Hurst)

The Carmelite. Trag. 7m 1w LS4

The Choleric Man. Com. 9m 3w (John Bell)

The Fashionable Lover. Com. 10m 4w sprs BP2

The Jew. Com. 6m 4w (Dicks)

The Mysterious Son. Trag. 6m 3w sprs

The West Indian. Com. 8m 6w sprs (Dicks)

The Wheel of Fortune. Com. 17m 4w (Longmans, Hurst)

Dibdin, Charles, The Deserter. Mus. dr. 5m 3w sprs LS1

The Farmer's Wife. Com. opera. 11m 5w LS4

My Spouse and I. Farcial opera. 9m 3w LS4

The Quaker. Com. opera. 4m 3w sprs (Dicks)

The Waterman. Ballad opera 3m 2w (Lacy)

Dimond, W., The Broken Sword. Melo. 5m 5w 16 sprs (Dicks)

The Royal Oak. Hist. play. 12m 4w (Dicks)

Stage Struck. F. 5m 3w (Lacy)

Foote, Samuel, Dramatic Works. 2 vols. (Lowndes), See esp.

Taste. Com.

The Mayor of Garratt. Com.

The Lyar. Com.

The Patron. Com.

The Maid of Bath. Com.

The Devil upon Two Sticks. Com.

Garrick, David, Adapted works by Dryden, Jonson, Shakespeare and Wycherley—and wrote also:

The Guardian. Com. 4m 2w MBT BD1

The Irish Widow. F. 7m 1w sprs BD1

Miss in her Teens, or The Medley of Lovers. F. 5m 2w BD2

(A version by W. Graham Robertson is published by Nelson.)

Three Farces. (O.U.P.)

Goldsmith, O., The Good Natur'd Man. Com. 12m 5w (French, etc.)

(Should be revived much more frequently.)

She Stoops to Conquer, or The Mistakes of a Night. 10m 4w sprs (French, etc.)

Griffiths, Elizabeth, The School for Rakes. Com. 7m 3w BP27

Holcroft, T., Deaf and Dumb, or The Orphan Protected. Dr. 11m 3w sprs

He's Much to Blame. Com. 7m 4w LS4

The Road to Ruin. Com. 7m 4w (Dicks)

The School for Arrogance. Com. 8m 3w sprs (J. Bell)

Seduction. Com. 5m 5w sprs LS4

A Tale of Mystery. Melo. 9m 2w sprs LS2

rray, W. H., *Dominique the Deserter*. Com. dr. 9m 4w sprs (French)

   Mary Queen of Scots. Hist. dr. 7m 7w (Dicks)

Hara, Kane, *The Golden Pippin*. Burletta. 5m 5w (T. Becket)

   Midas. Burlesque. 12m 4w LS1, BD1

Keeffe, J., *Wild Oats*, or *The Strolling Gentleman*. Com. 14m 3w (Dicks)

ynolds, F. Author of over 200 dramatic works. Typically of this period, the first play he wrote was a translation of *Werther*; his most successful *The Caravan*, or *The Driver and His Dog*—a dog drama at Drury Lane, in which a real dog rescued a child. Examine:

   The Dramatist, or *Stop Him Who Can!* Com. 8m 4w (O.U.P.)

   How to Grow Rich. Com. 14m 3w

   Life. Com. 12m 4w

   Notoriety. Com. 8m 3w

eridan, Frances, *The Discovery*. Com. 4m 5w (Davies, Dodsley) (Version by Aldous Huxley, 6m 8w, Chatto and Windus).

eridan, Richard Brinsley, *Plays and Poems*. Ed. R. Compton Rhodes (Blackwell, Oxford), inc.

   The Rivals.

   St. Patrick's Day. (F. 5m 2w sprs)

   The Duenna. Com. opera. 9m 3w sprs

   A Trip to Scarborough. Com. 12m 6w sprs

   The School for Scandal.

   The Critic.

   The Camp (Musical entertainment 10m 5w sprs)

   Pizarro (From Kotzbue. Melo. tr. 15m 3w 1b sprs)

   The Forty Thieves (operatic romance, 8m 6w sprs)

     Other collections by Nelson, Dent, Jenkins.

     Many separate editions.

owneley, James, *High Life Below Stairs*. F. 8m 4w sprs LS1, BD2

For reference:

outhern, R., *The Georgian Playhouse*. Pleiades Press

arton, M., *Garrick* (Faber)

vans, Bertrand, *Gothic Drama* (O.U.P.)

ibbs, L., *Sheridan* (Dent)

icoll, A., *A History of English Drama*. Vol. 3 (C.U.P.)

ROMANTICISM—EARLY NINETEENTH CENTURY

-Beckett, G. A., *The Man with the Carpet Bag*. F. 10m 3w (Lacy)

   The Postillion. Com. op. 4m 2w (See R. W. Peake)

   St. George and the Dragon (with Mark Lemon). Burl. 14m 5w sprs (Johnson)

Home, John, *Douglas*, or *The Noble Shepherd*. V. trag. 5m 2w sprs etc.

Hoole, J., *Cleonice, Princess of Bithynia*. V. trag. 8m 2w sprs (Bell's Cyrus. V. trag. 6m 2w sprs (Bell's Plays)

Inchbald, Elizabeth: Writer of sentimental drama, including:
    The Child of Nature. Dr. 7m 2w LS2
    Everyone Has His Fault. Com. 8m 4w (Dicks)
    I'll tell You What. Com. 8m 4w (Robinson)
    The Midnight Hour. Com. 6m 4w LS1
    Such Things Are. Com. 10m 3w sprs LS1
    Wives as they Were and Maids as they Are. Com. 6m 3w LS2

Jackman, Isaac, *All the World's a Stage*. F. 9m 2w BD2, etc.
    Hero and Leander. Operatic Burl. 5m 3w sprs BD1

Jephson, R., *Braganza*. Trag. 13m 2w sprs
    Count of Narbonne. Rom. V. trag. 5m 3w LS3
      (Based on Horace Walpole's *Castle of Otranto*.)
    Law of Lombardy. Trag. 9m 2w sprs

Joddrell, Paul, *Select Dramatic Pieces*. (W. Lowndes)
      Some comedies and farces worth examination, inc.
    The Boarding School Miss. 15m 4w sprs

Kelly, Hugh, *False Delicacy*. Com. 5m 5w sprs POTR
    School for Wives. Com. 11m 6w (John Bell)
    A Word to the Wise. Com. 6m 6w (Bell's Plays)

Kotzbue, A.F.F., Important in translation and adaptation for his development of romantic theatre in Britain.
    Deaf and Dumb, or *The Orphan*. Hist. dr. 8m 3w
    Lovers Vows, or *The Natural Son*. Dr. (trans. Thompson)
      (Vernon and Hood)
    Rollo, or *The Virgin of the Sun*. Dr. 10m 4w sprs (Vernon and
    The Stranger. Dr. 8m 6w 2b 1g sprs POTR

Lee, Sophia, *The Chapter of Accidents*. Com. 7m 6w sprs LS2.

Lessing, C. E. (Important as an influence on theatre themes and
    Emilia Galotti. Tr. 5m 3w sprs (tr. Thompson) (Vernon and

Macklin, Charles, *Love à la Mode*. F. 7m 1w (John Bell)
    The Man of the World. Com. 10 m 5w (John Bell)

McNally, L., *Fashionable Levities*. Com. 7m 7w

Murphy, Arthur, *All in the Wrong*. Com. 7m 6w LS2, etc.
    The Apprentice. F. 4m 1w (Vaillant)
    The Citizen. F. 7m 2w LS1
    The Grecian Daughter. V. trag. 10m 2w BD1, BP13
    Know Your Own Mind. Com. 7m 5w LS2
    The School for Guardians. Com. 7m 3w BP33
    Three Weeks after Marriage. Com. 4m 4w sprs LS1
    The Way to Keep Him. Com. 6m 6w (O.U.P.)
    Zenobia. V. trag. 6m 2w sprs BP30

Almar, George, *The Tower of Nesle*. Melo. 12m 5w (8 sets) (French)

Baillie, Joanna, *Dramas*. 3 vols. (Longmans, Rees)

 (Artificially "Shakespearian" verse dramas, but "some scenes of merit" according to Nicoll.)

Barnett, C. Z., *Dominique the Deserter*. Dr. 8m 3w sprs (Dicks)

Barnett, Morris (with Charles Matthews), *Serve him Right*. Com. dr. 5m 3w (Lacy)

Barrymore, W., *The Secret*. F. 4m 2w (Lacy)

Bayly, T. H., *Comfortable Service*. F. 5m 3w (Dicks) (and other farces).

 The Ladder of Love. Mus. Dr. 3m 2w (Dicks)

 The Swiss Cottage, or *Why Don't She Marry?* Burl. (Lacy)

Bernard, W. B., *The Boarding School*. F. 6m 5w (French)

 A Storm in a Tea-cup. Com. 3m 2w (French) (and other farces).

 The Farmer's Story. Com. 9m 3w (French)

 The Round of Wrong, or *A Fireside Story*. Dr. 9m 3w sprs (Webster)

Buckstone, J. B., *The Green Bushes*, or *A Hundred Years Ago*. Dr. 21m 9w sprs (9 sets) (Dicks)

 Jack Shepherd. Dr. 14m 4w sprs "Constant changes of set". (French)

 Josephine, the Child of the Regiment. Mus. com. 11m 3w sprs (Lacy)

 (He also wrote many one-act farces which can be found in old play collections—*Our Mary Anne*, *Popping the Question*, *A Kiss in the Dark*, etc.)

Byron, G. G. (Lord), wrote the following plays, all worthy of consideration for production, to be found in most editions of his works: *Manfred*, *Marino Faliero*, *Sardanapalus*, *Cain*, *Werner*. *Manfred* lends itself to imaginative treatment, and looks forward past Shakespearian imitation to the verse drama of today.

Carr, J. W. Comyns, *King Arthur*. Dr. 13m 5w sprs (Macmillan)

Coleridge, Samuel T., *Remorse*. (In most editions of his works.)

Colman, George (the younger), *The Battle of Hexham*, or *In Days of Old*. Hist. play with songs. 20m 4w sprs (Longmans, Hurst)

 The Heir at Law. Com. 10m 3w (French)

 The Iron Chest. Tr. 18m 5w (Lacy)

 John Bull, or *The Englishman's Fireside*. Com. 14m 3w (Lacy)

 The Mountaineers. Drama. 22m 3w sprs (Longmans)

 The Poor Gentleman. Com. 10m 4w sprs (Longmans)

 The Review, or *The Wags of Windsor*. Mus. F. 8m 4w (Cumberland)

 Sylvester Daggerwood. F. 2m (Dicks)

Courtney, J., *Time Tries All*. Dr. 6m 2w (Lacy)

Coyne, J. S., *Everybody's Friend*. Com. 5m 5w 1b (Lacy)

 The Hope of the Family. Com. 9m 7w (French)

 The Secret Agent. Com. 5m 3w (Lacy)

 Binks the Bagman. F. 5m 5w (Barth)

 What Will They Say at Brompton? Com. 5m 3w (Lacy) (and other comedies and farces.)

Dance, C., *The Country Squire*, or *Two Days at the Hall*. Dr. 9m 4w sprs (Dicks)

  Naval Engagements. Com. 4m 2w (Chapman and Hall)

Dibdin, T. J., *Harlequin and Mother Goose*, or *The Golden Egg*. Panto. 16m 2w 4 ch. sprs

  (See Beaumont. *History of Harlequin*.)

  Paul Jones. Melo. rom. 15m 10w sprs (Lacy)

  Suil Dhuv, the Coiner. melo. rom. 7m 4w sprs (Dicks)

  Two Faces under a Hood. Com. op. 10m 6w sprs (Appleyards)

  What Next? F. 7m 3w sprs (Dicks)

Dickens, C., *The Village Coquettes*. Op. burl. 7m 2w (Dicks)

Fitzball, E., Writer of melodrama and spectacular plays including:

  The Inchcape Bell. Nautical dr. 7m 3w

  The Innkeeper of Abbeville, or *The Ostler and the Robber*. Dr. 7m 2w (Cumberland)

  Jonathan Bradford, or *The Murder at the Roadside Inn*. Melo. 10m 2w 2g. (An early example of stage division into several box set "rooms".)

  Lurline. Op. libretto—music by Wallace. 7m 3w sprs

  The Flying Dutchman. Melo. See RBD

Heartwell, H., *The Castle of Sorrento*. Com. op. 7m 2w LS4

Hoare, Prince, *Lock and Key*. Com. 4m 4w (Longman.)

  No Song, No Supper. Op. F. 6m 3w LS4 also TEF

Horncastle, H., *The Infant Phenomenon*. F. (After *Nicholas Nickleby*) 8m 9w 1b (Dicks)

Jerrold, Douglas, *Blackeyed Susan*, or *"All in the Downs"*. Nautical melo. 14m 2w sprs (Dicks)

  Collected Comedies. (Bradbury and Evans)

  Fifteen Years of a Drunkard's Life. Melo. 10m 4w (Dicks)

  Nell Gwynne. Com. 9m 3w (Dicks)

  Paul Pry. Com. 7m 2w sprs (French)

  Sally in our Alley. Dr. 8m 2w (Dicks)

Johnstone, J., *Ben Bolt*. Melo. 7m 2w sprs (Lacy)

Kemble, J. P., *The Farmhouse*. F. 5m 2w sprs LS2

  The Panel. Com. 7m 4w sprs LS4

Kenney, C., and Albert Smith, *The Wood Demon*, or *One O'Clock*. Burl. 8m 9w sprs (T. Trettell)

Kenney, James, *Raising the Wind*. F. 7m 2w (Lacy)

  Spring and Autumn, or *Married for Money*. Com. 4m 3w (Lacy)

  Sweethearts and Wives. Com. 5m 4w (French)

Knight, T., *The House of Thieves*. F. 9m 3w sprs LS1

Knowles, J. Sheridan. (The most famous professional writer in the Elizabethan tragic "style" during the period.)

  Dramatic Works. (Routledge), inc.

  Virginius (trag.)

  William Tell (dr.)

The Hunchback (com.)
The Beggar of Bethnal Green (com.)
John of Procida, or *The Bridals of Messina* (trag.)
Lemon, Mark, *Domestic Economy*. F. 2m 5w 1c (French)
    Grandfather Whitehead. Dr. 6m 2w 1b (French, N.Y.)
    Hearts are Trumps. Domestic dr. 7m 3w (French)
Lewis, M. G. (Famous for his Gothic romances.)
    The Castle Spectre. Rom. dr. 10m 3w (Lacy)
    Timour the Tartar. Rom. dr. 9m 4w sprs (Lacy)
    (Both extremely popular on the stage.)
Lovell, G. W., *Love's Sacrifice*, or *The Rival Merchant*. Dr. 9m 4w (Dicks)
    The Provost of Bruges. Trag. 22m 2w (Dicks)
    The Wife's Secret. Dr. 9m 3w (French)
Lunn, J., *Family Jars*. F. 5m 2w
    Fish Out of Water. F. 6m 2w (Dicks)
Lytton, Edward Bulwer (Lord), *Dramatic Works*. (Vol. IX) (Collier, N.Y.), esp.
    The Duchess de la Valliere (rom. hist. v. dr.)
    The Lady of Lyons (rom. com.)
    Richelieu, or *The Conspiracy* (hist. v. dr.) and
    Money—one of the earliest naturalistic comedies: 17m 3w sprs
Maria Marten. Famous melo. 8m 3w (French)
    Another version by Slater is published by Lane.
Matthews, Charles. (Famous comedian.)
    The Adventures of a Love Letter. Com. 8m 6w (Lacy)
    My Wife's Mother. Com. dr. 4m 3w sprs (Lacy)
    Two in the Morning. Com. 3m 1w (Fairbrother)
    Who Killed Cock Robin? F. 2m 2w (French, N.Y.)
    And several one-act pieces.
Milner, H. M., *The Hut of the Red Mountains*, or *Thirty Years of a Gambler's Life*.
    Dr. 12m 3w sprs (Davidson)
    Turpin's Ride to York, or *Bonny Black Bess*. Equestrian dr. 12m 5w (Dicks)
Moncrieff, W. T., *The Bashful Men*. F. 8m 3w sprs (Lacy)
    The Cataract of the Ganges, or *The Rajah's Daughter*. Melo. 8m 4w sprs
        (Richardson)
    Eugene Aram. Dr. 16m 6w sprs (Dicks)
    The Heart of London, or *The Sharper's Progress* 21m 3w sprs (Dicks)
    Monsieur Tonson. F. 9m 2w sprs LS3
    The Red Farm, or *The Well of St. Marie*. Dom. dr. 6m 4w sprs (Dicks)
    The Somnambulist, or *The Phantom of the Village*. Melo. 5m 4w sprs
        (Cumberland)
    Tom and Jerry, or *Life in London*. Op. extrav. 12m 5w sprs (many sets)
        (Dicks)
Morton, Thomas, *The Children in the Wood*. op. 9m 3w 1b 1g (French, N.Y.)
    A Case of Heartache. Com. 15m 3w (Cumberland)

The School of Reform, or How to Cure a Husband. Com. 11m 5w (Cumberland)

Speed the Plough. Com. 11m 4w (O.U.P.)

The Way to Get Married. Com. 20m 4w (Dicks)

The Writing on the Wall. Melo. 13m 5w sprs (Lacy)

Peacock, Thomas Love, Plays (D. Nott), esp.

The Dilettanti. mus. farce. 7m 5w

Peake, Richard Brinsley, Amateurs and Actors. Mus. F. 7m 2w (French, N.Y.)

The Bottle Imp. Melo, rom. 10m 3w (Sherwood, Gilbert and Piper)

The Devil in London. Satirical dr. 13m 5w 16 sprs (Dicks)

Frankenstein. Rom. dr. 10m 4w sprs (Dicks)

Planche, James Robinson, a prolific writer of extravaganzas, burlettas, vaudevilles, he was also an authority on heraldry, costume and setting, and a considerable power in nineteenth-century theatre through his theories and personal influence.

The Extravaganzas. 4 vols. (French)

Included are the extravaganzas:

The Sleeping Beauty in the Wood. 9m 15w sprs

Beauty and the Beast. 3m 4w sprs

The White Cat. 16m 6w sprs

Graciosa and Percinet. 12m 6w sprs

The New Planet, or Harlequin out of Place. 10m 15w sprs

The Island of Jewels. 9m 12w sprs.

The Yellow Dwarf and the King of the Golden Mines. 6m 6w sprs

The New Haymarket Spring Meeting. 4m 6w

Burlettas include:

Olympic Revels. 13m 7w

The Paphian Bower, or Venus and Adonis. 7m 20w sprs

Riquet with the Tuft. 21m 12w sprs

Bluebeard. 5m 5w sprs

The Golden Fleece. 4m 2w 2b sprs

Opera bouffe—Orpheus in the Haymarket. 8m 10w

Other plays:

The Jacobite. Com. 3m 3w (French)

The Loan of a Lover. Vaudeville. (Originally with Madame Vestris in the lead.) (French)

Knights of the Round Table. Dr. 13m 4w (Lacy)

Reputations. V. dr. 17m 10w (Andrews)

Pocock, Isaac, The Magpie or The Maid? Melo. 8m 2w sprs (Cumberland)

Rob Roy Macgregor. Op. dr. 21m 7w sprs (French)

The Miller and His Men. Melo. 9m 3w sprs

(Probably the best known of all melodramas, which influenced through the "penny-plain, twopence coloured" sheets of characters and settings for toy theatre (amongst others) the young R. L. Stevenson. It is still obtainable, in reprint, with book of words, and is very valuable evidence of décor, presentation, movement and gesture, in the theatre of the earlier nineteenth century.)

Rogers, W., *Jack's the Lad*, or *The Pride of the Ocean*. Dr. 7m 2w 1b sprs (Dicks)
A Soldier and a Sailor, A Tinker and A Tailor. Interlude. 4m 2w (Dicks)

Schiller, F. The more emotional and romantic work of this writer had some influence and repute in translation and actual performance in early nineteenth-century theatre. From his works (Bell) the following may be noted:
Mary Stuart. Hist. dr. 15m 4w sprs
The Maid of Orleans. Hist. dr. 20m 6w sprs
The Robbers. trag. 15m 1w sprs
The Death of Wallenstein. (trans. S. T. Coleridge) 21m 4w sprs
William Tell. (trans. Sir Theodore Martin) 40m 6w sprs
His themes are still, as will be noted, part of the material of popular melo-dramatic theatre (film and television).

Scott, Sir Walter. In addition to many adaptations of his work which enforced the Gothic influence on early nineteenth-century theatre, one may note that he produced a version of Goethe's first "sturm und drang" tragedy, which again emphasised the romantic trends in drama:
Goetz von Berlichingen with the Iron Hand. 33m 17w 2b sprs. Two adaptations may be noted:
Guy Mannering, or *The Gipsy's Prophecy*. Mus. play. 13m 7w 1b sprs (Cumberland)
The Maid of Judah, or *The Knights Templar*. Dramatised by Lacy, music by Rossini. Op. 18m 2w sprs (Cumberland)

Selby, Charles, *Ask No Questions*. Burl. 7m 3w (Chapman and Hall)
Behind the Scenes, or *Actors by Lamplight*. Burl. 11m 7w 1b sprs (Duncombe)
And other one-act farces and interludes.
London By Night. Dr. 8m 1w sprs (Dicks)
The Marble Heart, or *The Sculptor's Dream*—"A romance of real life".
13m 11w sprs (Lacy)
Robert Macaire, or *Auberge des Abrets*. Dr. 9m 2w sprs (Lacy)

Shell, R. L., *Evadne*, or *The Statue* (adapted from Shelley). Tr. 7m 3w (Lacy)

Shelley, P. B., *The Cenci*. v. tr. 9m 2w sprs (Heath, etc.)
Prometheus Unbound. Lyrical dr. 11m 3w sprs (Dent, etc.)

Soane, George, *Zarah*. Rom. dr. 10m 8w sprs (Cumberland)

Somerset, C. A., *Home Sweet Home*. (fr. the German) Op. 5m 2w sprs (Dicks)

Telfourd, Sir T. N., *Tragedies* (verse) (Routledge), inc.
Ion. 11m 2w
The Athenian Captive. 7m 2w

Thompson, B., *The Stranger*. Dr. 8m 6w (Dicks)

Webster, G. N., *The Golden Farmer*. Domestic dr. 10m 3w (Cumberland)

Wigan, A., *A Model of a Wife*. F. 3m 2w sprs (Dicks)

Wilks, T. E., *The King's Wager*, or *The Camp, the Cottage, and the Court*. Dr. 16m 6w 2b sprs (Duncombe)
Michael Erle, the Maniac Lover. Rom. dr. 12m 3w sprs (Lacy)
The Roll of the Drum. Rom. dr. 8m 3w 1b sprs (Duncombe)

For reference:

Agate, J., *These Were Actors*: extracts from a newspaper cutting book, 1808-31 (Hutchinson)

Disher, M. W., *Blood and Thunder: Mid-Victorian Melodrama and its origins*. (Muller)

Laver, James, and Iris Brooke, *English Costume of the Nineteenth Century*. (Black)

Hunt, Leigh, *Dramatic Criticism*, 1808-31. (O.U.P.)

Nicoll, A., *Early Nineteenth Century Drama, 1800-50*. (C.U.P.)

Rice, Charles, *London Theatres: the 1830's*. (Society for Theatre Research)

Reynolds, E., *Early Victorian Drama, 1830-70* (Heffer)

Speaight, G., *Juvenile Drama*. (Macdonald) (Toy theatres and the plays prepared for it.)

Watson, E. B., *Sheridan to Robertson: a Study of the Nineteenth Century London Stage*. (Harvard Univ. Press)

ACTING METHODS

(*Important in interpreting the intention of play scripts.*)

Disher, M. W., *Mad Genius*. (Edmund Kean) (Hutchinson)

Herschel, *John Philip Kemble: The Actor in the Theatre*. (O.U.P.)

Toynbee, W., *The Diaries of W. C. Macready*. 2 vols. (Chapman and Hall)

Trewin, J. M. V., *Macready*. (Harrap)

(On the use of the terms "set piece", "set scene", and "setting" consult Richard Southern's *Changeable Scenery*, pages 249ff.)

NATURALISM AND PICTURE-FRAME. 1850—1900

PLAYS:

Albery, James, *Dramatic Works*. Peter Davies

Worth examination. Mainly full-length comedies with variable setting, e.g. *Fortune*. 9m 5w—4 sets: drawing-room, garden, studio, drawing-room. This is typical of many plays of the period.

Anstey, F. (Thomas Anstey Guthrie), *The Brass Bottle*. Com. 9m 6w sprs (5 sets) (Heinemann)

Vice Versa. Com. 6m 3w 9b 3g sprs (Smith, Elder)

Vice Versa (ad. Rose) 4m 2w sprs (French)

Bellingham, H., and Best, W., *Prince Camaralzaman, or The Fairies' Revenge*. Extrav. 9m 6w (Lacy)

Blanchard, E. L., *Hop o' my thumb and His Eleven Brothers*. Panto. (Thompson and Harrison)

Little King Pippin. Panto. and

Harlequinade (Jabez Tuck)

(Many other pantomimes survive from this period with large casts and varied settings.)

Boucicault, Dion, *Arrah-na-Pogue*, or *The Wicklow Wedding*. 14m 2w (13 sets) (French)

    The Colleen Bawn, or *The Brides of Garrytown*. Melo. 10m 6w sprs (12 sets) (French)

    The Corsican Brothers. (From Dumas) Melo. 13m 6w

    London Assurance. Com. 10m 3w (Lacy)

    The Octoroon, or *Life in Louisiana*. Dr. 14m 6w (Dramatic Publishing Company, N.Y.)

    The Shaugrhaun. Irish Drama. 12m 6w sprs (French)

    Flying Scud, or *A Four Legged Fortune*. Melo. 13m 3w (FAP)

Bowles, T. G., *The Blazing Burgee*, or *The Scarlet Rover*. Nautical melo. 6m (French)

Bradden, Mary E., *Lady Audley's Secret* (ad. Hazlewood) Melo. 4m 3w sprs (French, N.Y.)

Brough, W., *The Caliph of Bagdad*. Extrav. 9m 2w sprs chor. (Lacy)

    Conrad and Medora, or *Harlequin Corsair and the Little Fairy at the Bottom of the Sea*. Burl. and panto. 4m 8w sprs (French)

    Ernani, or *The Horn of a Dilemma*. Burl. extrav. 8m 3w sprs (Lacy)

    King Arthur, or *Days and Knights of the Round Table*. Extrav. 11m 6w (Lacy)

    Lalla Rookh, or *The Princess, the Peri, and the Troubadour*. Extrav. 7m 10w sprs (Lacy)

    Prince Annabel, or *The Fairy Rose*. Extrav. 6m 11w sprs (Lacy)

(This is a brief selection from the works of Brough. All give opportunity for scenic variety, dance, music, and adaptation by the modern producer. Other pieces by him have Pygmalion and Rasselas as central interest.)

Brougham, J., *The Game of Life*. Com. 6m 5w (Dicks)

    The Game of Love. Com. 8m 5w sprs (French, N.Y.)

    A Recollection of O'Flannigan and the Fairies. Extrav. 7m 4w sprs (Lacy)

Browning, Robert, *Poems and Plays*. 2 vols. (Dent). *Consider*:

    Paracelsus

    Strafford

    A Blot in the Scutcheon

    Colombe's Birthday

    Luria

Burnand, Sir F. C., *Acis and Galatea*, or *The Noble Nymph and the Terrible Troglodyte*. Extrav. 4m 6w sprs (Lacy)

    Betsey. Com. 7m 6w (French)

    Dido. Burl. 6m 13w sprs (Lacy)

    Helen, or *Taken from the Greek*. Burl. 10m 4w (Lacy)

    Proof (ad. from *Une Cause Célèbre*) Dr. 10m 9w sprs (French)

    Robin Hood, or *The Forester's Fate*. Extrav. 5m 10w (French)

    Rumpelstiltskin, or *The Woman at the Wheel*. Extrav. 10m 16w sprs (Lacy)

Byron, H. J. (A prolific writer of extravaganzas, burlesques, and pantomime.)

    Aladdin, or *The Wonderful Scamp*. Ext. 5m 5w sprs (Lacy)

    Ali Baba, or *The Thirtynine Thieves*. Burl. 4m 7w sprs (French)

Beauty and the Beast. Panto. 4m 5w REO
Blow for Blow. Dr. 12m 6w (French)
Bluebeard. Burl. 3m 6w (French)
Cinderella, or *The Lover, The Lackey, and the Little Glass Slipper.* Burl.
    4m 6w (Lacy)
Lady Belle Belle, or *Fortunio and His Seven Magic Men.* Ext. 15m 8w (Lacy)
La! Somnambula! or *The Supper, The Sleeper, and the Merry Swiss Boy.*
    Burl. 10m 3w (French)
Our Soldiers. Com. 6m 3w (French)
Our Boys. Com. 6m 4w (French)
Robinson Crusoe, or *Harlequin Friday and the King of the Caribee Islands.*
    Burl. 10m 3w (French)
    and many others including:
Sensational Dramas of the Back Drawing Room (French)—fourteen 15-minute
    burlesques

Carton, R. C. (R. C. Crotchett), *The Bear Leaders.* F. 9m 7w
    Lady Huntworth's Experiment. Com. 5m 4w 1b
    Liberty Hall. Com. 6m 4w
    Mr. Preedy and the Countess. F. 9m 4w (French)

Cheltnam, C. S., *A Lesson in Love.* Com. 3m 3w (French)
    More Precious than Gold. Com. 3m 3w 1b (French)

Daly, A., *Leah the Forsaken.* Dr. 10m 7w sprs (9 sets) (French)
    Under the Gaslight, or *Life and Love of these Times.* Dr. 14m 7w 3b sprs
    (10 sets) (Dicks)

Dubourg, A. W., *Four Original Plays* (Bentley), esp.
    Vittoria Contarini. Rom. dr. 9m 1w sprs

Dumas, Alexandre, Various adaptations from his stories were staged at this
    period. See BDLC page 213.

Esmond, H. V.
    Billy's Little Love Affair. Com. 7m 9w (French)
    One Summer's Day. Com. 6m 5w 1b (French)
    When We Were Twenty-one. Com. 9m 5w (French)

Falconer, E., *Extremes,* or *Men of the Day.* Com. 8m 6w (Lacy)

Gilbert, W. S., *Original Plays.* 4 series. (Chatto and Windus)
    Apart from Savoy Operas, notice:
    Pygmalion and Galatea
    Charity. dr.
    The Palace of Truth. Com.
    Engaged. (Farcical com. 5m 5w)
    Sweethearts. (Com. 2m 2w)
    Foggerty's Fairy. Fantasy dr. 9m 9w sprs
    The Fairy's Dilemma. Panto. 4m 4w sprs
    Brantingham Hall. Melo. 14m 3w
    Several of the above are published separately.

Grattan, Henry P., *Faust, or The Demon of the Drackenfels.* Rom. dr. 7m 7w
sprs (7 "romantic" sets) (Dicks)
    Packing Up. F. 2m 1w (French)
    The Plumbers. F. 2m 2w (French)
Grundy, Sidney, *A Bunch of Violets.* Dr. 9m 3w
    The Glass of Fashion. Com. 5m 3w
    The Late Mr. Costello. F. 4m 3w
    A Pair of Spectacles. Com. 8m 2w
    The Silver Shield. Com. 5m 5w
    Sowing the Wind. Dr. 8m 4w (French)
Harwicke, P., *A Bachelor of Arts.* Com. 8m 2w (Lacy)
Hawtry, Sir C., *The Private Secretary.* F. 9m 4w (French)
Hazelton, F., *Sweeney Todd, The Barber of Fleet Street.* Melo. 12m 3w sprs
(French)
Hazelwood, C. H., *Hop Pickers and Gipsies, or The Lost Daughter.* Dr. 11m 5w
sprs (Lacy)
    Lady Audley's Secret (from the novel by Elizabeth Braddon) Melo. 4m
    3w sprs (French, N.Y.)
    The Staff of Diamonds. Dr. 7m 1w sprs (Lacy)
    Jerry Vere, or The Return of the Wanderer. Domestic dr. 13m 6w sprs (Lacy)
Henley, W. E., and Stevenson, R. L., *Plays.* (Macmillan) (Also separate editions
by Heinemann.)
    Deacon Brodie. Melo. 10m 2w
    Beau Austin. Rom. com. 5m 3w sprs
    Admiral Guinea. Com. 3m 2w
    Robert Macaire. Melo. farce. 10m 2w sprs
(Good material—if carefully produced to offset the literary approach and
style.)
Howard, Bronson, *The Barber's Daughter.* Dr. 10m 4w 1g (FAP)
    Saratoga, or Pistols for Seven. 13m 11w sprs Dr. (French, N.Y.)
(American dramatist important in his day).
Ibsen, H. Several contemporary adaptations. See BDLC. The first performance
of an Ibsen play was staged by John Hollingshead in 1880 at the Gaiety
Theatre, under the title of
    Quicksands, or, The Pillars of Society (tr. William Archer.)
The outburst of some critics against *Ghosts* does not really represent the
Victorian judgment on Ibsen—or the Victorians themselves—although some
might like to think that it does!
Jones, H. A. Much of his best work falls within this period.
    Representative Plays. Ed Clayton Hamilton. (Macmillan), examine esp.
    The Silver King. Melo.
    Saints and Sinners. Dr.
    The Dancing Girl. Dr.
    The Case of Rebellious Susan. Com.
    The Triumph of the Philistines. Com.

Michael and His Lost Angel. Trag.

Mrs. Dane's Defence. Dr.

The last named was produced in 1900.

See also his one-act plays.

Jones, J. S., *The Carpenter of Rouen.* Rom. melo. 12m 3w sprs (Dicks)

Law, Arthur, *A Country Mouse.* Com. 6m 4w (French)

Lewis, Leopold, *The Bells.* Melo. (From *The Polish Jew,* by Erckman and Chatrian) 11m 3w (French). (Made famous by Henry Irving.)

MacCarthy, J. B., *If I Were King.* Rom. com. 18m 9w (French)

Marshall, R., *His Excellency the Governor.* F. 10m 3w

 A Royal Family. Rom. com. 7m 4w 1b sprs (French)

Marston, J. Westland, *Marie de Merano.* V. trag. 15m 3w 1b sprs (Mitchell)

 A Life's Ransom

 Life for Life

 The Favourite of Fortune

Merritt, Paul *Glen Gath,* or *The Man in the Cleft.* Dr. 10m 3w

 The Word of Honour. Dr. 6m 2w (French)

Morton, John Maddison. A prolific writer of one-act farces and "comediettas". The following are only a few of those issued by Lacy:

 Away With Melancholy. 3m 3w

 Brother Ben. 3m 3w

 Done on Both Sides. 3m 2w

 John Dobbs. 5m 2w

 My Wife's Aunt. 3m 4w

 Slasher and Crasher. 5m 2w (French)

 Aunt Charlotte's Maid. 3m 2w sprs

 Betsey Baker. 2m 2w

 Box and Cox. 2m 1w

 If I Had a Thousand a Year. 4m 3w

 My Precious Betsey. 4m 4w

  Longer plays include:

 The Muleteer of Toledo. Com. dr. 8m 3w 2b sprs (Lacy)

 The Barbers of Bassora. Com. opera. (Music by Hullah) 6m 3w sprs (Chapman and Hall)

Oxenford, John, *Pauline.* Dr. (From the French) 13m 5w (Lacy)

 Robin Hood. Opera. (Music by Macfarren) 6m 2w (Cranmer, Beale and Chappell)

 The Two Orphans. Dr. 12m 9w sprs (French)

 Uncle Zachary. Com. dr. 7m 2w (French)

 Timour the Tartar. (With C. W. S. Brookes) Extrav. 6m 4w sprs (Lacy)

Parker, Louis N. (He wrote over 100 plays. Much of his best work, at times sentimental, at times sensational, but always worth consideration, lies outside the period.)

 The Cardinal. Dr. 14m 7w sprs (French)

 Rosemary. Com. 6m 4w (French)

Payne, J. H., *Charles the Second*, or *The Merry Monarch*. Com. 4m 2w (Lacy)

Phillips, Watts, *Camilla's Husband*. Dr. 11m 5w sprs (French)

    The Dead Heart. Hist. dr. 11m 3w (French)

    Lost in London. Dr. 9m 3w sprs (French)

Pinero, Sir. A. W. (Much of his best work lies outside the period.)

    The Magistrate. 12m 4w (Heinemann)

    The Schoolmistress. 9m 7w (Heinemann)

    Dandy Dick. 7w 4m (Heinemann)

    The Cabinet Minister. 9m 9w (Heinemann)

    The Amazons. Farce-romance. 7m 5w (Heinemann)

    Sweet Lavender. Com. 7m 4w (Heinemann)

    Trelawny of the Wells. Com. 11m 8w sprs (French, etc.)

    (Valuable as a dramatic presentation of theatre history.)

    The Gay Lord Quex. Com. 4m 10w sprs (Heinemann)

    The Profligate. Dr. 7m 5w (Heinemann)

    The Second Mrs. Tanqueray. Dr. 7m 4w (Heinemann)

    The Notorious Mrs. Ebbsmith. Dr. 8m 5w (Heinemann)

Reece, Robert, *Dora's Device*. Com. 5m 5w (French)

    Mammon and Gammon. F. 5m 3w (Lacy)

    An Old Man. Domestic dr. 4m 3w 1b (French)

    Prometheus, or *The Man on the Rock*. Extrav. 7m 7w sprs (French)

Robertson, T. W., In some ways, he is the most important dramatist of the period. All his plays merit consideration for revival.

    The Principal Dramatic Works. (Sampson, Lowe), inc.

    Caste. Com. 5m 3w

    Dreams. Dr. 6m 3w

    Home. Com. 4m 3w

    M.P. Com. 7m 2w

    Society. Com. 16m 5w

    School, Com. 16m 5w

    Ours. Com. 7m 3w

    Several are issued separately, e.g.

    School by French.

Sardou, V. Translation and adaptation from this dramatist are characteristic of the later nineteenth century, e.g.

    The Black Pearl

    Fernande.

    His name occurs frequently in theatre magazines and actors' biographies.

Sharp, W. (Fiona MacLeod), *The Immortal Hour*. Legendary. v. dr. 6m 2w sprs (Heinemann)

Simpson, J. Palgrave, *Appearances*. Com. 5m 4w (French)

    Bianca, the Bravo's Bride. Legendary opera. Music by Balfe. 11m 2w sprs

    Daddy Hardacre. Domestic dr. 4m 2w (French)

    A Scrap of Paper. Com. 6m 6w (French)

    Time and the Hour. Rom. dr. 7m 3w (French)

Smith, A., *The Alhambra, or The Three Beautiful Princesses*. Burl. extrav. 12m
7w sprs (Lacy)
    Hop o' my Thumb, or The Seven League Boots. Rom. dr. 6m 6w 6b 7g sprs
    (T. Brettell)
Smith, W. M., *The Drunkard*. Melo. Acting version by Montague Slater. 13m
6w sprs (John Lane)
Stephens, H. P., and Yardley, W., *Little Jack Sheppard*. Burl. operatic melo.
15m 5w sprs (W. S. Johnson)
Stevenson, R. L. See Henley, W. E. *The Hanging Judge* (with Mrs. Stevenson)
Dr. 15m 2w in *Plays* (Macmillan)
Stirling, E., *Anchor of Hope*. Dr. 10m 3w (Duncombe and Moon)
    The Little Back Parlour. F. 3m 2w (Duncombe)
Suter, W. E., *The Adventures of Dick Turpin and Tom King*. Melo. 7m 2w (Lacy)
    (And other plays, including one-act farces.)
Sutro, Alfred, *The Barrier*. Dr. 6m 5w (French)
    The Builder of Bridges. Dr. 5m 4w (French)
    Far Above Rubies. Com. 7m 5w (Duckworth)
    The Firescreen. Com. 7m 2w (French)
    The Perfect Lover. Dr. 7m 7w (French)
    The Walls of Jericho. Dr. 12m 8w (French)
Swinburne, A. C., *Atalanta in Calydon, Erectheus*. V. tragedies. (Heinemann)
    Chastelard, Mary Stuart. V. tragedies. (Chatto and Windus)
Telfourd, Frances, *Alcestis Travestie*. Burl. 6m 3w (Lacy)
    Atalanta, or The Three Golden Apples. Extrav. 7m 9w sprs (French)
    Electra in a New Electric Light. Extrav. 5m 6w sprs (Lacy)
    Macbeth Travestie. Burl. 10m 4w sprs (French)
    The Miller and His Men (with H. J. Byron) Burl. melo. 8m 2w (Lacy)
Taylor, Tom, *Claude Duval, The Ladies Highwayman*. F. 3m 1w (Dicks)
    Fair Rosamund. Mus. burl. 5m 2w (James Pattie)
    The Fool's Revenge. v. dr. 7m 5w (French)
    The Overland Route. Melo. com. 11m 5w sprs (French)
    Still Waters Run Deep. Melo. com. 9m 3w (French)
    The Ticket-of-Leave Man. Melo. 9m 3w (French)
    An Unequal Match. Com. 9m 6w (French)
    Plot and Passion (with J. Lang) Dr. 7m 2w (French)
    Masks and Faces (with Charles Read) Com. 13m 6w (French)
    Historical Dramas (Chatto and Windus), esp.
    Jeanne D'Arc. Trag. 15m 4w sprs
    'Twixt Axe and Crown. Hist. dr. 11m 5w sprs
    Anne Boleyn. Tr. 15m 8w sprs
       and the naturalistic play:
    Arkwright's Wife. 10m 2w sprs with a plate showing the exact spinning-
    wheel to be constructed for stage use.
Tennyson, Alfred, Lord, *Dramas*. (Macmillan), inc.
    Queen Mary. Hist. dr. 36m 9w sprs

Harold. Hist. dr. 20m 3w sprs
Becket. Hist. trag, 23m 3w sprs
The Cup. Trag. 8m 3w sprs
The Falcon. Rom. com. 2m 2w
The Promise of May. Tr. 9m 4w sprs
The Foresters. Past. com. 12m 3w sprs
Wilde, Oscar, *Plays.* (Nelson)
    Lady Windermere's Fan. Dr. 7m 8w
    A Woman of No Importance. Dr. 8m 7w
    An Ideal Husband. Com. 8m 6w
    The Importance of Being Earnest. Com. 5m 4w
    The Duchess of Padua. V. dr. 10m 2w sprs (Methuen)
    Salome. (French text) 11m 2w (Metheun.)
      (English version John Lane)
    Salome and Other Plays. (Penguin Books)
    A Florentine Tragedy. (with T. Sturge Moore) 2m 2w (Methuen, pub. with
    Salome.)
Williams, T. S. Prolific writer of one act farces. See BDLC.
Wood, Mrs. Henry, *East Lynne.* Melo. 8m 7w (Dicks, etc.)

Bibliography

Bibliography

REFERENCE: GENERAL

British Drama League, *The Players' Library*. (And supplements)
Brook, D., *The Romance of the English Theatre*. (Rockliff)
Cole, T., and Chinoy, H. K. (Eds.), *Actors on Acting*. (Pitman)
    Directing the Play. (P. Owen and Vision Press)
Craig, G., *On the Art of Theatre*. (Heinemann)
Crafton and Roger, *The Complete Acted Play*. (Harrap)
Ellis-Fermor, U. M., *The Frontiers of Drama*. (Methuen)
Hartnoll, Phyllis (Ed.), *Oxford Companion to the Theatre*. (O.U.P.)
Hazlitt, W., Dramatic Essays. (In *Complete Works*. (Dent).)
Heffner, H. C. (and others), *Modern Theatre Practice*. (Harrap)
Lawrence, W. J., *Old Theatre Days and Ways*. (Harrap)
Laver, J., *Drama: Its Costume and Décor*. (Studio)
Motter, T. H. Vail, *The School Drama in England*. (Longmans, Green)
Nicoll, A., *Theory of Drama*. (Harrap)
    Development of the Theatre. (Harrap)
    Masks, Mimes and Miracles. (Harrap)
    The English Theatre. (Harrap)
    British Drama. (Harrap)
    Readings from British Drama (Harrap)
Odell, G., *Shakespeare from Betterton to Irving*. 2 vols. (Constable)
Short, E., *Introducing Theatre*. (Eyre and Spottiswoode)
Simonson, Lee, *The Art of Scenic Design*. (Harrap)
Southern, R., *The Open Stage and the Modern Theatre* (Faber)
    Changeable Scenery: Its Origin and Its Development in the British Theatre. (Faber)
Sprague, A. C., *Shakespeare and The Actors*. (Harvard)
Ward, A. C., *Specimens of English Dramatic Criticism*. 17th to 20th centuries. (O.U.P.)
Williams, R., *Drama in Performance*. (Muller)

DÉCOR AND SETTING

Burris-Meyer, H., and Cole, E., *Scenery for The Theatre*. (Harrap)
Cookson, K., *Small Stage Properties and Furniture*. (Allen and Unwin)

Forman, R., *Scene Painting* (Pitman)

Komisarjevsky, T., and Simonson, L., *Settings and Costumes for the Modern Stage*. (Studio)

Leeper, J., *Edward Gordon Craig's Designs for the Theatre*. (Penguin)

Melville, A., *Designing and Painting Scenery for the Theatre*. (Associated Trades Press)

Napier, P., *Curtains for Stage Settings*. (Muller)

Simonson, Lee, *The Art of Scenic Design*. (Harrap)

Southern, R., *Proscenium and Sightlines*. (Faber)

Whistler, R., *Designs for the Theatre*. (Batsford)

For a complete bibliography, including American publications and periodicals, see Richard Courtney: *Stagecraft*.

LIGHTING

Bentham, F., *Stage Lighting*. (Pitman)

Hartmann, L., *Theatre Lighting: a Manual of the Stage Switchboard*. (Appleton)

Ost, G. *Stage Lighting*. (Jenkins)

Ridge, C. H., and Alfred, F. S., *Stage Lighting: Principles and Practice*. (Pitman)

Williams, R. G., *The Technique of Stage Lighting*. (Pitman)

COSTUME

Barton, Lucy, *Historic Costume for the Stage*. (Black)

Brooke, I., *Western European Costume and Its Relation to the Theatre*. 2 vols (Harrap)

Calthrop, Donald, *English Costume*, 1066–1820. (Black)

Chalmers, H., *Clothes on and off the Stage: A History of Costume from the earliest times to the Present Day*. (Appleton)

Fernald, M., and Shenton, E., *Costume Design and Making: A Practical Handbook*. (Pitman)

Green, J. M. C., *Period Costumes and Settings for the Small Stage*. (Harrap)
    Planning the Stage Wardrobe. (Nelson)

Truman, N., *Historic Costuming*. (Pitman)

Wright, M. C., *Biblical Costume with Adaptations for use in Plays*. (Macmillan)

PRODUCTION AND DIRECTION

Boyd, A. V., *Technique of Play Production*. (Harrap)

Browne, E. M., *Production of Religious Plays* (Allan)

Fernald, J., *The Play Produced*. (Deane)

Jeffreys, M., and Stopford, R., *Play Production for Amateurs and Schools.* (Methuen)
Kelly, M., *How to Make a Pageant.* (Pitman)
Napier, F., *Noises Off.* A Handbook of Sound Effects. (Muller)
Purdom, C. B., *Producing Shakespeare.* (Pitman)
Rose, A., *Stage Effects.* (Routledge)
Stanislavski, K., *Stanislavski Produces Othello.* (Bles)
Stewart, H. D., *Stagecraft from the Stage Director's Point of View.* (Pitman)
Watkins, R., *On Producing Shakespeare.* (Joseph)

STAGE EQUIPMENT

Bell, S. (and others), *Essentials of Stage Planning.* (Muller)
Bradbury, A. S., and Howard, W. R. B., *Stagecraft.* (Jenkins)
Brandon-Thomas, J. *Practical Stagecraft for Amateurs.* (Harrap)
Corry, P., *Stage Planning and Equipment for Multi-purpose Halls.* (Strand Electric)
Courtney, R., *Stagecraft.* (Union Publishing Co. Huddersfield.)
Wilson, R. A., *The Small Stage and Its Equipment.* (Allen and Unwin)

ACTING

Battye, Marguerite, *Stage Movement.* (Jenkins)
Boleslavsky, R., *Acting: The First Six Lessons.* (Dobson)
Carroll, S. W., *Acting for the Stage: Art, Craft and Practice.* (Pitman)
Chisman, L., and Raven-Hart, H., *Manners and Movements in Period Plays.* (Deane)
Coquelin, C., *The Art of the Actor.* (Allen and Unwin)
Coffin, L. Charteris, *Stage Speech.* (Jenkins)
Darlington, W., *The Actor and His Audience.* (Phoenix House)
Laban, R., *The Mastery of Movement on the Stage.* (MacDonald and Evans)
Mackenzie, Frances, *The Amateur Actor.* (Nelson)
    (A valuable and practical book with many exercises and immediate relevance to stage work.)
    Approach to Theatre. (French)
Mawer, I., *The Art of Mime: its History and Technique in Education and the Theatre.* (Methuen)
Oxenford, Lyn, *Playing Period Plays.* (4 vols.) (Garnett Miller)
    (Indispensable. Movement, gesture, dance, manners, are all discussed and related to practical work.)
Reeves, J., and Culpan, N., *Dialogue and Drama.* (Heinemann)
Seldon, S., *First Steps in Acting.* (Harrap)
Seyler, A., and Haggard, S., *The Craft of Comedy.* (Muller)
Speaight, R., *Acting. Its Idea and Tradition.* (Cassell)
Stanislavski, K., *An Actor Prepares* . (Bles)
    Building a Character. (Reinhardt and Evans)
    On the Art of the Stage. (Faber)

Turner, J. C., *Voice and Speech in the Theatre*. (Pitman)
White, E. A., *Problems of Play Acting and Production*. (Pitman)
(For a fuller bibliography, see R. Courtney *Preparing to Act*: Union Publishing Co., Huddersfield.)

MAKE-UP

Bamford, T., *Practical Make-up for the Stage*. (Pitman)
Lane, Y., *Stage Make-up*. (Methuen)
Sequeira, H., *Stage Make-up*. (Jenkins)
Ward, E. A., *A Book of Make-up*. (French)

MUSIC

As drama in the broad sense was the basis and origin of the other arts, so it synthesises these in presentation, relating them to its own practical needs in the fully organised experience of theatre. Music, for example, can rarely be excluded from dramatic work.

For plays in period begin by listening to the various recordings in the H.M.V. *History of Music in Sound*, and secure the explanatory booklets which accompany this. These recordings are indispensable for medieval and early Renaissance plays. Also useful are the various dances and jigs issued by H.M.V. under the auspices of the English Folk Dance and Song Society (e.g. B.9577). Excellent, too, especially for Renaissance and Elizabethan music are Archive Productions (Heliodor Record Company). Miss Lyn Oxenford has many stimulating suggestions on music as an accompaniment to period movement in *Design for Movement*.

The tape recorder is a great help to the producer. "Live" music, the small orchestra, has, of course, a quality and impact which can never be equalled by the recorded, however good the reproduction. But the tape recorder enables all effects, including door slams, crackling flames, incidental music, "melodrame", horses' hooves, explosions, to be prepared beforehand, to be arranged in order, and to be given with "spot-on" accuracy by a single stage hand—especially if the machine has a "counter". Where space is limited this method of supplying music and effects is invaluable, and the volume available is sufficient for a small theatre or hall. If, of course, further amplification is needed, artificiality intrudes. One warning—tapes tend to stretch a turn or two, and if one is using a counter, check positions before each performance.. Always record more "effect" than will be needed if there is a sustained sound. One has then margin for fading out or bringing in smoothly.

Index

This is a working index for production, including direction, acting, and décor. The references are therefore, in the main, to practical tasks and problems. Accepted terms are listed as used, e.g. "comic opera" rather than "opera, comic".